The Stock Market Investor's Computer Guide

Michael Gianturco

President and Editor, *High Technology Investments*

McGraw-Hill Book Company
New York St. Louis San Francisco Auckland Bogotá
Hamburg Johannesburg London Madrid Mexico
Milan Montreal New Delhi Panama
Paris São Paulo Singapore
Sydney Tokyo Toronto

This book is for Alexander Gianturco.

Library of Congress Cataloging-in-Publication Data

Gianturco, Michael.
  The stock market investor's computer guide.
  Includes index.
    1. Investment analysis—Computer programs—
Purchasing. 2. Electronic digital computers—
Purchasing. I. Title.
HG4529.G52 1987   332.6′028′5416   86-20937
ISBN 0-07-023186-9

1234567890 DOC/DOC 893210987

ISBN 0-07-023186-9

*The editors for this book were William A. Sabin and Jim Bessent,
the designer was Naomi Auerbach, and the production supervisor
was Thomas G. Kowalczyk. It was set in Baskerville by Techna Type, Inc.
Printed and bound by R. R. Donnelley & Sons Company.*

*Portions of Chapters 6, 16, 17, and 18 of this book are adapted from
articles previously published in* PC Magazine.

The author has made every reasonable attempt to ensure that the descriptions
and the prices of the computer hardware and software printed in this book
are as accurate and up to date as possible. However, because of the fast pace
at which innovations and modifications occur, the reader is advised that
changes in specifications and prices may have occurred after the publication
of this book.

    Please also note that the recommendations and opinions of the author do
not necessarily reflect those of McGraw-Hill, and McGraw-Hill does not necessarily endorse or recommend any of the products described in this book.

Contents

Part 4 Fundamental Analytical Software

Part 5 Portfolio Management and Fully Integrated Software

Part 6 On-Line Services

Preface

In 1983, we retired a big minicomputer we had long used for our investment advisory service and shifted our work to a COMPAQ microcomputer. A year later we added an IBM-PC. We weren't the only investors moving to microcomputers. A dam had broken somewhere.

The computer power (and it is precisely that—power) which had long been cloistered within the "big machine centers" of the investment community was suddenly being made available for sale in stores to investors who could—and would—put it to work from the tops of their kitchen tables. Among financial professionals, microcomputers began to proliferate on desktops, and they have become simply indispensable.

This wide new diffusion of stock market information and processing power is a wonderful thing, and it continues to gain impetus. The purpose of this book is to help you put this new and eminently useful technology to work in your own investment program.

Many investors sense there is a great deal a computer can do for them, but they hesitate. They don't yet know exactly how to approach the problem. Computer and software salespeople are knowledgeable about computers, but only a helpful few are well informed about the investment side of the story. And books about computers don't help investors, who are rarely much interested in computers. A case in point. I once watched an acquaintance, who is under normal circumstances an icily logical speculator in options contracts, strike his brand-new computer with the full force of his open hand. He was trying to bring it to life in the traditional way one would swat an unreliable old radio.

Hence this book. *The Stock Market Investor's Computer Guide* is designed to let you know just which devices and programs are essential and how to make them work. If you are looking for concrete detail, it is here. If you are impatient with detail, this book provides short shopping lists that itemize what to buy.

Running a computer comes down to pushing buttons and watching the screen. If you push the right buttons and correctly interpret the screen, your computer can make you rich. This book talks about computerized investing in terms of which buttons to push. It includes 70 illustrations of computer screens. Your computer can convert densely detailed numerical data (12 years of historical earnings, for example) into an instantly understandable graph on the screen—a railway line into the future. Much of the computer's value to investors follows from this delightful ability to make pictures out of numbers.

You can spend $2000 to $3000 on computer equipment, justifiably, for managing your investments. Investment computer systems are not like ordinary computer systems. If you were to buy the standard model business computer off the display floor of a computer store, you would be off to a pretty bad start. For reasons that are not at all obvious, even to experienced computerists, you could misspend a third of your money and get stuck with a computer that is hard on your eyes. This book is designed to help you spend well on specialized investment hardware and software.

The software you select must mirror your own style of investing. It must help you get results. The major software presented in this book has been tested and evaluated in the turbulent everyday working environment of our investment advisory service, High Technology Investments. I *have not* attempted to include all the software packages available. There are hundreds. I *have* intensively examined several widely marketed packages—the software which appears most useful for most investors. The selection is subjective, and the treatment of each program is detailed. Where possible, I interviewed the writers of the software. I also visited many of them at their workplaces.

For the many technical charting programs, standardized summaries of features are provided. Use them to directly compare the charting ability of one program with that of each of several other programs.

It is a good time to get started in computerized investing. The technology has matured. You can focus on your investments and let the computing machinery run itself, very much in the background. The new low-cost FM radio and TV cable quote services will virtually put your computer on the exchange floor and leave it there continuously, all day, every day, monitoring your stocks. I think you will be very pleased indeed with what it can accomplish for you.

Michael Gianturco

PART 1

Catching Up on Computerized Investing

1
Introduction

Why Buy a Computer?

If you invest or trade in stocks, bonds, or options, you should buy a computer. The reasons are safety and victory. The machine will help you keep your investment program or trading strategy out of trouble, and it will help you win.

First, consider safety. You can justify the purchase of a computer as you might the purchase of an electronic security system or a good watchdog, i.e., in terms of personal property unlost. A computer is not infallible, of course, but neither is a burglar alarm or a dog. It is wiser to have one than not. Your computer system should cost from $2000 to $3000 and last 10 years. At $200 to $300 per year, the cost of a computer is in line with the cost of insurance. You cannot buy insurance on stock market investments, but you can buy a computer. It is the sensible thing to do.

Computers do not make money. Assets make money. If your assets suddenly begin producing a lot of money in response to a successful computerized investment or trading strategy, so much the better. But the machine's first purpose is to keep your assets from ebbing away in the marketplace for no good reason. The machine is perfect for this task because it is more watchful than a human being.

The computer will also keep you constantly informed about the value of your stocks, both in the absolute sense of value projected from balance sheet strengths and earnings growth and in the very different sense of market value as it is understood by traders. Real safety lies in seeing your stocks from both points of view.

On Winning Big

Safety is not the feature which draws most people into computerized investing. They want to get into the game, hit the jackpot right away, and keep hitting it. Everyone shares this fantasy. It is like a treasured childhood story. No one would dispute that it is in fact a fantasy, nor would anyone want to just forget it. It persists in the back of one's mind.

Can a personal computer transfigure the fantasy into reality? Can it achieve for you a dazzling grand slam? A healthy attitude toward this question is one of suspended skepticism. There is no point ruling out the possibility of achieving vast personal wealth overnight, easily, through the clever application of a small computer. It is possible, as you know. The odds are solidly against it, but you know that too. In this book you will learn about some of the computer programs that have been developed to improve those odds. If you are in the market at all, you are in it to win. It follows logically and directly that you should be using a computer.

What to Realistically Expect

Speculation aside, a computer will help your investment program by keeping you informed about the market, about your own stocks, and about what the market thinks of your stocks. Turning on the computer is like opening an instant newspaper, written and published in real time, dealing with your stocks.

You will do a better job of investing and trading stocks with a computer than you could ever hope to do without it. You will always know a little more a little sooner than the investor who relys on faith, the advice of well-meaning friends, and the print media. A few percentage points have always accrued to investors who take the trouble to keep themselves exceptionally well informed about their portfolios. Here is what computerized investors are able to do with their special knowledge.

1. They buy well.
2. They keep track—not merely of how their stocks are doing but of how attractive their stocks look to the market from day to day.
3. They don't overmother or constantly fiddle with their portfolios.
4. They view the market in terms of profit and loss instead of rightness and wrongness.
5. They are able to determine quickly, without personally involving

themselves in tiresome arithmetic, whether a given stock still pays a return big enough to justify the risk they took in buying it—and the risk they continue to take by holding it.

6. They know when to sell. The computer can even be made to beep loudly when that time comes.

7. At the end of the year, they figure the taxes on their portfolios by pushing a button.

Some Results

A novelist who has been involved in computerized investing for several years has been making as much as 40 percent per year on his stock portfolio. A retired dentist in Washington, D.C., launched a career in computerized investing with an initial stake of $2000; he has parlayed it into $80,000.

These clearly outstanding performances are just that, however. It is not yet possible to compare the median performance of computerized investors with that of conventionally informed investors. No one has assembled the statistics needed to support such a study. What you can pick up on this subject is in the nature of cocktail party anecdotes and must be evaluated as such. I know from my experience in the field that it is sometimes possible to try something experimentally with the computer and watch in delighted amazement as the idea blossoms into spectacular profit.

One idea that happened to work like that for our advisory service was simple and qualitative. No heavy financial or technical analysis was involved. It occurred to me that since stock selection is a process of elimination, those stocks which did not neatly fit into standard industry categories would be eliminated early, and unjustly, in any methodical computer screening process. Such screens are widely used in the financial community. New types of technology stocks are often screened out because they fit no existing industrial category; this occurs simply because no category has yet been defined. A company like this might be lumped by analysts into a general category, e.g., electronics, where it could well be an apple competing against oranges with regard to financial performance. More likely than not, it would fail to meet the group norms and would be eliminated from consideration as a buy in a very early screening step. One expects this sort of undervaluation of any special quality. It results automatically from institutional thinking and recalls Einstein's teachers' view of him as a mediocre and unpromising student. They simply had no class or category set up for geniuses like Einstein.

The Einstein Hunt

Given a problem like this—finding stock market misfits—you can use the computer's power to scan industry groups. For this particular strategy, tell the computer to list companies which appear in more than one industry group (hard to classify) and in miscellaneous categories. You can also tell it to ferret out companies whose key financial data are utterly beyond the norms and ranges of the group in which they happen to appear, *wild* points, in other words.

I found a pair of misfits by using procedures like these. Both turned out to be government contractors. Contractors do so many assorted things, it is difficult to categorize or summarize what they do. The two companies were strikingly profitable. One had been lumped into three different industry categories, including the one for garment manufacturers (the company made bulletproof clothes, it turned out). The other was misfiled under software services; it was a think tank. I guessed from their financial performance that the two companies were undervalued and that their earnings would eventually make them shine in their obscurity. That turned out to be a good guess.

The "garment manufacturer" rather quickly appreciated 15 percent, and we took the profit. The think tank went up 85 percent before we recommended its sale. I then watched in awe and some regret as it ascended steeply and without much hesitation to the 600 percent level, splitting twice en route. At the end of the year, *The New York Times* ranked it among their top 10 "superstocks" for that year. Finally, at long last, it plummeted.

There are two observations to be made. First, with the help of the computer I did indeed discover some winning stocks I would certainly have missed on my own. Second, the overcautious machine told me to sell much too soon. I get the credit, and the computer takes the blame; the computer does not notice this.

Computer Technology versus People

There is a widespread feeling that any technology is dehumanizing, and the computer is always easy to seize upon as an emblem of this conflict—the most dehumanizing technology of all. Apple has fought a decadelong uphill battle against this deeply rooted cultural prejudice. This is why personal computers are so insistently marketed even today as warm, cuddly, child-oriented, user-friendly, and—well, personal.

But it seems to me, as a stock market investor, that the great appeal of my computer lies precisely in its inhumanity. The computer is utterly disinterested. It doesn't panic, suffer melancholy, experience elation, bellow in anger, or get frivolous hunches and gut feelings. It is a cool, implacable robot intelligence, and I trust it the way Captain Kirk trusted Mister Spock. It protects my investments from the wilder gyrations of the market, true enough, but its crucial role probably lies in protecting my investments from me. If you have played the market, you should know exactly what I am talking about.

The Bottom Line

Here is what your computer should accomplish for you: preservation of assets above all, plus a few percentage points of extra appreciation, and the peace of mind that comes with immediate access to valid information. This is what you should expect from and demand of your machine.

As for fabulous wealth extracted from the market (and the villa above Lugano, the antique Aston-Martin, and the personal Cray supercomputer with the cryogenic option), such a coup could follow only from hysterically aggressive trading and amazingly good luck. You'd be crazy to try it with a computer.

But it is also true that you'd be crazy to try it without a computer.

2
What Investment Computers Do

The Three Things

Computer systems designed for investors do three things primarily: fundamental analysis, technical analysis, and portfolio management. Each of these major pursuits is supported by software packages. You can purchase a few of these packages in stores. For others, you should do business directly with the software company.

Portfolio Management Programs

Most investors are familiar with portfolio management on paper. It is basically a bookkeeping problem. A portfolio management program, often called simply a portfolio manager, will display your portfolio on the screen in tabular form. Typically the program indicates the size of your positions (both long and short), dates of purchase and sale, cumulative profits and losses, percentage profits and losses, and percentage changes in value since purchase and since yesterday. In addition, a portfolio manager will keep a record of realized short- and long-term capital gains and help you assess the tax consequences of both real and hypothetical transactions. A good one will also keep an eye on commission expenses, cash positions, transactions on margin, and buying power.

There are two things to be done with this type of information. One is to store it on a disk for quick reference. The other is to keep it up to date by entering current prices and positions. In most cases a change in position is entered by hand using the keyboard. Prices, however, usually can be updated automatically by bringing in price data over the telephone or FM radio link. This is a nice convenience. Some portfolio managers have access to a built-in communications program to accomplish the downloading of prices. With others you may have to use a stand-alone communications program to download prices.

Portfolio management programs are easy for programmers to write; if you are interested in programming or learning to program, you may wish to create one of your own. The difficulty and expense in writing such programs for commercial distribution lie in making them comprehensive enough to cover the needs of every conceivable investor. Thus, when you purchase one in a store, you must typically pay for more of a program than you really need.

If you do not program but happen to have a spreadsheet, you can often prepare a portfolio management file that precisely suits your investments. Spreadsheet templates can be purchased to do the job for you. Spreadsheets can also be made to accept data from a telephone, TV cable, or FM link. Finally, portfolio managers are sometimes thrown in with technical or fully integrated analysis packages, so you may not need to purchase separately or create a portfolio manager program.

Do not, incidentally, allow a portfolio management program offered as part of another technical or fundamental package to weigh overmuch in your decision to buy. Focus on the meat of the package, the power to run technical or fundamental analyses. You can always pick up a portfolio manager to suit you. They are like ballpoint pens—indispensable. But at the same time they are no big deal, unless you are in the investment business.

The great difference between microcomputer programs created for the financial community and those created for individual investors can be seen in the area of portfolio management. A good program for brokers will have the capacity for multiple portfolio management, performance per risk analysis, and more comprehensive accounting features. If you are an individual investor, you should avoid professional-type portfolio managers, which chiefly deliver excess capacity.

If you are interested in the risk/reward problem or in immunization, you can attack (but not necessarily solve) these problems with separate programs. They operate to some extent on portfolio data, but they are not typically provided as components of portfolio management programs for private investors.

If, on the other hand, you are a broker or investment adviser, you may find the private investors' small-scale packages of little use, since they cannot keep track of enough portfolios. What you are after is a portfolio management system conjoined with a database management system, a library rather than a page.

Technical Analysis Packages

These products are at present the bread and butter of the investment software business. They use historical and current price and volume data to create stock charts on the computer screen. The charts can be brought up to date monthly, weekly, daily, hourly, or in one very expensive case, almost instantaneously—the price chart actually wriggles along in real time as the underlying issue is traded. Charts can be used to track options, stocks, and indexes such as the Dow Jones industrial average, the Standard and Poor's (S&P) 500, or the New York Stock Exchange (NYSE).

The advantages of using a computer in technical analysis are clear. If you use charts, this is a way to get them into view and keep them current without plotting them yourself or waiting for printed versions to reach your desk. The computer also enables you to experiment casually with various techniques and variations of techniques that would tax your endurance if you were doing the work by hand. Some of the programs will sort through hundreds of charts according to your own preset technical criteria. Using them, you can automate the process of discovering technically interesting stocks and then focus your analytical attention on these few potential winners. The most interesting of the newer programs evaluate various buy and sell strategies in an effort to pin down that strategy which appears most appropriate to a particular stock.

Technical analysis appeals most strongly to traders. The accelerated work pace that follows from computer automation seems to draw many of them into options trading. There is some specialized software available for options traders. It helps one define an acceptable guessing range for the true value of an option. Most such programs automate the Black-Scholes concept.

Investors, many of whom look askance at technical analysis and its practitioners, will find that the computer makes it so easy to check the charts that it is hard to resist doing so, if only to assess what today's technical consensus might be regarding one's favorite stocks.

Fundamental Analysis
Software

At this point in the development of computerized investing there is a great deal of software for traders but a paucity of software for investors. There are two reasons for this: (1) Traders are more interested in a medium which delivers market information right away, whereas investors are patient by definition, and (2) the data which support computerized trading—chiefly price and volume data—are cheap. You can fill a floppy disk with these data over the telephone for about $100.

The data which support fundamental investment analysis (anything other than price and volume data), including balance sheets, income statements, calculated values, earnings projections, and qualitative information, are hugely expensive to download into computers. To fill a 360K floppy disk with this type of information over the telephone, figure on spending about $6000.

Some new ways to get around this price barrier have emerged in the past year. Fundamental programs are now offered in conjunction with floppy disk subscription services which deliver, on a floppy rather than over the wire, information on as many as 10,000 publicly traded issues. This approach puts the price of fundamental analysis roughly on a par with that of technical analysis. The price-related data on the floppies, which change every trading day, can be updated by phone using the newest programs.

Another approach has been pioneered by Value Line's supplier for database services, Interactive. Interactive prepackages fundamental data and downloads the data over the phone to subscribers in a single swift rush. The cost is in line with that of a floppy disk service.

Investors define fundamental analysis in various ways. I like to distinguish between extensive and intensive analysis. In intensive analysis you look very closely at the performances of just a few companies. You can do this very well using a calculator. In extensive analysis you make comparative evaluations among thousands of companies. Extensive analysis requires the power of a computer to sort, rank, and classify. Wanting a machine that could "do sorts," I bought my first microcomputer with this specific task in mind. The computer's ability to run extensive fundamental analyses distinguishes it from an advanced electronic calculator. It is what justifies the computer's price and represents its key competitive advantage. It will also, and not incidentally, do the same things a calculator does.

In looking over the available software for fundamental analysis, you will find that it falls rather naturally into the two classes of extensive and intensive. An intensive analysis program will ask you to enter the key data on the company under study. It will evaluate and perhaps project earnings data, scrutinize accounting ratios, and report on how the company measures up against certain preset standards. It may give the company some sort of grade.

In extensive analysis you start with an idea rather than a company. You might ask the program to tell you the name of the fastest-growing company in Massachusetts. The computer will rank the growth of all the companies in Massachusetts and select the first-ranking company.

Canned Expertise

There are such things as "expert systems," programs which attempt to emulate the response of a human expert to a given situation. These have been applied with interesting results to stock market analysis. However, there is an expertise of a lesser order that is built into every stock market program you can purchase. This is the expertise of a numerical technician.

You may know very well how to wade through the preparation and synthesis of a calculation of a least-squares fit to a linear regression. If so, you know that it takes time and, because it is a lengthy procedure, offers many opportunities to make mistakes. If you are like me, it is probably not your idea of a Saturday pastime.

Suppose you have a chart on your computer screen and shotgunned into it are points representing the closing prices of a stock over the past month. A good way to connect the dots—to see a trend—is to run a least-squares fit. You push a function key. A straight line appears as a spine among the dots. It rises from the lower left of the screen to the upper right at an angle of about 12 degrees. From a peppering of dots you have extracted the information that the stock has been trending up nicely for a month. You can use this information without ever worrying through or worrying about the technique used to derive it. All you need to know is the number of the function key.

Similarly, you may not be particularly interested in the arcana and minutiae of financial analysis. What you are after is a result, a basis for judgment about how a certain company is doing. The computer can show you the company's position on six or seven indexes of performance so that you quickly learn how it is doing today relative to every other company in your area of interest. You may not have a quick feel for the importance of a price/sales ratio of, say, 2, but if the computer shows you a ranking of PSRs, you'll notice quickly enough that 2s and 3s are close to the top of one stock group but close to the bottom of another.

In short, as you feel your way into stock market analysis with the computer, you will find that you quickly pick up the essential lore. It's quick because the computer is taking care of all the drudgery so that you can focus on end results.

Asserting Order

Investors and traders alike accumulate mounds of paper. We are pack rats. Each pile has some sort of guilt associated with it or it would have been dumped out long ago. Take, for instance, that dusty pile of annual reports from two quarters ago that are waiting patiently to be read. Face it. You'll never read them.

One of the things you can do with a computer is use it as an excuse to throw away every pile of paper in your nest. You can be confident that should you ever need to review anything printed about an investment or potential investment, you will be able to retrieve it from a database with your computer.

Also, as new reports come in, you can enter the pertinent numbers from them, then throw away the printed original. You can save quite a bit of money by loading your own data into the computer (see Chapter 18 on setting up a private database). But the most gratifying results are gains in desk and shelf space, plus a slight reduction in ambient guilt.

The Latest Trends and Technology in Computerized Investing

Until very recently the growth of computerized investing was restricted by the cost of the data. The advent of FM radio modems and TV cable information services is changing this picture dramatically. Using FM, it is possible for an individual investor to use the computer to monitor the performance—continuously, all day, every day—of up to 350 stocks as they are traded. It costs very little. The computer and FM radio modem can even do the job unattended. With a TV cable-to-computer link, one can actually monitor 8000 stocks in real time—essentially the whole market. This illustrates the point made above that the computer can be more watchful than any human being. It is curious that this transforming technology has come from outside the computer field, which is famous for ongoing technological advances. FM radio and cable television links seem by now to be quite commonplace technologies, but their impact on computerized investing will far exceed that of any recent break-through in computer hardware or software per se. Both FM and TV cable are rebroadcasting techniques for signals distributed nationwide by satellites. As such, they distribute the cost of satellite transmission and are thus much more economical for individuals than a straight satellite-to-computer link could be. Direct satellite links are available, and some professionals rely on them, but FM radio and TV cable can bring the stock market home to private investors as no other media can.

Another area of technological progress is that of software integration. Several investment analysis software companies are working their way, module by module, toward a completely integrated package of four components: a technical analysis program, a fundamental analysis pro-gram, a portfolio manager, and a communications utility. The first such fully integrated program was made available by Interactive Data of Bos-ton, and other software developers are not far behind. A higher level of integration is being experimented with. This involves putting the charting utilities of technical analysis programs to work in displaying fundamental indicators and trends. Telescan leads in this area. Telescan also leads in a unique new method of data transmission. Instead of transmitting numbers over the phone and then using these numbers to construct charts, Telescan simply transmits the graphic information re-quired to put a chart directly on the screen of the receiving computer. The method is fast and relatively inexpensive and is being used for both fundamental and technical data.

Fundamental data are getting less expensive, though it is still costly enough to weight the field of computerized investing heavily toward the relatively inexpensive pursuit of technical analysis. Fundamental data are now being made available in prepackaged form for rapid-fire down-loading via Interactive Data from Value Line. Some people call this a "whoosh" download, since it is a quick one-way transmission that is not interrupted by the query-response procedures more typically used to transfer data over the phone from mainframes to micros.

Value Line and three other sources (Savant, Gibson & Sons, and Stand-ard & Poor's) all offer fundamental data diskettes on a subscription basis. Preprogrammed downloading and floppy subscriptions are reasonably priced, and interest in fundamental analysis is increasing as a result.

The advent of high-capacity Bernoulli disks and (ultimately) optical disk storage suggests that we will one day be able to buy encyclopedic historical databases on disk. At that point we will be able to dispense with recovering data over the phone from mainframes. It will be possible to use Bernoulli or optical disks for historical data, and FM, TV cable, or satellites for continuous updates.

In software, the technology is advancing largely through refinements, but there is one area where a few software writers are breaking new ground. This is in the field of strategy optimization. By inclination, most people tend to look for a "good" stock to buy, evaluating it as good or not by using various yardsticks, or indicators, of performance. The assumption behind an optimization program is that you can make money on any stock provided that you know which of many possible indicators most reliably predicts its turns. An optimization program focuses on a single stock, and after a long spell of computing—sometimes a day or more—it tells you which indicator has in the past best predicted the turns of the selected stock. These programs are primitive but obviously hold great promise. The strategy optimization problem is worthy of a mainframe, but given plenty of time, your micro can attack it. Software from Summa Technologies, Inc., now provides a basic optimizer as a feature of Summa's standard technical analysis package, Winning on Wall Street. Two other optimization programs are available as accessory packages to work with conventional technical analysis programs. A major stand-alone optimizer called Swing Trader is also available. This seems rather a jazzy name, but it is representative of the highest technology you can get this year in personal computerized investing.

Finally, it should be noted that the whole computer field has been maturing. We are well into a second generation of hardware, and the most current software takes full advantage of the powerful processors which have become standard in microcomputers. After almost a decade of energetic and persistent tinkering, the bugs are out. Computerized investing has really begun to click.

PART 2

Computer Hardware Especially for Investors

3
Which Computer Should You Buy?

You Are Special

Because you intend to use your computer for investing, you have specialized requirements that can be met by only a few machines. IBM, Compaq, and AT&T are good choices. The selection of a particular model is not easy, and this chapter will cover the distinctions among the various machines.

Your special requirements include, above all, compatibility with specialized investment software. You will need monochrome graphic display capability and twice the communications ability offered on more conventional computers. You will also want to leave an avenue open to expand your computer, as technology and your finances permit, to display extremely high resolution color graphics.

No computer will meet all your requirements out of the box. Once you decide which computer to buy, you will have to stipulate precisely to the dealer the ways you would like to have it "fitted out" to meet your needs. This is a process similar to picking the options for a new car, but it is more selective. You can't just say "fully loaded." You have to know exactly what you want and make sure you get it.

It is essential to become acquainted with the options needed, as they markedly affect the price you will pay for the computer. A bargain personal computer may turn out to cost more, fully equipped, than a model advertised at a higher price which offers more comprehensive standard equipment. However, no matter which computer you choose, you must regard the basic machine as an incomplete computer kit. You'll have to add some things to make it work for investment management.

What to Buy

If you intend to buy a new computer, get an IBM PC, an IBM XT, any Compaq, or an AT&T model 6300. If you prefer a used machine, the Apple II and the TRS-80 are attractively priced, and a great deal of early investment software was produced for each of them. However, they are obsolete. Obsolescence for a computer is like obsolescence for a fine camera. You can continue to get excellent results, but the stream of technology that supports the product gradually narrows to a trickle. In the end you can no longer find fresh film for the camera or fresh software for the computer.

Computerized investing is a competitive game, and it will help you to start out with equipment that gives you a competitive advantage—not just now but also during the period of several years over which you intend to amortize the cost of the hardware. Your competitive advantage comes not from the computer but from the software that happens to run on that computer. Some of it has not even been written yet. Pick a computer with software in its future.

A majority of the most useful investment software to date has been written originally for the IBM PC and its compatibles or has been written on an Apple II and then rewritten and uprated (rather than merely converted) for the IBM machines. The best new software builds upon the experience gained in the first generation of investment computers and takes full advantage of the power of the newer hardware.

At a recent Micro/Invest Tech industry show in New York, one of the major gatherings for software producers and their customers this year, the display hall was alight with booth after booth of IBM PCs and their compatibles, chiefly Compaqs. The computers were not being offered for sale. All were set up by investment software companies for the purpose of demonstrating their products. I noticed one Apple II and not a single Macintosh.

The Reason for Choosing
IBM Compatibility

The impression one might receive from the Sunday newspaper supplements is that computerized investing has become a big thing. It is in fact an industry, but it is a tiny, specialized industry serving a limited market. Of the 12 million or so individual computer owners, a little over 750,000 actually use the computer to obtain financial information. The active market for stock market analytical software is probably (my own guess) well under 100,000 units, total.

Computerized investing may be growing exponentially, but it is still a small field, and the major investment software producers are still small businesses. They cannot afford to create multiple versions of their software to broaden their market to include a wide range of computer systems. Instead, they have concentrated on the largest professional and corporate market, which is dominated at the moment by the IBM PC and its compatibles.

Producers of broad-market software products, such as spreadsheets, word processors, database managers, and even accounting packages, adapt their programs to work on many different computers, including the many IBM-like "compatibles." But investment packages run on IBM PCs, the 100 percent compatible Compaqs, and other highly compatible machines. I have tested many of them on the AT&T 6300, which is perhaps only marginally less than 100 percent compatible, with good results.

IBM and Its Compatibles versus the Macintoshes

The 32-bit Apples of the Macintosh series, with their clearly superior graphics, have strong appeal for stock chartists, but at this writing not many investment programs have appeared to take full advantage of the machine's unexploited capability. One of the major producers of investment software went into business with the intention of coding for the Apples but shifted its product to IBM after trying it. At that time, there were real obstacles to programming the Macintosh, and some observers feel that the computer missed its launch window in consequence. This situation has changed. There are a few software packages for the Macintosh (Dow Jones's among them), but there is no broad range of Macintosh software to consider in the investment field.

Three Favorite Investment Computers: An Overview

IBM, Compaq, and AT&T are obviously establishment choices among computers, but they are being suggested here for practical reasons. Recall that the primary purpose of an investment computer is to sound an alarm. Imagine your computer benched and waiting for service during the week preceding a major rally or, worse, a major retreat—no computer, no warning. When an IBM, a Compaq, or an AT&T needs help, help is at hand—parts too. This matters even more to investors than to mainstream business computer users.

We Use Our Machines to Take Risks

Take the same conservative approach in selecting your computer that you might take in selecting a personal airplane. You are going to depend on it heavily in a risk-intensive environment. Spend an extra nickel or two up front. Safety first.

Microcomputers have come to us in waves. The first wave brought the Apple II and the TRS-80; the second wave brought IBM and its clones; and the third wave is bringing the IBM AT, the UNIX computer, and some superclones. There is no clear progression here from good to better to best. Instead of 1, 2, 3, we have something like 1, 2, 2a.

The newest computers are personal computers only incidentally, since they are intended for use in groups and clumps. They are built around the Intel 80286 microprocessor. Their technological power is dedicated to clustering. They appeal chiefly to corporations because of their networking ability. But most investment computers, including brokers' and analysts' machines, will never fit neatly and happily into a network or coalition. This has more to do with investors than with computers. Investment machines tend to be stand-alone computers for stand-alone people, people who cannot afford to wait their turn in a networking environment. The hard disk versions of these new computers tend to be faster than most second-wave computers, but there have been reliability problems. The 80286 generation of corporate computers might form the basis for a new generation of personal computers, but the transition to the newer 80386 computers is already under way.

The second-wave computers are at their zenith technologically, and it is a particularly good time to buy one. Some are heavily discounted because of the hundreds (literally) of manufacturers who hoped to do well by IBM compatibility and flooded the market with clones.

The IBM PC was the earliest of these computers and the least sophisticated. The Compaq portable is more advanced in the sense that it is more complete, and the Compaq Deskpro model 2 is at the top of its generation in regard to quality, compatibility, technology, and price.

The AT&T 6300 is very much like many other compatibles, but it is newer than most, reflects the experience of a whole generation of computers, and uses the technology of the moment to good advantage. Other than price, there is no single outstanding "superfeature" that makes the model 6300 unusually exciting, but the excellent detailing and the long list of standard features add up to a very attractive machine.

AT&T does not make the 6300. Olivetti, in which AT&T bought a substantial interest, is the actual manufacturer. The 6300's distinguishing qualities are speed, the AT&T logo, and price. With a numerical coprocessor, it is faster than a similarly equipped IBM AT. It is also a supreme bargain. AT&T is forcefully willing its way into the computer business, and the bargain price of the 6300 is an instrument of that will. The 6300 also comes closest to being a finished computer, requiring only the addition of communications capability.

Does Portability Matter?

I first purchased a Compaq portable and then, later, an IBM PC. Given the choice, I eventually parked the Compaq at home for occasional use and for business began using the IBM PC exclusively. The decision made itself. The IBM has a bigger, higher screen which is much easier to read. Unfortunately, it has to be specially adapted to display charts.

In the past the Compaq portable enjoyed a 20 percent price advantage over the IBM PC, but with discounting, the absolute price differences have dwindled. The Compaq portable is nominally a portable, and the IBM PC is a desktop, but this is not a distinguishing difference. They are both desktop computers. That's where you use a computer—on top of your desk.

When I purchased my Compaq, I had the notion that it would be less costly to have one computer that I could shuttle back and forth between home and office than to keep one computer in each place. I never had much interest in a "home computer," but I do need a computer, a fully compatible one, at home.

The Compaq shuttle never worked out. I simply left it in the office and moved my portable self to the office whenever I wanted to use it. In practice, you must make three lugging trips to transfer a Compaq from office to car and three more to install it in your house: one trip for the computer, one for the printer, and one for the floppies, cabling, paper supplies, and your hat.

It takes just two more trips to move an IBM PC, because it has a separate monitor. The point is, you have your choice between a six-trip computer and an eight-trip computer, which means there is no real basis for choice at all. If you plan to move either computer frequently, buy a little cart or tip truck from the hardware store. This is not exactly jaunty-looking, but it will save your back and your computer as well. For the Compaq, folding aluminum luggage carts sold in airport gift shops are great.

The Compaq will travel with you on an airplane, but I avoid traveling with mine. It's easier to carry a floppy disk and plan to find or arrange to rent a compatible computer at one's destination. From personal experience, I would say that portability in computers is a quality which appeals chiefly to thieves.

IBM versus Compaq: A Question of Visibility

The real differences between the two machines involve the monitor screens. One concern is graphics, or the machine's ability (or inability) to display both text material and graphs on the screen. A standard monochrome IBM PC is intended to reproduce only text material: crisply displayed letters, numbers, and symbols selected from a preset repertoire. It will not draw pictures or elaborate graphs such as stock charts.

For a technical stock market analyst or a fundamental investor who uses graphs as an evaluation tool and also may want to check price-volume charts now and then, a text-only PC is completely unacceptable. Compaq comes with graphic capability at no extra cost. It is sometimes called a *dual-mode* computer because it handles both text and graphics. To get both crisp numbers and pictures on a monochrome IBM PC you must install a monochrome graphics adapter card from a third-party manufacturer. Allow $250 to $350 for this option, which you should purchase in lieu of the IBM monochrome adapter card typically supplied with the machine. Alternatively, you can install an IBM color/graphics board. It will (despite its name) draw pictures on a monochrome monitor, but the quality of the text is dismal in my opinion. Finally, you might install an enhanced graphics adapter (EGA) board. It is expensive and will run only a limited range of investment software, though it provides both acceptable text and graphics. The Compaq, in contrast to the IBM machines, is ready to run both heavily numerical and graphic investment software without the necessity of plugging in special graphics boards.

The other difference between the two computers is screen size. The Compaq portable's screen is too small. It is also positioned immediately over the keyboard so that one tends to crouch over the machine, peering down into the little screen. It really does seem to affect one's back and eyes after a while. You can solve this problem in two ways. One is to buy a separate monitor for $120 to $150 and set it up on top of the computer. The separate monochrome monitor, however, is driven from the standard Compaq by a composite video signal, which means it won't be as readable as an IBM monochrome monitor. With the pair of monitors you sit before two electron guns, one pointed at your heart and one pointed at your head. This bothers some people. Perhaps the best thing to do is to elevate the portable Compaq several inches above your tabletop on an inexpensive printer stand and just live with the small screen. Stands cost $20 and make a surprising improvement in ease of use.

IBM PC versus Compaq Deskpro Model 2

It would seem that for investors, the optimum answer might lie in the Compaq Deskpro model 2, which has both text and graphics displayed on a big, readable full-sized screen. But the price becomes a factor, since the Deskpro is an upmarket computer and has not been drawn quite so deeply into the discount wars as the Compaq portable and the IBM PC. It would be less expensive to get an IBM PC and add an extra-cost monochrome graphics card in order to display both text and graphics. As a matter of fact, the marketing promise of the Deskpro seems to have been fulfilled by the AT&T model 6300, which provides both graphics and text on a big screen—and at a more competitive price. But the 6300 is less compatible (formally speaking—not in ways you are likely to notice), and anyway, discounting may change this. At equivalent prices the Compaq Deskpro 2 would be preferable to similarly configured IBM and AT&T machines.

Some Tangible but Invisible Compaq Advantages

AT&T does not have a track record like Compaq's in the IBM-compatible computer business. In fact, there are reasons to surmise that AT&T does not care deeply about IBM compatibility except as a wedge into the market. They have it all right—the 6300 runs PC programs—so there is no cause for alarm here. But what AT&T really wants is for IBM to achieve AT&T compatibility.

At Compaq, the concept of IBM compatibility has assumed the dimensions of a faith. When Compaq was being launched in 1982, its principals were able to put together an immense fund of venture capital—about $25 million. They assembled a superb team of engineers and software designers and put them to work to create a product which, in its essential features, had already been completed and documented by IBM's engineers. What more could Compaq do?

Quite a lot. Compaq took the design of the IBM PC and polished it, and the firm has been polishing it ever since. Not even IBM does such a magnificent job of engineering IBM-compatible computers.

The AT&T Model 6300 versus IBM and Compaq

AT&T came along last, and so their IBM-compatible model 6300 has been designed with the advantage of hindsight in regard to their competitors' work. IBM, at the outset, offered what amounted to a skeletal computer. To fill it out, an investor interested in technical analysis would have had to add one or more disk drives, a lot of memory, an asynchronous port, a modem, a printer, a clock, a color graphics card, and a monitor.

Compaq shortened this catalog of missing components somewhat by offering integral monochrome graphics and additional on-board memory, but it is still something of a computer kit, to be assembled (by the dealer or by you) with add-on circuit boards in accordance with your needs.

AT&T noticed not only what its competition was doing but also what the aftermarket suppliers were doing to help fill in the option slots in the IBMs and Compaqs. The mainstays of the aftermarket suppliers have been the graphics board and the memory board. The graphics board, as noted, adapts the IBM PC to display monochrome graphics. The memory board adds memory (RAM), plus a few bells and whistles, typically a battery-driven clock and calendar plus an asynchronous serial port. Sometimes a board will include an extra parallel port as well. The AT&T 6300 includes the bells, the whistles, and the graphics (it's a dual-mode computer, like the Compaq). It also provides enough sockets on the mother board to let you expand the RAM all the way to 640K. In short, if you buy the 6300, you will never have to buy either of the standard expansion cards. Just add RAM chips if you need extra memory. But be careful. If you let the dealer plug in the chips for you, the expense will cut deeply into the bargain you gained by purchasing the 6300. Do it yourself.

Graphics and Text Made Plain

At this point, we have examined the available hardware in its essential details. The question of text versus graphics arises again and again, and none of the manufacturers provides a perfect answer.

With a conventional IBM PC, you can get the best text available or you can get graphics, but you can't have both. With the dual-mode computers, you get good graphics and slightly compromised text, but most important, you get both. Finally, you can get an IBM machine fitted with the EGA adapter, which provides both good text and good graphics and costs over $500 fully rigged, not counting the price of a color monitor.

If you buy a dual-mode computer, you can consider the problem adequately and economically solved and forget it. Many informed investors have been buying Compaqs and 6300s for this reason alone.

If you buy IBM's PC or XT, you must arrange to convert it into a dual-mode machine. The actual mechanics are simple: You plug in a circuit board or ask your dealer to do so. But the selection of an appropriate board is amazingly complex. (See Chapter 4 for help in selecting graphics boards.) If you take the trouble to install one of these boards, you may well come up with a better solution than that offered by the dual-mode computers, and at only nominally greater expense.

At this point, while we are considering the purchase of the computer itself, there are three key points to bear in mind.

1. Don't buy color.

2. If you buy an IBM, specify a monochrome monitor. Do not let your dealer install the standard monochrome adapter. Unless otherwise instructed, the dealer will probably do this as a matter of course, since you want monochrome. The adapter costs about $250, and you will have to replace it immediately with a dual-function board.

3. Do not be hurried through the selection of the proper graphics board for your IBM PC or XT. The one your dealer may urge upon you almost reflexively is the Hercules, but this is not necessarily the best card for all investment work. For some applications it is certainly the superior choice, but for most investment programs it is at the time of this writing the wrong card. Study Chapter 4 on graphics boards before you make up your mind.

But What about Color?

If you walk into a computer store, you will notice that most top-of-the-line machines on the floor are displaying full-color graphs, games, signs, landscapes, animated psychedelia, or some other powerful visual design. This is good promotion, and if you like what you see, you may actually buy a color monitor and the card that supports it. You will find that this adds $800 to $1000 to the retail price of the machine. You may also find when you get home that letters, numbers, and symbols—text material—are hard to read on a color monitor. The numbers will hurt your eyes, and as an investor you are going to be scrutinizing lots of numbers.

You may become puzzled over the color problem, because most investment software is sold with a note on the box specifying a "color/graphics card." This makes it seem that a color monitor is imperative. It isn't.

Third-party hardware manufacturers were quick to invent monochrome graphics cards, and their whole purpose lies in saving you the price of color and the poor text readability that goes with it.

Another way to avoid buying color is to select, instead of the IBM PC, a dual-mode computer such as the AT&T 6300 or any Compaq. These computers run investment software without modification at the cost of a very slight (but in some cases noticeable) sacrifice in the quality of the text.

The Future of Color

If you are much involved in technical analysis of charts, you will eventually want a color monitor. As you work on a chart, it can deteriorate quickly into a tangled web of thin lines on the screen. Color coding helps you tell the lines apart. This functional use of color is a feature of several major charting packages, including Interactive, Dow Jones, Telescan, and Savant (EGA version only). Functional color will be adopted gradually by the other software vendors as well. In the meantime, it is possible to get along without color, and I think it is a good idea to do so for two reasons, as follows:

1. The only major benefit of color is in distinguishing between superimposed lines on charts. Programs which offer functional color also provide graphic devices to help your eye distinguish between lines if you are using a monochrome monitor. In monochrome you notice dotted versus solid versus dashed lines. This is quite sufficient. To get functional color with an IBM color/graphics card and the very small added convenience that comes with it, you must accept and live with fuzzy textual

material all the time. If you do much word processing or spreadsheet analysis, you will soon regret the decision.

2. If you buy more advanced technology in the form of an IBM EGA card or one of its compatibles, you can get good text along with functional color graphics. It will cost a great deal and does not appear to be the last stop in the development of color technology. My preference would be to wait for truly high resolution color.

Two investment software packages, Savant and Telescan, are now compatible with the IBM enhanced graphics card, but enhanced graphics seems to be just a station along the way to excellent graphics.

Color monitors are changing. The latest and best of them offer extremely high resolution (640 × 400 lines) as opposed to a typical value of 640 × 200 lines in the current generation of monitors. When resolution is high enough, a color graphics monitor can reproduce quite acceptable text in addition to graphics. Various new graphics cards plug into any compatible computer to support these higher-quality graphics monitors, but this is not a time, in an admittedly conservative view, to commit money in this direction. When they get it all sorted out and the full range of investment software finally catches up to the emerging generation of new color hardware, I will move up to color and retire my monochrome monitor and the card that runs it.

Planning for Obsolescence

If you own a dual-mode computer, when the time comes for super-high-resolution color, you can probably just add it. This can be done by plugging whichever card has the victorious technology into an expansion slot to bring your machine up to date. With the IBM PC you will find it necessary to throw away the $150 to $350 monochrome graphics card, which will become obsolete with the newer color technology. You will have enjoyed in the meantime, however, the satisfaction of crisp, clear, large text. I consider this an even trade-off.

Hard Disks and Power Supplies

A hard disk is a mass storage device that is typically installed in place of a floppy disk drive. It works faster than a floppy drive, and you notice the improved speed in terms of quicker response to commands. It holds from 10 to 70 megabytes of data on a typical system and can thus replace several boxes of floppy disks. Having installed one, you very rarely need to feed floppy disks in and out of drive doors. This is a major convenience.

If you do technical analysis, you can probably get along quite nicely without a hard disk. Technical analysts typically focus on groups of stocks, and if you assign each group to a floppy, it is easy enough to keep them sorted. Selective updating is also facilitated by separate disk storage. The latest investment software supports hard disk storage, but much earlier software does not. Eventually, you'll probably want the speed and operating convenience that come with a hard disk, but this is not an essential item.

If you emphasize fundamental stock analysis, which may involve comparisons among thousands of companies (for each of which you may wish to accumulate balance sheet, income, and calculated data spanning a period of years), you will be happiest with a hard disk. If you are an investment professional, sooner or later you will probably have to have one or more hard disks. It costs about $500 to put one in.

If you want to wait before making up your mind, do not buy an IBM PC or Compaq portable. Their power supplies are not up to the extra load imposed by an ordinary hard disk. Low-powered hard disk drives are available, but even without them, investment computer systems draw an unusually large amount of power because they depend heavily on extra option cards. To install a full-power disk drive, you probably need a 150-watt power supply in the IBM PC. This is twice the output of the unit installed at the factory. Thus, to put in a proper hard disk, you need to pitch out the existing power supply and install a brand-new 150-watt unit, which looks just like the original. The IBM XT has the high-output power supply and the hard disk already installed. This is the fundamental difference between a PC and an XT.

If you want a hard disk, it makes sense to buy an XT system unit rather than a PC in the first place. The hard disk need not be installed when you purchase the computer since you can add it later. For similar reasons, if you want a hard disk in a Compaq portable, it makes sense to get a factory-installed Rodime shock-mounted hard drive in a Compaq Plus.

If you want a hard disk someday but would prefer to wait as the prices decline (and they are still coming down), you will find it easiest to upgrade an XT or one of the newer computers, such as the Deskpro model 2 or the AT&T 6300. These have designed-in power supplies of enormous capacity. Hot, feeble power supplies were the weak design element in some of the earlier computers of this generation, and in the later computers the problem has been solved with a vengeance.

It may be, too, that some marketing person noticed that stereo sound systems sell on power output, as cars used to sell on horsepower, and adapted the notion of raw power to the selling of computers. Let's not be drawn in by this. A 200-watt power supply does not give you a powerful computer. It just keeps the computer from blinking out on you.

The Bernoulli Box

If you are a professional with a substantial database that must be kept secure, you can leapfrog past the clanking, sputtering, whizzing technology of hard disks and backup tapes and buy instead a Bernoulli box. These beautiful mechanisms store and retrieve data from 10-megabyte cartridges. You can back up one cartridge onto another in four minutes. The cartridges are cheap, and when you need another 10 megabytes, you just add another cartridge. To accomplish this expansion of storage with a hard drive, you would have to add another hard drive. The Bernoulli boxes are the best of the mechanical solutions to the mass storage problem. They are stand-alone desktop machines and cost about as much as a PC.

Coping with Computer Stores

A retail computer store is a good place to buy a computer. You have some assurance that if you take delivery of a lemon, they will make it right.

You can also have your machine serviced at a computer store. Typically, they trace the problem to the level of the circuit board and then replace the whole board. In my view this is not unlike replacing the engine of your automobile in order to correct a fouled spark plug. But the computer retailing business is precisely that: a retailing business. Knowing this, you should ask yourself what you gain by doing business with such stores. The answer is that it is a good question.

I am inclined to feel that the retail stores are more trustworthy than discount sources. They have a continuing relationship with the manufacturers as well as a direct line of communication to them. The line of communication between a manufacturer and a discounter may be somewhat tenuous. It is also true, however, that the discounters are becoming more established as computers come to be regarded as commodity items. In some areas they have virtually seized the marketplace. Many of them are fully as dignified as the "name" stores and are fully prepared and equipped to service what they sell.

Service

In my experience, service is very rarely required. It is at the point of system start-up that you may wish for technical support from a dealer, for if the equipment is going to fail, it usually fails right away. You can get technical support from discounters and even from mail-order houses, but in the case of mail-order suppliers it is not easy to use these services.

There are many independent service technicians with the skills, instruments, and documentation it takes to fix computers. If you can find one who will trace the problem to the level of a chip or component rather than sell you a whole board, keep in touch with that person.

How to Buy a Computer
without Wasting Any Money

If you would like to approach the problem as I did, here is how to proceed.

1. Know exactly what you want. List the cost of each feature as advertised by discounters. Look at the 47th Street listings in *The New York Times* or the mail-order ads in the major computer magazines. Decide how much tinkering you are willing to do.

2. From a retail store, buy the most stripped-down, basic, no-chrome loss leader of a discounted computer system. Usually the best deal entails a basic package purchase, including a computer with 256K RAM, a pair of floppy disk drives, a monitor, and a keyboard. Make sure you get the most current model available. An older one may have less RAM (you need at least 192K; 128K is insufficient), single-sided disk drives, or just one disk drive. The dealer should burn-in and test the system for you. Test this basic system again at home so you know everything works.

3. For the rest of your system—modems, serial ports, memory expansion cards, graphics cards, hard disks, software, and perhaps even a monitor—use discount computer sources. If there is no discount store in your area, go to the nearest major metropolitan area and find one. Failing that, use mail-order suppliers. For some of the equipment and software you will need as a computerized investor, you have no choice but to use mail-order firms or, preferably, manufacturers who sell directly to you.

4. Installing circuit cards in computers is not more demanding technically than installing a quarter in a parking meter. A circuit board is

an electronic device, but the business of installing it is purely mechanical. You will save hundreds of dollars if you do it yourself. Two cautions: (1) unplug the computer, and (2) even though it is unplugged, stay out of the boxed high-voltage anode supply for the monitor tube.

You must weigh the initial savings against the possibility that you may void the warranty by opening the computer. It seemed to me that once the computer had been demonstrated to work by the dealer, I probably would not need further protection. What the warranty protects, perhaps primarily, is the dealer's opportunity to sell you optional circuit cards.

5. If the computer doesn't work, get help from a technician, either at your dealer or from an independent.

This approach saved me several hundred dollars on each computer system. On a comprehensive system it can save you over a thousand dollars. It also assures that you will get exactly what you need without duplication of capabilities.

Dealers will prefer to sell you what they happen to have for sale. This is seldom just right. You have to go shopping, and it follows from this that you will have to open up the computer to install your purchases.

You don't have to get this involved. You can make a list of the hardware you need, take it to a computer store, let them plug together a complete system and burn it in and test it. Write a check, take the computer home, and turn it on. This will limit you to the type of hardware the store happens to handle, but that's okay. If you prefer this course of action, you should probably buy the AT&T 6300 because there is so little to add to it. It is almost finished as is.

Avoid Mass Market Computers

Dealers are not in business primarily to sell computers tailored to stock market investors. This is why you should be prepared to go to a little trouble to set up your own computer. The dealer is in business to sell a rather standardized basic computer system. It's an IBM PC with one or more of the three major commodity-type programs: word processors, spreadsheets, and database managers. All these programs can be helpful in managing your investments, and I use all three for this and that. None is specialized for investors, though spreadsheets and database managers can be customized (by you) for stock analysis. If you plan to use the machine only for private investing, you can probably get along nicely without buying any of the three major programs.

Recommended Systems

Here is a list of computers, each configured to achieve a basic level of performance for computerized investors. This means that most portfolio management and analytical software will run on the system and that it will have access to both "live" and historical stock market information. Some computers require more optional equipment than others.

IBM PC

Basic System:

256K RAM
Two 360K floppy disk drives

Monitor:

Monochrome monitor

Added features that are essential:

Third-party color/graphics card. Paradise, Genoa, or Everex. Be careful with those requiring special versions of standard software packages, i.e., software patches. Try to get one with a parallel port for your printer.

Parallel dot-matrix printer. IBM, Epson, Okidata, or equivalent. A dot-matrix printer—as opposed to a letter quality printer—is essential if you wish to print charts and fast if you are running out rankings. It requires a parallel port. Do not be creative in selecting a printer. Most investment software drives only IBM and 100 percent compatibles.

1200-baud internal modem with serial output port. The purpose of the serial port is to drive the FM radio modem or TV cable decoder. If you prefer to use a Hayes 1200B, which is the industry standard but has no serial port, you can add a separate serial port card. The cost is $80 to $100. Serial ports are also provided as components of some monochrome graphics cards and many RAM expansion cards. A small AT-type serial port may require a connection adapter to run FM or TV cable.

FM radio modem or TV cable decoder. Typically supplied along with software by quote service. An expensive alternative is a satellite receiver.

Remarks:

This computer was the prototype and is the model, or standard, for its generation, but it is rather primitive and slow compared with its most recent competitors. The standard disk drives are big, and this is considered unfashionable now. (It is as if the machine had been equipped with great clumsy feet.) These big drives sputter and clank, but you can specify multiple svelte half-height drives in their place. Finally, the computer must be specially configured (i.e., modified with non-IBM circuits) to display both clear text and graphics on a monochrome monitor. Investors require both, but it is an easy problem to solve. The low speed and early style are not very important in the real world. If you think you will ever want a hard disk, get an XT instead.

Compaq Portable

Basic system:

256K RAM
Two 360K floppy disk drives

Monitor:

Monochrome monitor built into computer. A dual-mode machine. No separate monitor is necessary, nor are display adapter cards needed.

Added features that are essential:

Printer stand. Use it to elevate the system unit for better screen visibility and comfort.

Parallel dot-matrix printer. Epson or equivalent. Dot matrix is essential if you wish to print charts and fast if you are running out rankings. It requires a parallel port, which is supplied as standard equipment on a Compaq.

1200-baud internal modem with serial output port. The purpose of the serial port is to drive the FM radio modem or TV cable decoder. If you prefer to use a Hayes 1200B, which is the industry standard but has no serial port, you can add a separate serial port card. The cost is $80 to $100 for the port alone. A small AT-type serial port may require a connection adapter to run FM or TV cable.

FM radio modem or TV cable decoder. Typically supplied along with software by quote service. An expensive alternative is a satellite receiver.

Remarks:

This is both the best and the worst of computers for an internal modem. Since Compaq's industrial designer managed to fit everything into a single neat box, it seems a shame to compromise the integral design (and portability) with an external modem. But a technical problem can arise with an internal modem in this machine. It arose in mine, at any rate.

The Compaq portables' power supplies (at least on the earlier models) apparently did not have adequate heat dissipation. Some of them destroyed their power transistors, according to the technician who "repaired" my own parboiled power transistor by replacing the entire power supply. Internal modems produce quite a bit of internal heat, and this can only aggravate the situation. I removed my internal modem and transferred it to our IBM PC. To be on the safe side, you might select an external modem driven by an internal asynchronous port. One asynch port would serve both the FM (or TV cable) feed and the telephone modem, and the internal heat would not rise. If you travel with a Compaq, however, it makes sense to take an internal modem and accept the risk that comes with it. Do not conclude from this that the Compaq portable is unreliable. In several years of very hard use, this is the only thing that has ever gone wrong with it.

If you are considering a hard disk, get one immediately, factory installed. The Compaq portable equivalent of the IBM XT is the Compaq Plus. The hard disk features a unique shock mounting system to withstand those sharp bangs down onto the runway.

Compaq Deskpro Model 2

Basic system:

256K RAM
Two 360K floppy disk drives

Monitor:

A Compaq monochrome monitor should be purchased with the computer. This is a dual-mode machine; no display adapter cards are required.

Added features that are essential:

Parallel dot-matrix printer. Epson or equivalent. Dot matrix is essential if you wish to print charts and fast if you are running out rankings. It requires a parallel port, which is supplied as standard equipment on a Compaq.

1200-baud internal modem with serial output port. The purpose of the serial port is to drive the FM radio modem or TV cable decoder. If you prefer to use a Hayes 1200B, which is the industry standard but has no serial port, you can add a separate serial port card. The cost is $80 to $100 for the port alone. A small AT-type Compaq serial port will require a connection adapter to run FM or TV cable.

FM radio modem or TV cable decoder. Typically supplied along with software by quote service. An expensive alternative is a satellite receiver.

Remarks:

In my subjective opinion, this is the most desirable computer for investment work. It is at this writing more costly than the AT&T model 6300 at equivalent levels of capability, but the discount wars may change this situation. It is of course supremely compatible. Although it uses the 8086 processor and is thus in the same speed class as the AT&T 6300, it also emulates at lower speed the old 8088 processor of the IBM PC. At the flip of a switch, you can recover compatibility with any older program that won't run on the 8086. Programs that won't work at 8086 velocity are typically shoot-'em-up video games, which the faster processor and its clock accelerate beyond the range of human reflexes. As an investor you may never have to use the 8088 compatibility switch, but it is reassuring to know it is there.

The power supply limitations of the earlier portables are gone. The power supply of the Deskpro model 2 has a 200-watt output. Figuratively speaking, this should be sufficient to drag stumps out of the ground. You can support great chunks of optional equipment with this much power, and the expansion of the basic model 2 has been worked out for you in advance by the computer's designers. As you add hard disks, tape backup, ports, and so on, your model 2 evolves into a model 3, 4, 5, 6, or 7.

AT&T Model 6300

Basic system:

256K RAM
Two 360K floppy disk drives

Monitor:

An AT&T monochrome monitor should be purchased with the computer. A dual-mode machine; no display adapter cards are required.

Added features that are essential:

Parallel dot-matrix printer. Epson or equivalent. Dot matrix is essential if you wish to print charts and fast if you are running out rankings. It requires a parallel port, which is standard.

1200-baud internal modem. A serial output port is provided as standard equipment. If you wish to use a Hayes 1200B, which is the industry standard but has no serial port, you need not add a separate serial port card to support FM or TV cable reception. AT&T has an optional Voice-Data modem you might look at. A small, AT-type serial port may require a connection adapter to run FM or TV cable.

FM radio modem or TV cable decoder. Typically supplied along with software by quote service. An expensive alternative is a satellite receiver.

Remarks:

This computer requires the least modification to adapt for investment purposes. It comes with dual-mode graphics and both a serial and a parallel port. It has sockets on the mother board to fully expand the RAM. You will not have to purchase any expansion board other than an internal modem at the outset. At some time you may wish to purchase high-resolution color, which requires a monitor and an expansion card.

Compatibility is good. I have not found any problems with it, but it runs the high-speed 8086 with a fast clock (8 MHz) at all times. There is no slowing it down and adapting it to accommodate older 8088 software, as with the Compaq, so you may run into a compatibility problem sometime. I doubt it, but you might. The Dow Jones Market Analyzer program was written with some timing loops that were accelerated by the fast processor, but RTR, which wrote the program, fixed the problem soon after the 6300 appeared. Savant, among others, is also fully compatible.

AT&T has an 800 number you can call to confirm compatibility before you invest in software.

The computational speed is impressive, but you may notice it less in actual operations than the fast refresh rate for the screen. The screen is nonglare and easy to read.

The power supply is sufficiently big to handle a hard disk if you decide to add one later. Installation of a hard disk at the outset can be done at a reasonable price.

AT&T's commitment to IBM compatibility as a concept is not as fierce as Compaq's, so the 6300 could be just an anomaly, not really part of a product line progression from basic to advanced or from past to future. On the other hand, the 6300 is a great bargain and a perfectly reasonable alternative to the Deskpro model 2.

It has elegant half-height disk drives and is easier to look at (both aesthetically and ergonometrically) than any of the alternatives. Tilt and swivel for the monitor costs nothing extra, though it is a $90 option on some computers.

The New IBM?

A successor to the IBM PC is overdue, as you can see by comparing the specifications of the venerable PC with those of its 8086-based competitors. Probably the new machine will be a dual-mode computer with a fast clock. The successor is not, however, the IBM AT, which goes a bit beyond the popular notion of a personal computer. The AT is a corporate computer which can be accessed by many people, and it can be thought of as more mini than micro. It is certainly more "powerful" than the PC, but the power is not particularly useful in applications for individual investors.

4
Graphics Boards

For IBM Only

If you select a dual-mode computer such as a Compaq or the AT&T 6300, you need not be concerned with the problem of selecting a graphics board. If you intend to buy or already own an IBM PC or XT, you may find this chapter helpful. Graphics boards are probably the most complex and therefore time-consuming option to consider. Salespeople in computer stores who have not schooled themselves in this area are not qualified to help you. Plan to make your own way through this thicket of specifications.

The answer for you, as a computerized investor, is going to be a circuit board of the type manufactured by Genoa, Paradise, or Everex. Generically, you should insist on a "monochrome graphics card that is IBM-graphics-compatible (rather than, or in addition to, Hercules-graphics-compatible) and that uses the full screen for graphics display." But to begin at the beginning . . .

Graphics versus Text

IBM designed the PC to be set up for you by a dealer in either of two quite different configurations. One writes words, or text. The other draws pictures, or graphics. Each task calls for a specific adapter board to be plugged into one of the option slots of the PC. The IBM monochrome adapter sets the computer up to display sharp, high-resolution letters, numbers, and symbols from a preset repertoire of characters. The IBM color/graphics adapter enables the machine to display graphics (drawings, graphs, charts, and pictures). Graphics are typically displayed in color on a full-color monitor.

An IBM PC which has been set up for monochrome display of text is incapable of displaying pictures. The color/graphics machine is able to produce both pictures and text, but the text that comes with color graphics is second-rate. The numbers and letters are poorly resolved, fuzzy and hard to read.

Investors routinely work with both text and charts of various kinds, and investment software is designed to display information in text form (tables, rankings, and portfolios) and in pictorial form (graphs, price-volume, growth curves, pies, and bars). One usual way to get both text and graphic displays to appear on an IBM monitor is to buy the color system. Most investment software, in fact, calls for a color system (or a Compaq). The color is pretty but costs a great deal. Moreover, the current color technology is obsolescent. It is not a good time to buy into it.

An uncompromising solution technically would be to use both adapter cards and a pair of monitors, one monochrome for text and one RGB for graphics. Almost no one does this because it is technically difficult and costs too much. A more plausible solution is to buy the IBM color/graphics board but use it to drive a monochrome monitor. This works for graphics, but the text which appears on the screen is as fuzzy and hard to read as that obtained with a color monitor. I recently phoned the IBM product center and asked if they had devised some better way. "Buy a Hercules card," said the person at IBM. Perhaps she meant I should buy a *monochrome graphics card.*

The prototype for such cards was the Hercules, and the name is used almost generically for a monochrome graphics card (not to be confused with the similarly named, text-only IBM monochrome adapter card). The Hercules card plugs into an option slot inside your IBM PC or XT. You plug it in instead of the IBM monochrome adapter and thus save the price of the text-only IBM card. The Hercules card converts the IBM computer into a dual-mode machine. The standard IBM top-quality text is supported by the monochrome graphics card, and it also displays graphics on the monochrome screen. Different colors are represented by different shades of green. This is exactly what you want, but you may have some problems if you take too literally the IBM salesperson's advice to buy a Hercules card.

Hercules Graphics Cards

The Hercules card is the established standard in monochrome graphics cards. Its purpose, as with all such cards, is to display color graphics on a monochrome screen. The Hercules card takes full advantage of the high resolution of the IBM monochrome screen, which is markedly superior to the resolution available from the IBM color monitors. Unfortunately, software must be specifically designed or adapted to work with the Hercules card. Many of the major commodity-type software packages are available in Hercules-compatible versions. For example, Lotus 1-2-3, which is useful in many important investment applications, is available in a Hercules-compatible form. The Hercules card will also support graphics produced by programs written in IBM's BASIC programming language. Many BASIC programs have been produced by and for investors. Some of them are in the public domain, and some are commercially available.

Almost all commercial applications programs specifically designed for investors call for IBM graphics, not Hercules graphics. Telescan is the important exception—it does both. Two things may be expected to happen: (1) Hercules may create an IBM-graphics-compatible card, because there is now competitive pressure suggesting they may wish to do so, and (2) manufacturers of investment software may, one by one, adapt their existing programs to take advantage of the superior resolution of Hercules graphics.

But what should you do right now? The best course would seem to be to seek out monochrome graphics cards that offer IBM graphics compatibility. There aren't many. If the card you select happens to offer Hercules graphics compatibility in addition to IBM, that's a nice bonus feature, but IBM graphics compatibility is essential. Avoid cards that offer high-resolution Hercules-compatible graphics *exclusively* and thus cannot run the lower-resolution IBM-type graphics. A salesperson may tell you that Hercules graphics are better. They are. The trouble is, most investment software *does not support* Hercules graphics. Plainly put, such programs won't run on a card that is strictly Hercules-compatible.

Enter Paradise

An alternative is the Paradise graphics card. It runs IBM graphics on a monochrome screen and retains (almost) the fine IBM text mode. It costs about $280 undiscounted. When you get ready to add color, you can do so simply by adding a color monitor. An RGB (red, green, blue) color monitor can be driven by it, and no additional or add-on circuit cards are required. For a suggested retail price just slightly above that of the IBM text-only monochrome adapter card, you get text plus graphics—a dual-mode computer. The monochrome graphics are not as high in resolution as those delivered by the Hercules card. However, since the card is IBM-graphics-compatible, it will run most investment programs.

If you intend to use your machine for investment graphics, this is a good choice. The only difficulty with the Paradise and similar cards is that they do too much, too soon. The color capability is nice, but it serves the color technology of 1986. In 1987 and 1988, as high-resolution color is finally realized, the type of color graphics supported by the card may become obsolete. In practical terms, this means that when the time comes to upgrade your system to color, you may have to throw this card away and replace it with whatever finally emerges as the best ultra-high-resolution color graphics card. When ultra-high-resolution color comes true, however, you will be able to find some real bargains in RGB monitors with specifications at the now-current level of resolution. If you don't mind being one iteration behind on graphics technology, Paradise may suit you perfectly over the lifetime of your current computer system. Right at this moment, it seems the optimum choice if you use the computer strictly to run investment software.

As options, you can get a parallel port for your printer or a serial port for your modem. A second series of options includes a clock and 256K RAM. You'll need a parallel port to make up for the one you didn't get when you did not buy an IBM text-only monochrome adapter. You may have secured a parallel port in some other way, however. I have one that came as a component of a RAM expansion (multifunction) board. If you do need a parallel port, the option may bump the price of this board as much as $75, and that is at discounted levels.

Exit Gemini

There used to be a board called the Genoa Gemini. It has been superseded but is helpful to consider if you are trying to make sense of these multifarious graphics boards. The idea of the Gemini's designers was to combine Hercules compatibility (meaning high-resolution 720 × 348 line monochrome graphics) with IBM graphics compatibility (meaning it runs any non-Hercules color graphics program you happen to pick up, without modification, but the graphics appear in relatively lower resolution than the Hercules-compatible programs). The name Gemini evidently came from the power of this single board to duplicate the various capabilities of a pair of cards, namely, the Hercules graphics card and the IBM color/graphics adapter.

The Genoa Gemini concept delivered one thing you cannot get with a Paradise card: high-resolution (720 × 348) Hercules-compatible monochrome graphics. The ability to handle both monochrome and color is common to all Genoa and Paradise cards, as is the ability to reproduce high-resolution IBM-like text. Gemini has been superseded by a newer product from the same company, the Genoa Spectrum card.

The Genoa Spectrum

The Genoa Spectrum is almost a do-everything card. It handles high-resolution (720 × 348) monochrome graphics so that you can take advantage of those programs available in versions specially modified for this purpose, e.g., Lotus, Symphony, and Framework. It will run color when the day comes that you want to add an RGB monitor. It will run, in monochrome, programs written for the IBM color/graphics adapter, and this means it will run most investment programs that use graphics and charting. A printer port is standard.

How to Choose Which Card to Buy

To choose between the Genoa Spectrum and the Paradise card, decide first whether you will be using spreadsheets intensively, either for investment analysis or for other work. If you like spreadsheets, get a Genoa Spectrum and a high-resolution version of Lotus, Symphony, or Framework to exploit its capabilities. The word processing program The Word is also available in Hercules-compatible form. Spectrum provides 132 columns of text in both monochrome and color displays. This will nicely expand your window onto a spreadsheet problem. If you use spreadsheets in monochrome, you will probably prefer the Genoa card. If you add a color monitor (a shift up in price, down in resolution), the 132-column capability is the only noticeable distinction that will remain between the Genoa Spectrum and the Paradise cards.

If you don't care deeply about spreadsheets (as an investor you will discover specialized programs more suitable than spreadsheets for most investment applications), the Paradise card will do nicely. At this writing, a telephone survey of various dealers indicates that the two cards are comparably priced if you get the Paradise card with the extra-cost parallel port. (The parallel port is standard on the higher-priced Genoa Spectrum.) If you already have a parallel port and don't do spreadsheets, you can save money by selecting the Paradise card. Moreover, the price of Paradise is coming down. Most of the market probably does indeed want high-resolution and 132-column monochrome spreadsheet graphics, which means Genoa is ahead of the game for the moment. Paradise is competing on the basis of price. As an investor, you can respond to the favorable price of the Paradise card without losing much in the way of useful investment analysis capability.

Do You Really Need a 132-Column Spreadsheet?

In the past spreadsheets proved particularly helpful for two tasks in our field: portfolio management and intensive fundamental analysis. In addition, a spreadsheet can be used to chart stocks in a primitive way. For each of these tasks, however, there are specific applications programs for investors that will do the given job better, quicker, and more easily.

The new and at the moment quite important application for spreadsheets is as a buffer, or temporary parking place, for data captured with an FM radio modem or TV cable decoder. I use spreadsheet files to accumulate 250 days of high, low, close, and volume FM data on about 20 stocks per file. The data can be uploaded into specialized programs for stock charting. Presumably, specialized programs will be developed to capture FM data, but at the moment you need a spreadsheet to do this job.

If you have an experimental or playful turn of mind, you'll probably find yourself involved in spreadsheets sooner or later. They are close to irresistible.

It does not follow, however, that you need a Hercules card. IBM graphics are adequate in this application, although they cannot provide the 132-column format Hercules offers. You probably will not be using the graphics capabilities of a spreadsheet often enough to really appreciate the superb Hercules graphics resolution.

The Levels of Resolution

The Paradise card will display on your monochrome monitor stock charts generated by investment programs originally written for the IBM color/graphics board (i.e., most major investment programs) at the equivalent of the highest currently conventional RGB resolution, which is 640×200. This is one notch down from the Genoa Spectrum's largely useless, for us, Hercules-emulation level of 720×348. It is not very useful because so little investment software is Hercules-compatible.

When the Genoa Spectrum emulates IBM color on monochrome (as it must to run most investment software), it uses 16 shades of gray at a resolution level of 320 × 200. At this level of resolution Paradise does likewise. This is the level at which you will view any investment software that actually uses color on either card. It is also the resolution level at which you can play video games. However, very little of the existing investment software actually uses color in a functional way. The programs call for the IBM color/graphics card because they need access to graphics capability in order to draw stock charts. The color is incidental. The Paradise board offers monochrome emulation of color graphics at 640 × 200 with no gray scale. This is twice the resolution of the IBM color emulation on the Genoa board. Genoa does not advertise a monochrome graphics capability at this higher level of resolution, where most investment software is at home.

I bought a Paradise card for my own IBM PC. I think there is a slightly perceptible deterioration in the quality of text display going from the IBM monochrome adapter to the Paradise card. In word processing and in some investment text-type applications, it has an odd and extremely annoying quirk when it gets hot. When it is supposed to display an *s* followed by a comma, on my terminal it instead displays an *s* followed by a parenthesis. An *s* followed by a period is displayed with the period surmounted by an asterisk which blinks at high frequency—twinkle, twinkle. I was able to alleviate most of these problems in my case by repositioning the Paradise board in the option slot farthest from the internal modem, which generates a great deal of heat.

Because of the size of the IBM monochrome display, the screen seems easier to read in both text and graphic applications than that of the Compaq portable. Text display on the Genoa Spectrum and the Everex, because of their inherent higher maximum level of text resolution, should be identical to IBM's and slightly better than that of Paradise.

Installing the card entails the usual switch resetting on the mother board of the computer. There is, in addition, some software installation work. This sounds like an imposing task, but it isn't. To accomplish it, you basically shuffle disks in and out of drives. Aside from changing disks, it is a highly automated procedure and should be carried out on each program you use frequently.

After this initial installation, your programs will boot and reinstall the graphics capability automatically. It is a process you will not repeat manually or even notice happening in daily operation. The automatic installation does not work for DOS 1.1, so if you have some older programs, you'll have to follow an installation procedure each time you load them. It is easy and quick.

Neither the Genoa Spectrum nor the Paradise card can handle the "next-generation" color resolution of 640 × 400 or higher. This new high watermark in color resolution is still about 5 percent lower than the resolution of the Hercules mono. It is high enough, however, to make color desirable and worth waiting for. By buying a monochrome graphics adapter card today, you can avoid buying a 600 × 200 color monitor for $500 or so that is clearly slipping into obsolescence. If you wait, you can expect to purchase a contemporary-style color monitor at discounted prices or pay the full price and get a new, far higher level of resolution. I would urge the latter course. Of paramount importance here is your own vision.

Everex and Its Edges

There is a third contender. At the time of this writing, Everex is advertising a product which seems comparable to the Genoa Spectrum but has not yet been made available for sale. Everex's previous product, the Graphics Edge, was evidently not a full-screen display card. According to their dealer, The Edge (as opposed to the now passé Graphics Edge) is going to be a full-screen card.

Full-screen capability is something to ask for. Several monochrome graphics cards use only about two-thirds of the display area available on the face of the monitor. Genoa, Paradise, and the new Everex are all "full-screen" graphics monitors.

Monochrome Graphics Cards I Would Avoid

Most monochrome adapter cards use the Hercules-compatible 720 × 348 resolution scheme. Most people who buy these cards do so in order to run spreadsheet graphics. You can get cards of this Hercules-compatible type for as little as $125. They will run only the specially adapted programs; almost none of the major investment packages are suitable for them. I say "almost" because there is some very good Lotus and Lotus-based software for investment work. The Telescan technical and fundamental analysis program will run with a Hercules card, but that's about it.

It is a shame that in order to get broadly compatible monochrome graphics, you must buy color graphics capability as well (you may never use it), but that seems to be the case. The dual-mode computers are similar in this respect to IBMs which have been converted with cards for dual-mode display; Compaqs and AT&T 6300s will also run color with no further ado.

The Enhanced Graphics Card

IBM offers a relatively new card called the Enhanced Graphics Adapter (EGA). The term *enhanced* means, of course, better than before. It does not mean terrific. Two important investment programs will run on the EGA: Savant and Telescan. In the case of Savant, it makes a real difference. With an EGA, the Savant program will draw lines which are distinguished by different colors or by different graphic styles on color and monochrome monitors, respectively. The version of the program which runs on conventional IBM graphics does not distinguish one line from another in any way and thus sometimes produces stock charts which are difficult to read.

Nevertheless, the EGA represents an expensive investment in a technology that strikes me as a side road to someplace I don't much want to go. I am inclined to wait for truly high resolution color.

If you feel that the EGA is or may become important enough to force conformity to its specifications among programmers, consider Genoa's most recent offering, the Spectra Card. It is universal. It supports software designed for the EGA, the original IBM color/graphics card, the Hercules card, and the IBM monochrome adapter card. It costs about the same as IBM's EGA card but comes with 4 times as much RAM on the board. If you buy one, you'll want a color monitor. NEC's MultiSync color monitor is, like the Genoa Spectra card, almost omnicompatible.

Before You Write a Check for an IBM PC or XT . . .

The cost of converting your IBM for dual-mode display is not significantly greater than the cost of setting it up with an IBM monochrome adapter for text only.

The trick is to buy your monochrome graphics card as original equipment. It supplants the IBM text-only monochrome adapter, does the same job and graphics too, and costs about the same. If you already have an IBM monochrome adapter card, you'll have to extract and replace it. You'll have no further use for it unless you can trade it in. As promotions, some card manufacturers offer (typically) a $50 trade-in allowance for one's old IBM monochrome text-only adapter. If you happen across one of these promotions, it can take away some of the economic sting associated with converting an IBM PC or XT into a dual-mode computer.

However, you may wish to keep your IBM monochrome adapter, as I have, and reinstall it in place of a Paradise for heavy text applications in hot rooms. The other graphics boards should not make you want to do this, but they have other limitations. This whole chapter could, in fact, be construed as a strong argument in favor of buying a Deskpro or a 6300 dual-mode, large-screen computer as your original equipment instead of an IBM PC or XT. If I had it to do over, that's what I would do. One can probably assume that IBM's next computer will be a dual-mode machine and that henceforth the very term *dual mode* will pass into disuse. Let's hope so.

Manufacturers, List Prices, and Specifications

THE EDGE
Everex
47777 Warm Springs Blvd.
Fremont, CA 94539
415-498-1111

List price: $399

Resolution: 720 × 348 and 640 × 200

Remarks: Parallel port standard. Avoid similarly named earlier card, which was not full-screen.

GENOA SPECTRUM (specifications below)
GENOA SPECTRA (EGA-compatible)
Genoa Systems Corporation
73 E. Trimble Road
San Jose, CA 95131
408-945-9720

List price: $459

Resolution: 720 × 348 and 640 × 200

Remarks: Parallel port standard.

PARADISE MODULAR GRAPHICS CARD
Paradise Systems Inc.
150 N. Hill Drive
Brisbane, CA 94005
415-468-6000

List price: $395

Resolution: 640 × 200

Remarks: Parallel or serial port optional. Other options include 256K RAM expansion and clock-calendar, or a combination floppy controller and parallel port.

Note that if you use this card to replace an IBM monochrome text adapter card, you will need to provide a parallel printer port to replace the port supplied as standard with the IBM card.

Text readability is good but not quite as good as with a 720 × 348 resolution card.

HERCULES GRAPHICS CARD
Hercules Computer Technology
2550 Ninth Street
Berkeley, CA 94710
800-532-0600, ext. 401, for dealer name

List price: $499

Resolution: 720 × 348

Remarks: Parallel port standard. Of the charting packages reviewed in this book, only Telescan's is compatible with Hercules graphics.

IBM COLOR CARD
International Business Machines
Old Orchard Road
Armonk, NY 10504
914-765-1900

List price: $244

Resolution: 640 × 200

Remarks: Runs graphics in monochrome, but text resolution is not good. Many programs recommend this card because of its essential graphics capability, but the first three cards named above will provide both monochrome IBM-compatible graphics and crisp, readable text.

IBM ENHANCED GRAPHICS ADAPTER
International Business Machines
Old Orchard Road
Armonk, NY 10504
914-765-1900

List price: $199 to $524

Resolution: 640 × 350

Remarks: Carries 64–256K RAM. The Telescan and Savant programs run on this card.

5
Telephone Modems and Asynchronous Ports

About 15 percent of the computers sold to individuals are equipped with a device called a modem. The purpose of a conventional modem is to enable the computer to receive and send information over a telephone wire. Some of the information you will need as an investor is accessible over the telephone. About half the people who have modems use them to gain access to financial information.

You can use a modem to collect current news items about companies, i.e., earnings, management changes, insider trading, current stock quotes, complete price and volume histories of individual stocks over the span of the past decade or so, and comprehensive balance sheet and income statement data.

The sources of the information are various data services, which maintain it on their own mainframe computers. The modem connects your computer, via the telephone, to the mainframe. This is called going *on-line* to or *downloading* from the mainframe. The services which collect and sell the information (Dow Jones, Warner Computer, Dial Data) are called on-line services or on-line databases.

How Investors Use Modems

The modem is a delivery system. Once you have used it to gain access to a mainframe, you can quickly download the information you want into your own computer and store it there. Once the information has been captured and stored in a file, you can break the telephone connection. At your leisure, you can then read the news wire items or process the financial data you have captured.

The database service will bill you for the time your computer was connected via modem to theirs. Some investors use their modems to browse through the databases of the various services and examine current information while they are still connected. This is a rather expensive practice, but sometimes it is unavoidable.

Although the databases you need reside in mainframes that may be a thousand miles away, you will probably not have to pay long-distance phone charges. Most major databases are accessible via local phone numbers in medium to large U.S. cities. If you live in a remote area, you can sometimes arrange for an 800-number link.

The mechanics of linking your computer to the mainframe can be so fully automated that you don't even have to dial the phone. Instead, you just push a button on the computer's keyboard. Communications software embedded in the major investment packages will automate the linking process, as will communications programs made available by the modem manufacturers.

Software supplied with the modem is useful in communicating with on-line brokerage services (see Chapter 23). These services enable you to enter buy and sell orders and typically provide access to on-line databases and quote services. Some provide analytical services as well.

Shortcut

Having read this far, you now know enough about modems to buy one. The one to buy, if you don't want to dip any deeper into this admittedly dry subject, is a freestanding Haye's 1200 Smartmodem. This is the most conservative choice, and it is the standard specified for most investment software. If you have an AT&T model 6300 or already have an asynch port in some other type of computer, you may prefer a Hayes 1200B internal modem.

There are, however, about 125 alternative modems. Some won't do at all, but among them are a few you may find more convenient than the Smartmodem in regard to investment applications and/or a good deal less costly. They are "Hayes-compatible," so investment software should run on them. The balance of this chapter deals with the subject of modem selection in some detail.

Why You Need Two Different Modems

As a computerized investor, you will need two modems. One is the conventional type, discussed in this chapter, which puts your computer on the telephone. The other may be one of two types, an FM radio modem or a TV cable decoder. Either will enable your computer to receive stock market data broadcasts. A broadcast service is essential if you want to limit and predict your monthly cost of monitoring the market and wish to monitor it continuously without running up colossal bills. The radio hardware will in most private installations pay for itself in terms of reduced on-line data charges in just over a year. There is no purchase cost for a TV decoder, which is essentially on loan to you for as long as you use the service. The monthly charges are therefore higher for TV cable than those for comparable FM services.

If you rely exclusively on the telephone for data, there is a good chance the whole enterprise of computerized investing may come apart in your hands. As the bills for on-line access mount, you may find yourself doing less and less work with the computer. But the computer can do useful work only in proportion to the amount of usable information it gets to work on. If it gets less information, it will eventually stop earning its keep. At that point you could sell it at a loss, grumbling righteously that you didn't get enough use out of the machine to justify its high initial cost. Alternatively, you might let it just sit. One wonders how many of those 15 million-plus personal computers are just sitting.

To save your computer from this rather common spiral into sloth, spend a few dollars initially to make it compatible with an FM radio modem or a TV cable decoder. The broadcast services will keep your data costs down and your spirits up. The matter is raised in this chapter because the need for a second unit, a radio modem or decoder, now or later, can affect your choice of a telephone modem.

Incidentally, these considerations are unique to investors. Nobody else needs two modems, and your dealer may not have encountered the problem before. It thus merits some detailed home study, as follows.

Why Not Just Rely on the Quote Broadcasts?

The FM radio modem or TV decoder will essentially put your computer on the exchange floor and leave it there. Data broadcasting is a breakthrough which allows continuous low-cost computer monitoring of stocks and options. But it is brand new, and it is useful chiefly because of its timeliness. It gives you the moment—but nothing else.

Stock market analyses of both major types, technical and fundamental, are based on scrutiny of historical data. To get historical data, you must use the phone. FM radio and TV cable broadcasts will tell you how you're doing this instant, but to examine, say, the 12-year cyclical growth pattern of a particular company's revenues, you need to interact with a mainframe over the phone. *Interact* means that you can send specific instructions over the phone wire and receive specific data in return. FM is a one-way medium, as is TV cable. They broadcast everything they've got, and your FM modem or TV decoder must scan the ticker broadcast to extract data on your particular stocks or options contracts.

What Is Asynch?

Asynch (ā-sink) is short for *asynchronous communications*. You need an asynchronous communications adapter in order to receive cable or FM stock quotes. It is also called variously and imprecisely a serial communications adapter, a serial card, and a serial port. To get asynch capability, you can install an IBM asynchronous communications adapter card in one of the option slots of your computer. There is a connector built into the card. The connector will protrude from the back or side of your computer. Run a cable from the connector to your FM radio modem or TV decoder and you can begin to receive broadcasts of stock quotes. The necessary wiring is included with the purchase of the FM modem and is installed along with a decoder at no extra charge. However, the asynch card must be provided by the computer owner. If your computer does not have an asynchronous card, or "serial port," installed as standard equipment, you must come up with one. At this writing, only the AT&T 6300 provides a serial port as standard equipment.

Serial Ports and Internal Phone Modems

A few years ago serial ports were universally required to hook up phone modems, just as they are required today to hook up TV decoders and FM radio modems. Evidently the manufacturers of phone modems decided to throw a wing over the market for asynch cards, which was so closely associated with the market for their own products, so they began packaging both a serial port and a phone modem on a single circuit card which they continue to call a modem. Now, if you need to purchase a phone modem, what you can get is this neat combination of a serial port and a modem—there is nothing else to buy. These combination units are all internal modems. The circuit board is installed in one of the option slots inside your computer.

Many internal-type phone modems provide a connector so that you can tap their built-in asynchronous communication circuitry to drive something other than the phone modem. This serial port connector is chiefly intended for hooking up letter quality printers, some of which require a serial output from the computer. However, it will also connect to your TV decoder or FM radio modem.

You need two modems, one to get data from the phone and the other to get data from the broadcast services. If you select an internal phone modem which provides a serial port, you are saving the price of an extra, duplicate serial port. The asynchronous communication circuitry provided with the internal phone modem does the job for both radio and phone modems.

Internal versus External Modems

External modems are slightly passé. They belong to the period when personal computer installations resembled small cliffside villages—boxes stacked upon boxes. In fact, another term for external modem is *stack modem*. As microcomputers evolved, they tended to become integral units with everything neatly packaged in a single box. The Compaq portable is the paradigm. The newer computers (newer than the IBM PC, that is) also provide plenty of slots and interior space for option cards.

With this recent background in style and technology, most of the newest modems are internal. They are built onto a single printed circuit card. Once one has been installed inside your PC, you never have to see it again. The fact one can derive from these observations is that the newest technology seems to come with internal rather than external modems. In some respects, this is a shame.

Modems draw a good deal of power and turn much of it into heat. Microcomputers, particularly the older designs, do not need extra internal heat to dissipate and do not have excess power to lavish on a modem. External modems come with a separate power supply. One pays for this, but one should do so happily. As an added benefit, the separate power supply can be turned on and off independently of the computer. This means that you can reset the modem without resetting the whole system. I have never encountered a situation that calls for a separate reset, but you never know.

Another argument against going inside with the modem is service convenience. You can take an external modem to be repaired more easily than you can take the whole computer, theoretically. However, this argument is specious. To quickly isolate the problem, it is usually best to take in the whole computer system, from the plugs out, and this is slightly less troublesome if you own an internal modem.

Most external modems are about the size of a book, and they look nice. Some have status lights that are decorative. One is built into a telephone. One looks like a little plastic tuber on the cabling that serves it.

External modems typically have no asynchronous adapter. This is important. The adapter must be purchased separately and installed inside the computer. The AT&T 6300 has an asynchronous adapter as standard equipment. Most memory expansion multifunction cards and some graphics cards provide serial ports, or you can just buy one.

I think it is a good idea to try to get the most current technology. Modems are better than they used to be, and it is wise to get one that is fully compatible with the most currently available communications software. This requirement for newness directs our attention to the internal modems. The further requirement for TV decoder or FM modem support suggests that among internal modems, those with serial port connectors should be favored. Finally, if we select an internal modem, we have decided, without actually taking up the question, in favor of a 1200-bps unit, because that's the speed at which most of them run. Let's back up and consider the matter of speed.

300 Baud versus 1200 bps versus 2400 bps

The 300-baud modem is going to become obsolete. If you use one to access a database, it will cost, typically, half what it costs to bring in data at 1200 bps. However, the 1200-bps modem operates four times as fast as a 300-baud unit. You come out ahead at 1200 bps. At one time the higher initial cost of the 1200-bps units severely offset their lower operating expense, but competition and technology have brought down the price. In the meantime, the software writers who produce investment packages have pretty much made the choice for us. Some of the best of them call for 1200 bps.

As this is being written, 2400-bps modems are beginning to be advertised at prices within the range of realism, at least for business and professional applications. I do not recommend buying one. There is as yet no established standard, and by the time one is set, the technology may have moved along to 4800 bps. The 4800-bps level is generally regarded as a practical upper limit imposed by the inherent noisiness of the phone system. In the meantime, not all data services have made the leap to 2400, and none of them are about to abandon 1200.

The $75 Modem

When I first confronted the problem of selecting a modem, the Hayes 1200B had just been introduced and was priced at around $600. I already owned an asynch port, which I had purchased to drive an old Texas Instruments printer left over from a prior involvement in minicomputers. Thus equipped, I elected to gamble on a battery-operated $75 external 300-baud modem for my Compaq.

Over the course of that hot summer, the installation of the little $75 modem became my hobby. I purchased a specially made cable to connect it to my asynch port and, when that did not work, began creating cables of my own. These did not work either. I came to know the technical support people who answered the modem manufacturer's hot line on a first-name basis. They actually gave up before I did and sent me a new modem—a slightly fancier one—which also did not work. I tried the new modem (as I had the old) on a different computer and a different asynch port to rule out problems having nothing to do with the modem. No luck. Finally I gave it away. I lugged my Compaq to the Computerland store and asked them to please install the most expensive modem they had and burn it in and test it and guarantee it and so forth. They did. The Hayes 1200B worked immediately, and it has worked faithfully ever since. The net (counting the price of the two modems and my many useless cables, experimental work on the part of various paid technicians, and phone bills) exceeded $1000. You can get an excellent 1200-bps internal modem for half that, and I urge that you do so. Cheap 300-baud modems, however, now sell for $50, and there are new insights available about how to actually make them work. My own problem seemed to revolve around a communications protocol called handshaking. You solve it and I shall be honored to shake your hand.

Selecting a Modem

Although any of the modems listed below will work with an IBM-compatible computer, the selection of a specific modem will depend to some degree on which computer you own.

If you have an earlier computer (i.e., one with an 8088 processor, such as the IBM PC and the Compaq portables), the most conservative course would be to get an external 1200-bps modem. In the case of the Compaq, this is problematical, since an internal modem is best for travelers. But the external modem does not tax the computer's power supply and adds no heat to the interior of the computer. Internal modems borrow power and return internal heat.

Assuming that you do favor an external modem, you will need an asynchronous communications port as well. The port can be used to hook up a phone modem, an FM radio modem, or a TV cable decoder. You cannot hook up two at once, however.

If you have a Compaq Deskpro, the selection of a modem may depend on the other options that have been installed. If an asynchronous port has been purchased singly (or as part of a dual-function clock/port card), you will not need any other serial port to support a TV decoder or FM modem. If your Deskpro is a stock model 2, which provides no serial port, you may want to select one of the internal modems which do provide a serial port. (You are not likely to pick up a serial port along with a RAM expansion card for this computer, because you can expand the RAM on the mother board. Nor are you likely to get a port with a graphics card, because the Deskpro is a dual-mode computer.)

If you prefer an internal modem (as I would—the Deskpro power supply is more than equal to the task), pick a Hayes-compatible modem with a serial port to drive your external FM radio modem or TV decoder. The advantage of using an internal rather than an external phone modem is a matter of operating convenience. With an internal phone modem you won't have to plug and unplug cables to shift the system from FM or TV reception to telephone communications. There is a price advantage in most cases as well.

Compaq provides a serial port with some of the more fully optioned Deskpros. It is a small connector, AT-type port. Neither the Telemet nor the Lotus Signal FM modem will plug into it; probably the TV cable decoders won't fit either. A cable connection adapter could be created to fix the problem. I tried to hook Signal to a Deskpro using a "standard" adapter provided by a computer store. It didn't work. You may have to wire one of your own until the various manufacturers discover one another.

If you have an IBM XT, you have plenty of power to run an internal modem. You also have a number of opportunities to pick up a serial port. Graphics cards and multifunction expansion cards typically provide asynchronous communications. If you already have a port, you can use the Hayes 1200B internal modem, which does not provide one. If you don't, select a modem with a serial port so that you can run your FM radio modem or TV cable decoder from it.

If you have an AT&T model 6300, you can run any modem you want. The serial port for your FM or TV link is built in as standard equipment, and the power supply is equal to the demand of an internal modem if you prefer one. You can get an AT&T communications card with this computer. It is a fancy modem, as one might expect from AT&T, and it provides for both voice and data transmission. With this special modem you can accomplish something called phone management if you need to.

If you are using the AT&T 6300 system for investment purposes only, you can save a bit by plugging in a basic Hayes or Hayes-compatible instead of the standard AT&T. The computer is fully hardware-compatible with IBM's, so no problems arise from making this choice. The Hayes 1200B internal modem offers no serial port, but you won't need one. Another internal modem is the Qubie PC modem, which costs about $300 and is available only by mail order. The price is $200 under that of the most nearly comparable modems. It is Hayes-command-compatible.

Manufacturers, List Prices, and Specifications

There are at least 125 modems available for sale, but the selection for investors is limited. The modem must be (1) Hayes-compatible, (2) IBM-PC-compatible, (3) 1200 bps or 1200/300, and (4) a direct-connect rather than acoustically coupled modem. In addition, it helps if the modem has a serial input/output port. Software to accompany the product is usually free. Most investment software is packaged with a communications module, so you may not need the modem manufacturer's software to download quotes or data. When you want to use your computer as a "dumb" terminal to a mainframe, however, it will come in handy. Typically, you would communicate with an on-line broker or news wire in this mode.

SMARTMODEM 1200B (internal)
SMARTMODEM 1200 (external)
Hayes Microcomputer Products
5923 Peachtree Industrial Blvd.
Norcross, GA 30092
(404)449-8792

List prices: $599 for the internal modem
                  $699 for the external modem

Requires: The external modem requires a serial port. These currently cost $80 to $100 purchased separately. A serial port is commonly provided along with a RAM expansion card and is a standard feature of the AT&T 6300. The internal model has a built-in serial port for its own use only. You would need a separate serial port to plug in an FM radio modem, a TV cable decoder, or a serial printer.

Remarks: The industry standard. Smart Com II communications software included with purchase. These are elegant, expensive products you can count on.

IDEAcomm 1200 (internal)
IDE Associates, Inc.
7 Oakpark Drive
Bedford, MA 01730
(617)663-6878

List price: $545

Remarks: Includes a built-in serial port for its own use, but it is also accessible, when the modem is not in use, by other peripherals, such as a serial printer, a TV cable decoder, and an FM radio modem.

QUBIE PC MODEM 212A/1200 (external or internal)
Qubie Distributing Inc.
4809 Calle Alto
Camarillo, CA 93010
(800)821-4479

List price: $139 internal, $149 external

Remarks: Supplied with PC-Talk III, a public domain communications program. You should send $35 in a contribution if you use it. Mail order, no-frills. I would check on current warranty policy before commiting to this modem, but it is a clear bargain. Circuitry is similar to the IDEAcomm 1200 noted above. Provides serial port.

PC212A (1200-bps, internal)
Rixon, Inc.
2120 Industrial Pkwy.
Silver Spring, MD 20904
(301)622-2121

List price: $539, dual-port model

Remarks: Dual serial ports, one for this modem and a second for options— a good configuration for investors with separate FM modems or TV cable decoders. Supplied with Rixon communications software.

SMART CAT PLUS (external or internal)
Novation, Inc.
20409 Prairie St.
Chatsworth, CA 91311
(800)423-5419

List price: $499

Requires: External version requires a serial port.

Remarks: Supplied with Novation's communications software, called Mite. Internal modem hooks up to IBM's built-in loudspeaker. Regarded as a technically advanced modem, though the software is basic. Compatible with other major communications software.

PC MODEM/1200 (internal)
Ven-Tel, Inc.
2342 Walsh Ave.
Santa Clara, CA 95051
(408)727-5721

List price: $499

Remarks: The Ven-Tel model which offered an extra serial port has been discontinued, unfortunately for FM modem, TV cable decoder, and serial printer users. A half-card model is offered which fits into the short slot of the IBM XT. The modems are supplied with the CROSSTALK XVI communications program. This is probably the top communications package for microcomputers.

PC:INTELLIMODEM (internal)
Bizcomp, Inc.
532 Wedell Drive
Sunnyvale, CA 94089
(408)745-1616

List price: $499

Remarks: Company holds patent on "intelligent modems," and this is one. Voice and data. Supplied with PC:IntelliCom communications program. Compatible with other popular communications software. Technically advanced modem.

6
FM Radio Networks: Continuous Live Stock Quotes at Popular Prices

Vigorous stock and option traders can make and/or lose thousands of dollars in the course of a choppy day on the market. For these traders, the stock market quotes reported in the next day's morning paper are of archival interest only. Traders must be alert to transactions as they occur. They need continuous quote services. Now, for as little as $1 per trading day, traders with PCs can receive quotes continuously via FM radio.

The relatively new FM-to-PC quote services broadcast a stream of quotes straight from the exchange floors to your PC. To receive the broadcasts you need a radio modem, appropriate software, a subscription to a service, and a password. Hook the radio modem to your PC and you can watch the screen as your own options, futures, and stocks drift, spike, plummet, and surge—all day, every day.

Traders are a relatively small group of market participants. Investors, who by definition do not trade frequently, can also benefit from continuous monitoring of stock quotes. The chief benefit to investors is safety. The radio modem can be set up to watch your portfolio for you. If anything really frightful happens to one of your stocks, the PC can sound an alarm in plenty of time for you to cut your loss. For a serious investor, the cost of an FM-to-PC link should be justified not in terms of spectacular winnings but in terms of dollars unlost. Investors install FM in a conservative spirit. It is rather like an electronic burglar alarm for the preservation of assets.

A second advantage to serious investors follows from the new analytical power that can be tapped with their PCs after a massive downloading of low-cost FM data. The cost of bringing down quotes via FM is the same for a thousand stocks as it is for one stock. The monthly charge for the FM quote service is fixed, regardless of usage. Individual investors can thus easily afford to track the performance of whole groups of stocks and then watch to see how their own select few stocks are performing within and relative to those groups. FM also makes it economically feasible to keep the price-related items in a large fundamental database up to date on a daily or hourly basis.

In short, FM brings large-scale market analyses within the price range of individual investors with PCs. Suddenly, you can luxuriate in price data. For investors with an analytical interest in the market, the real-time availability of FM quotes is a nice fillip. However, the truly important benefit of FM is the incredible volume of data it delivers into the PC at low cost.

Market professionals make up a third group to whom FM-to-PC links appeal. Quote display terminals, sometimes called *quote machines,* are indispensable to brokers, money managers, investment advisers, and some analysts. The terminals are the shop windows of the investment business. Quote delivery is a big, strikingly profitable pursuit. Before being bought out, Quotron Systems, Inc., the dominant domestic supplier of stock market quotes, reported revenues of $190 million and netted $27 million on an installed base of 72,000 terminals. Quotron has about two-thirds of the business. Quote display terminals are typically fed by leased telephone lines used exclusively for this purpose.

Now that PCs have become commonplace in the financial services industry, it seems an obvious step to dispense with quote machines and feed quotes directly into the PCs. A PC can be used variously for quote display, multiple portfolio monitoring, and analyses in depth that exceed the capabilities of a dedicated quote machine. Quotron and others have introduced dial-up and dedicated phone line quote services for PCs. Nevertheless, the new FM radio services now provide the least costly direct link between the marketplace and the microcomputer. FM reception cannot be made absolutely reliable, and the services which provide it do not offer a dial-up backup service. For this reason the leased-line quote services, which are precisely as reliable as our phone lines, will persist. They have probably begun to notice, however, the competitive pricing of the FM-to-PC services. Additional price pressure is coming from the new, low-priced quote services made available via cable TV data broadcasts to home and office computers.

How the FM-to-PC Link Works

Commercial FM radio stations broadcast, within their allotted wave bands, the programming you receive on your personal radio, but they also broadcast subcarrier signals that the radio ignores. Ordinarily these signals are just wasted segments of the frequency spectrum, but they can be used to transmit information to specialized receivers. Some FM stations therefore make their subcarriers available for lease as a source of extra revenue. The subcarriers are most commonly leased by the marketers of that bland, meandering background music one hears in elevators and supermarkets.

In recent years FM stock quote services have been building networks by leasing the subcarriers of commercial FM broadcast stations in every major city in the United States. In most big cities there are now two or three stations that broadcast quotes from the competing quote services.

For several years, the three major FM quote broadcasting services were Bonneville Telecommunications, Telemet America, and Dataspeed. Then Dataspeed was bought out by Lotus Development Corporation; this service now operates as the Lotus Information Network Corporation. The sudden appearance of Lotus as a major player in this field changed the complexion of business: After a decade of development in relative obscurity, FM data broadcasting technology is now finding wider acceptance.

Each quote service maintains a central computer which gathers trading data from the stock exchanges. The data are initially transmitted from the service via satellite to receivers at FM stations in various cities. The satellite signal is then retransmitted on a leased subcarrier by the participating commercial FM station in each city.

To pick up the FM signal at your PC, you need a radio modem. Two of the three FM quote broadcasters now offer radio modems for the PC: Lotus and Telemet America. They will supply you with a modem when you subscribe to their quote services. Bonneville Telecommunications, which pioneered in the business, currently broadcasts to dedicated display terminals but has a radio modem under development.

A radio modem looks like any other external modem. It is a black box about the size and shape of a book. It uses its own power supply rather than the computer's and thus must be plugged into a wall outlet. The radio modem communicates with your PC via a serial port. A cable is supplied with the modem for this, but you must provide the port. The modem also requires an antenna.

Electronically, the "front end" of a radio modem is an FM radio tuned to the narrow subcarrier of the station in your city. The signal is detected, amplified, and used to drive a built-in modem. From this point, it is just as if the signals had arrived via telephone. The modem converts the incoming signal into a series of bits intelligible to the PC.

The Quote Broadcast

Stock, options, and futures quotes are broadcast and received in an alphabetically ordered stream of ticker symbols and their associated price-volume data. When the complete list of tickers from A to Z has been broadcast, the process begins anew at the top of the list. In practice, this ticker "tape" loops every two to eight minutes.

The radio modem is equipped with some on-board memory, typically 64K of RAM. It stores the ticker symbols of the stocks, options, or futures of particular interest to you. The modem watches the ticker loop and extracts from it only the prices of these designated stocks, much as you might pluck your children off a merry-go-round. The most current quotes are stored in the modem's RAM, where they are held available for display on your PC's monitor. The ticker loop is broadcast over and over again, so the modem RAM is steadily refreshed with data from the market.

An eight-minute loop is too slow a refresh rate to provide real-time market data. A priority interrupt technique speeds up the process. Whenever a stock is traded, the new quote for that stock is instantly inserted into the loop, immediately perceived by the modem's RAM, and displayed on the terminal right away. As the trading day progresses, actively traded stocks are constantly pushing up in line on the ticker loop. The trader watching the screen is kept continuously aware of their price fluctuations and accumulating volume.

The practical result of all this technology is a display screen you can consult any time you wish in the course of a trading day. A basic screen lists your stocks (or options, indexes, or commodity futures) down the left-hand column and presents tabulations of their current prices (high, low, last), the tick, the change since yesterday's close, bid and asked, and volume data. Both Lotus and Telemet America, the two suppliers of FM-to-PC services, will provide you with essentially the same basic product, using the same basic technology. Many additional features and points of difference will be discussed below, but first let's look at the advantages and limitations of the technique itself.

How Reliable Is FM Reception?

The major advantage of FM is the low cost. The major objection is unreliable reception; you may lose your quote feed altogether in a thunderstorm. Occasionally the FM signal grows so feeble that it stops updating the quotes on your screen. For many market professionals, this means FM must be used in tandem with a high-reliability service, probably via a leased line. When the FM service is up, which is virtually all the time, you can save substantial sums in usage charges on other quote terminals. When it is down, the modem alerts you immediately. If there were an automatic dial-up access to the ticker loop, it would help one's peace of mind. For advisers, analysts, and most individual traders and investors, however, it seems that FM is sufficiently reliable to be used as a stand-alone system.

Indoor antennae will work, though neither of the indoor antennas supplied with the two FM systems reviewed here was adequate. I hooked up rabbit ears for this evaluation; they make the computer look preposterous. Some people are able to use tiny antennae fashioned from paper clips; these are more socially acceptable. The most common reception problem arises from multiple signal paths produced when FM signals bounce between downtown buildings. This can be solved with a circular polarizing antenna.

If you live beyond the transmitting radius of a major city, FM is not for you. Consider a cable TV link or a direct satellite link instead. PC Quote in Chicago and Bonneville Telecommunications in Salt Lake City can tell you more about satellite links. Chapter 7 of this book discusses the TV cable services.

Signal

Signal includes Lotus's radio modem and the software which supports it. Signal is aptly named and beautifully packaged. The documentation is thorough, clear, and impressive. The radio modem downloads quotes in real time on up to 20,000 stocks, options, and futures. It has sufficient on-board RAM to track 250 issues at a time. (If you want to track a different set of 250 stocks, you must erase the existing set and then wait a few minutes for the ticker to update the quotes on the new collection of 250.) High and low price alarms can be set on any stock. A uniquely attractive feature of Signal is the off-line alarm. If you are using your PC for some other purpose, such as word processing, the modem will continue to watch over your stocks. If one suddenly heads south, the modem will beep. You can then reload the Signal program, examine the report screen, and discover precisely which stock is in trouble.

Signal has changed, since its previous incarnation as Dataspeed's Modio, in at least two respects which are quickly evident: price and software. The price is somewhat higher; the software is somewhat more promising.

Consider software first. Dataspeed used to offer for free a rickety little bridge program to download quotes from the modem into Lotus 1-2-3. Lotus has so completely automated this process that the transfer of quotes into the spreadsheet can be accomplished almost instantaneously. If you own Lotus 1-2-3 or Symphony, the practical benefit is as follows. You can set up a portfolio management worksheet for your stocks using the spreadsheet and then, from within Lotus 1-2-3, update your portfolio constantly by pulling in fresh quotes from the modem's RAM. The spreadsheet, since it is a spreadsheet, can automatically take care of expansions (100 shares $\times$ 23.88 per share = $2388 current value), calculate percentage gains and losses, and create totals. Instead of watching the simple tabulation of quotes provided by the basic Signal package, you can watch a Lotus worksheet in which your complete portfolio is kept up to date in real time.

It is up to you to configure the spreadsheet as a portfolio manager and to write macros to repeatedly scan the modem for fresh quotes. Some sample worksheets are included with the program to accomplish all this. When I reviewed Signal, the worksheets did not interact with the radio modem as the documentation insisted they should. I phoned the Signal technical support number for help, and they confirmed that the sample portfolio manager did not work and, in their view at least, could not be made to work. "Just write one of your own," they suggested. "It's easier." It is easy to create a simple portfolio monitor, but the promised performance of the sample worksheet went beyond that. It was supposed to have kept track of both realized and unrealized capital gains. It was probably just an isolated macro problem, and it may have been worked out by the time you read this. But check.

If you are a financial professional and/or don't wish to devote time to spreadsheet programming for your Signal—or if you do not own Lotus 1-2-3 or Symphony—I suggest you look into the Window on Wall Street package from Bristol Financial Systems. It is a serious multiple portfolio manager that includes a historical price-volume database and a good stock-charting facility. It is wholly menu driven and runs right out of the box on FM quotes from Signal. It was originally developed for the old Modio, so the bugs are out.

The initial Signal package of hardware and software costs $595. It will cost $100 a month in fees to Lotus to keep it running. In addition, because it conveys only real-time quotes, you must pay exchange fees to whichever exchange is the source of the data. For individual investors these fees are not excessive ($7.50 per month for the NYSE, for example). Professionals pay more ($68 per month for the NYSE), as they would with every other quote carrier. Thus there is a minimum maintenance fee of $105 to $125 per month for individual investors, depending on the choice of exchanges.

Radio Exchange

This product seems to be a better value. The fully expanded version of the modem, with software and cabling included, costs about $200 less than Signal initially, and the monthly subscription fees are substantially lower. It keeps watch over 78 more stocks and futures at any given moment and offers more than just quotes, including corporate news items on specific companies, weather (if you are a commodities player), and even sports scores.

The software provides the standard tabulation of tickers, ticks, last prices, change since yesterday, high, low, close, bid and asked, and volume. It also calculates TRIN. You can choose from a menu in order to replace this basic tabulation screen with a valuation screen for your portfolio. It displays percentage and absolute gains and losses for individual issues and for the whole portfolio and updates these computed values as fresh quotes come in. Note that this portfolio monitor is inherent in the basic Telemet software—you need not move data into a spreadsheet to display the data.

If you do want to move the quotes into another program environment, you can download a data interchange format (DIF) file of current quotes and subsequently upload it into a spreadsheet or database manager. I have tested this feature by transferring quotes into Lotus 1-2-3, which is a DIF-compatible program. Within the spreadsheet I set up a quote accumulator. It is run once a day to stack up daily closing price and volume data for later charting and analysis. The quote accumulator is conceived as warehouse and forklift truck for cheap price and volume data on the 500-odd high-technology stocks we monitor as an investment advisory service. (I mentioned the notion of luxuriating in low-cost data. From a dial-up service, the closing high, low, close, and volume data on 500 stocks every day can range from $300 to $700 per month. Via Telemet it costs $20 per month.)

You can directly transfer Radio Exchange quotes to any DIF-compatible spreadsheet or DBMS. The transfer is less facile than Signal's instantaneous link to Lotus 1-2-3, but Telemet's DIF compatibility gives you alternative places to go with the data if you don't own Lotus 1-2-3 or Symphony.

Note that the DIF transfer is a one-way street. You cannot shift a list of tickers you want to monitor from, say, a database program into the Radio Exchange's memory. Such a list would have to be printed out and then keyed back in. Signal, in contrast, will let you move tickers from a Lotus spreadsheet back into Signal's RAM.

You can accumulate 30 days of data within the Telemet software, and a charting facility for the month's accumulated price-volume data is also provided as a menu item. If you find it useful to chart intraday index, stock, future, or option price movements, it will do that too.

The basic subscription fee is $25 per month for all exchanges. This entitles you to 15-minute delayed quotes. If you want real-time quotes, Telemet typically charges $10 per month plus an exchange fee. For NYSE and American Stock Exchange (AMEX) quotes in real time, this works out to about $48 per month for individual investors.

For my firm's purposes, I have found that the 15-minute delayed quotes are timely enough—and we often track options on OTC issues, which are notoriously slippery. If you subscribe to Telemet's service for three years, you get rate protection over that period and the monthly fee drops to $20 per month, or about $1 per trading day. Radio Exchange's RAM keeps watching your stocks while you are using your computer for something else, but unlike Signal, it will not issue an audible alarm on preset trigger prices. You must remember to boot the program at regular intervals to check for any alarms, which appear as flashing bars across the tabulation of stocks.

To solve this problem, Telemet offers—as a dealer—the excellent DesqView windowing software. When Personal Gains runs under DesqView, you can leave the whole FM system, hardware and software, up and running while you use the computer for other things. Suppose, for example, you are writing a letter with a word processing program. If you are suddenly seized with a need to know how your stocks or options are doing, you can pop open a window on-screen, right in the middle of your letter, and peer in on your portfolio. When you've satisfied your curiosity, you can close the window and go back to work. In the event a stock touches a preset trigger price, DesqView will "break through" whatever application software you may be running and alert you to the problem.

On balance, the Telemet Radio Exchange package strikes me as a more sensible investment than Signal.

Charting

The most direct means of charting FM data are provided by the Window on Wall Street program for Signal and by the Personal Gains software supplied for the Radio Exchange. The Personal Gains software will not plot more than a month's data. However, price data accumulated in spreadsheets can be plotted by several major charting packages if the data are correctly configured. MetaStock will chart spreadsheet data without much ado. Savant can chart spreadsheet data, but the data must be brought in via a translation program, the Technical Databridge. The Databridge costs $145. The Anidata Market Analyst, the precursor of the technical component of Interactive's Active Investor, could bring in data via a DIF upload. This feature was eliminated in the Active Investor version, unfortunately. If you have the old Anidata program, however, you can probably chart FM data. A preliminary copy of the current Dow Jones Market Analyzer Plus could upload DIF files. If the production version retains this capability, it may operate on FM data.

There is at this moment a clear market niche for a little database program coupled with some utilities to accumulate FM data for charting. Until somebody markets one, the most cost-efficient course is probably to download from Radio Exchange into a spreadsheet file and then plot the spreadsheet with MetaStock. See Chapter 20 for a free FM quote accumulator program for Lotus 1-2-3 users.

The Bottom Line

There are now two low-cost quote feeds accessible to individual and professional investors. One is FM, particularly as marketed by Telemet America. The other is via cable TV link to your computer. You should switch to either cable or FM, rather than continue to dial for price-volume data, when your total invoices from a dial-up database service touch $20 per month for quotes. By switching, you can cap these charges at $20 per month and gain access to an enormous reservoir of additional data at no additional charge. Bear in mind that the cost of accumulating broadcast data on a thousand stocks is the same as the cost for a single stock. There are no usage charges.

Manufacturers, List Prices, and Specifications

SIGNAL
Lotus Information Network Corp.
1900 South Norfolk Street
San Mateo, CA 94403
800-S-MARKET

List price: $595 for radio modem and support software. Follows 250 issues at once. Subscriptions to network and exchange fees are additional and as appropriate.

Requires: 320 RAM, at least one drive, serial card, monochrome monitor, DOS 2.0 or higher. Graphics card and color optional. Antenna. Lotus 1-2-3 or Symphony recommended if you want to take fullest advantage of the system's portfolio-monitoring capability. Runs on PC, XT, AT, or compatibles. AT-style asynch port connector will not accept a Signal connector, and a cable adapter is required. These smaller asynch ports are on the AT and the Compaq Deskpros.

RADIO EXCHANGE
Telemet America, Inc.
515 Wythe Street
Alexandria, VA 22314
800-368-2078; in Virginia
call 703-548-2042

List price: $199 for basic unit (follows 72 issues) or $279 for upgraded unit (follows 328 issues). Personal Gains software, $89. Subscriptions and exchange fees additional and as appropriate. Portfolio monitor and some charting capability are inherent in Personal Gains.

Requires: 128K RAM, serial card, monochrome. FM antenna. Same wide-style asynch connector as Signal; may require a cable adaptor for AT or Deskpro, with their new smaller asynch ports connectors.

WINDOW ON WALL STREET
Bristol Financial Systems
1010 Washington Blvd.
Stamford, CT 06901
203-356-9490

List price: $495 for basic program. Includes charting, scanning, and a historical database on 500 stocks. Package for multiple portfolio management additional.

Requires: Signal hardware, two drives, 384K RAM, graphics card for stock charts (preferably Hercules), serial port.

7
TV Cable: Quotes and News Direct to Your Computer

TV cable services transmit financial data to your microcomputer. Two of these services are now available. Your television set is not directly involved or affected by the installation of a computer service, except that it will share with the computer its access to the cable.

The advantages of cable links are similar but not identical to those offered by FM. You pay only a low fixed monthly charge for unlimited access to the data provided by the service. Your computer can monitor the market continuously, in real time if you wish. The advantage over FM is assured high-quality reception. The disadvantage is the ongoing monthly charge associated with the cable itself. If you already have cable and analyze stocks at home, cable is the better choice. If you live in a rural area beyond the range of metropolitan FM transmitters, cable should work best. If you don't want cable television or if you do your work in an office, you may prefer FM. If you work downtown, in most cities—Manhattan is an important exception—you may not be able to get cable installed. An FM link costs more up front because you must purchase a modem, but once you've paid for it, that's that.

Cable charges are billed monthly as long as you use the service. Installation of a cable may cost about $50. Monthly cable charges may range between $10 and $30 per month, and the cost of a cable quote service (about $20 a month at a minimum) will be charged as a premium over and above the basic cable service.

The Two Services

Two companies currently offer financial information via television cable. They are Data Broadcasting Corporation and X*Press Information Services. Both are cooperative ventures. Data Broadcasting transmits via the blanking interval of the Financial News Network (FNN). Their data source is Merrill Lynch. Merrill Lynch Investments owns a substantial percentage of the company. The service is called MarketWatch.

The X*Press Information Service is a partnership of Telecrafter, TeleCommunications, Inc., and McGraw-Hill. (It should not be confused with the very similarly named Investor's Xpress, which is the on-line brokerage service offered by Fidelity.)

The more realistically priced TV cable service is X*Press. The premium is $19.95 a month for stock quotes only. Data Broadcasting premiums range from $36 a month for a basic, closing-price quote service to $130 a month for a professional's continuous real-time stream of both options and stock quotes.

The Technologies

There are two different transmission technologies. Data Broadcasting uses part of the waveform of your cable TV signal, the vertical blanking interval, to convey stock quotes. These data are not visible on the TV, though the vertical blanking interval is familiar to viewers as that massive black bar that encroaches on the screen when the picture rolls. Data Broadcasting can load information into the blanking interval at 100,000 bps. This far exceeds the 300-, 1200-, and 2400-bps rates at which data can be moved over a telephone wire. The technology thus makes information available to the computer at a very high rate. Unfortunately, the computer can ingest information only so fast, and so there is a bottleneck on the receiving end. In other words, don't expect to jump from 300 baud to 100,000 bps when you shift from a dial-up service to cable.

To get the data into your computer, the TV cable is split to form a Y at your end. At the end of one arm of the Y goes your TV, and at the end of the other arm goes your computer. At the computer, a Data-Receiver box captures the incoming data. The data are then fed into your computer via the asynch port. The computer is used to display a portfolio monitor screen. Depending on the type of installation, you may or may not be able to use both the TV and the computer simultaneously. If you want to use both, make this clear to the installer.

The X*Press service does not "piggyback" on a video signal. Data are transmitted over the cable as a radio frequency signal in a segment of the frequency spectrum distinct from that used for TV signals. A decoder box detects the signal and feeds it into the computer via an asynch port. The transmission rate is 9600 baud. This is about as fast as a microcomputer system can communicate without buffering. TV sets connected to the cable are not affected in any way.

Hardware and Software

X*Press is being marketed via cable operators, who will be prepared to help you with installation. The decoder box costs nothing. If you try the service and don't like it, you thus have no commitment to hardware— they'll simply take the box back. The DataReceiver is obtained, along with the software which supports it, from Data Broadcasting. The company asks for a $50 deposit on the hardware, which is fully refundable upon its return in good condition.

The operating software for MarketWatch or X*Press is free. If you want to preview the MarketWatch system on your PC without actually installing it, you can obtain for $10 a demo disk which simulates the system. A demo disk is also to be made available for X*Press, although it was not ready at the time of this writing.

The MarketWatch Display

The MarketWatch screen is divided by ruled borders into five panels of information. The main panel, which occupies the top half of the screen, is configured as a tabulation of your portfolio. It displays tickers, along with the corresponding high, low, close, change since yesterday, bid and asked, and volume data. You can set alarms for high, low, and volume.

Your computer's memory is used to retain quotes. The DataReceiver does not do this with on-board memory as the FM systems do. The number of stocks and options you can watch is a function of the memory capacity of your computer. With 512K, you can follow 20,000 issues; with 384K, 10,000 issues; with 256K, 3000 issues.

At this stage in the development of the technology, you must essentially dedicate your computer to the monitoring task. The computer cannot both watch your stocks and run an applications program (e.g., a word processor or spreadsheet) at the same time.

A multitasking software package such as DesqView or DoubleDOS cannot free the computer to do other things while it watches your stocks "in the background." If you turn MarketWatch off to do something else with the computer and then turn it back on, you can be back up to speed in six and a half minutes. This is how long it takes the quote stream to loop during market hours. After hours it may take as little as two minutes. During this period, the system is refreshing its memory on the whole market—perhaps 8000 stocks in all. Contrast this with FM systems using outboard memory. They may watch just 300 to 400 stocks at any one time, but they'll do it in the background while you do other work.

The main portfolio display panel of MarketWatch can be used to present a continuously updated valuation of stocks on display, calculated on the basis of the numbers-of-shares data which have been entered by the user. A summary screen doubles the number of stocks which can be displayed in this panel and presents the ticker, the last price, the change, and the volume for each stock.

The lower half of the screen is divided into three main panels. One presents the NYSE ticker on six selected stocks. An adjacent panel presents the ticker on the most recently traded stocks in the monitored portfolio. A third panel presents portfolio valuation information, including initial value, appreciation, commissions, and current value.

Finally, a thin panel extending the full width of the bottom of the screen presents menu options. These are primarily triggered by function keys. Single stock or option quotes are also displayed, on retrieval, in this panel.

Statistical summaries are accessible indicating the 10 most active stocks, the 10 biggest percentage gainers, and the 10 biggest percentage losers for the exchanges, for the NASDAQ national market system, and for the Options Price Reporting Authority (OPRA). Subscribers with access to continuous data can watch these listings being refreshed every two minutes throughout the day. Indexes which can be monitored are recalculated every 1 to 10 minutes, depending on market activity. There are 19 indexes altogether.

The presentation is compact and puts a maximum of information on the screen all at once. Financial news is updated hourly, and this text material can be displayed in one of the panels. This is primarily a quote-monitoring system, however. Since the signal "rides" the FNN television signal, there is a good chance that you will be watching FNN for your news rather than reading it off the screen of your computer.

MarketWatch Services and Pricing

The MarketWatch service is actually a rather complex menu of services, with different prices for annual versus monthly subscribers, for different tiers of service, and, as is customary, for professionals and individuals.

The least costly service is called DBC/Summary. It delivers essentially the information you might use a dial-up database to obtain, namely, the day's closing quotes. It does not provide continuous monitoring. If you light up the system any time in the course of the trading day, you will read on the display screen the previous day's close. There is no limit to the number of issues whose closings you can look at for the fixed monthly charge to annual subscribers of $36. However, the service is not competitively priced. Newspapers are cheaper, and you can get continuous computer monitoring through the day from two other sources for about $20 per month.

For continuous quotes, annual subscribers pay $44 per month for stocks only and $60 a month for stocks plus options. These quotes are delayed 20 minutes. For real-time quotes, add a surcharge of $26 a month for stocks and $29 for stocks plus options. This brings us up to $89 per month for real-time stock and option quotes, total, before monthly cable charges. Professionals using real-time quotes must lay out another $20.

Prices change. Cable is a new field, and the services are still feeling their way into their markets. The DBC/MarketWatch is the most buttoned-down of the services in this field. You can receive the service anywhere you can get FNN, which is essentially nationwide. The software is finished and is very well designed. It provides an essential feature in my view: It enables you to download and, if you wish, to accumulate price-volume data in any DIF-compatible program, e.g., Lotus 1-2-3. This means you can accumulate historical data for subsequent charting, create indexes and mock portfolios to monitor group performance, and generally make the most of your investment in the computer. MarketWatch provides for the capture and downloading of quotes off the screen as a menu item. This is a big plus and a significant advantage that is not offered by the competitive service, X*Press.

Incidentally, since ticker data can be downloaded, it is possible to create a system to allocate the trade-by-trade data off the continuous ticker. Such a system would accumulate large institutional trades in one stack and smaller trades in another stack, noting the appropriate changes in price accompanying each trade. At the end of a week you could see whether the institutions were net buyers or sellers of a particular stock and compare this information with similar news about what the "little guys" had been doing with it. This is one of several useful things you can do with a continuous stream of market data. MarketWatch's downloading facility should make it a relatively easy problem to attack.

X*Press

This service is virtually brand new. It was tested initially in Hawaii and Colorado and was introduced in the San Francisco Bay area in late spring, 1986. The service will become more widely available as more cities are added, expanding generally from west to east, with early availability in major financial markets.

X*Press offers two outstanding features: its price, which is a $19.95 premium over the base cable charge, and its power to deliver financial and business news. It could in fact be characterized as a news wire and news-scanning service, with a quote stream included as an adjunct feature. You can follow a collection of 128 stocks. No options or futures are quoted. The quotes are continuous, but no real-time service is available. The quote stream is delayed for 15 minutes. The portfolio-monitoring software, which is called the Standard & Poor's Market Monitor, displays the usual tabulation of tickers, high, low, last, bid and asked, change, and volume. The ticks are also displayed. There is no valuation facility.

The Torrent of News

In the course of a single day, X*Press can pump through your computer over 100 million words of news in more than 3000 different categories. News wires from 26 different services are fed into the system. In addition to the regular news, the system has access to valuable sources of business, financial, and trade press reports.

In a few hours all this news fills up the computer's memory completely, spills over, and vanishes into oblivion. New news pushes out the old news. No news can be captured on disk; it can only be temporarily buffered in memory until the buffer gets full.

Given a key word, X*Press software will scout through all the news currently in memory and retrieve for display those stories in which the key word appears. If you are using this facility to scout for news of a particular stock, say Merck, you can enter "Merck" as the key word. Anything on Merck in the trade, financial, and business news wires will be displayed for you to read with the key word highlighted. In this way you can stay about a day ahead of the printed word on your favorite stocks.

Since old news is lost from memory in the course of the day, it is a good idea to restrict the appetite of the system's memory to business and financial data. The program provides for selective news monitoring. If you monitor only a few of the news wires, the computer's memory will be slower to fill, and it should be necessary to do a key word search only each four to five hours. Clearly the system cannot be left unattended all day. It would be better if the day's accumulation of key-word-related news—or at least the daily overflow—could be sponged into a floppy disk for review at the day's end. There are evidently legal reasons why capturing to disk would be unacceptable to the news wires.

Some of the news wire services accessible via X*Press are as follows: the PR news wire, Business Wire, Business Week, Associated Press, United Press International, McGraw-Hill, SportsTicker, Zephyr Weather Service, Electronic Media Services, Washington Post Writers Group, Copley News Service, TV Data, TASS, Sinhua (PRC), OPECNA (oil-exporting countries), Kyodo (Japan), Canadian Press, NOTIMEX (Mexico), DPA (West Germany), AFP (France), and CNA (Republic of China, Taiwan). Some of these services may be offered at a premium.

Third-Party Charting Software
for X*Press

The neatest fit at this point is a program from TSA Proforma, Inc., in Toronto: the Pro Monitor. It has been marketed in the United States under the name MultiQuote by Bonneville Telecommunications for use in conjunction with their FM network. It also works in conjunction with a satellite downlink quote service from CQI Comstock. The program is thus a proven one. The details of the link to X*Press have already been worked out for you. X*Press cannot, however, tap the full capacity of the program.

The program maintains a portfolio-monitoring screen listing 24 stocks per page. As many as 15 pages can be included in one collection. There is no wait if you decide to change collections; the system can watch over 30,000 issues in the background if you have the proper quote feed and sufficient memory. TSA says that 512K will do it. A 256K system is the minimum required. By watching the whole market, the system can note and report on the big percentage gainers and losers throughout the trading day, and it does so. You can set high, low, and volume alerts on any issue. There is no facility to evaluate portfolios. However, the Pro Monitor will pass data directly into Lotus 1-2-3, where you can construct a true portfolio manager very easily.

The system offers both intraday and historical charting. For intraday charts, it puts as many as 15 charts on-screen at once and keeps them up to date in real time. Less powerful systems may chart at intervals of every few minutes. A Pro Monitor chart responds to every trade the instant it is reported. With X*Press, this will be 15 minutes after the fact, but this would not bother me much.

For historical charts, the system provides a dial-up communication program for data retrieval from Dow Jones or other databases. Once you have built the file of historical price-volume data, you can keep it up to date with the daily closes from X*Press. The program automatically accumulates daily data, a key feature that is missing from most FM- and cable-based software. The default period for a chart is 150 days, but you can reset it for as long a period as you choose. Charting features are minimal but do include simple, weighted, and exponential moving averages. It will not multitask, meaning you must dedicate your computer to it. However, if you shut it off to do other things, it will recover its image of the market after a 25-minute loop of the X*Press service.

The program will display a ticker tape "crawl." If you have two monitors, you can display charts on one and data on the other. Pro Monitor costs $495. It can monitor many more data than X*Press can deliver, since X*Press will report only on stocks—no options or commodities. It is, however, a realized product you can plug in and use right away.

Other software is in prospect. A link to MetaStock is one possibility, though it is just that at this writing. McGraw-Hill cable has arranged for software for Apple and Commodore links as well as for IBM and its compatibles. Ashton-Tate will offer a link to its Framework software.

Finally, if you don't mind taking a do-it-yourself approach, you can try using Borland's Sidekick to capture screens from X*Press. Having stored one in a file, it will probably be necessary to write a BASIC program to reconfigure the data for your choice of charting packages. I am told this has been done successfully but have no idea how to do it myself. One hopes such a BASIC utility will become available in the public domain or as a product. It would solve a big problem with X*Press, which is precisely that of downloading data: It won't do it unaided.

Choosing between the Services

The choice should take FM into account. I would rank the four services in the following order: (1) FM from Telemet America, (2) X*Press cable from X*Press Information Services, (3) DBC/MarketWatch from Data Broadcasting Corporation, and (4) Signal from Lotus Broadcasting Corporation.

The first two choices are similarly priced services. Telemet provides more quote data, in real time if you want it, including stocks, options, commodities, and indexes. It charts, and it's easy to capture data and export the data to a spreadsheet. X*Press provides a more limited quote feed (stock data only). The news resource is tremendous, and the "reception" is bound to be perfect. But X*Press doesn't chart, and you can't extract the data from the system. You can solve both problems with third-party software or by developing special expertise, but this elevates the real price of the service.

Data Broadcasting has a complete quote stream. I think most brokers would prefer the 8000-stock monitoring capacity—and the instant access to any quote that comes with it. Downtown brokers (other than downtown Manhattan brokers) may not be able to get the service, however. MarketWatch delivers quotes in real time, and they have made it easy to capture and file the data. You will need third-party software to draw charts, and the quote stream is expensive. Signal is fourth because it costs a great deal of money and delivers no special capabilities. If one accepts for the sake of discussion a choice between a high-priced cable service and a high-priced FM service, cable seems more attractive—no reception problems. If price matters, and it does, then the choice lies between a low-priced FM service and a low-priced cable service, i.e., between Telemet and X*Press. Telemet offers most investors enough in the way of additional quote services and capabilities to offset the disadvantage of occasional reception problems.

It wouldn't hurt to get both Telemet and X*Press, actually. Between the news access and scanning capabilities of X*Press and the quote delivery capability of Telemet, you can cover the market. Moreover, you can use one to back up the other if either system has problems. You can have the pair for as little as $50 a month, plus installation and modem costs, and this compares quite favorably with the cost of just one of the other two competitive services.

Services, List Prices, and Specifications

DBC/MARKETWATCH SERVICES
Data Broadcasting Corporation
1951 Kidwell Drive
Vienna, VA 22180
703-790-3570

List price: Services range upward from $36 a month as a premium on existing cable service. Cable service itself and installation are additional expenses. There is no charge other than a refundable $50 deposit for the hardware, which is called a DBC/DataReceiver. Software is included at no extra charge. A software demonstration disk is available for $10.

Requires: IBM PC or compatible, at least 256K RAM, two floppy drives or a single floppy drive plus a hard disk, an asynchronous port, and a monochrome or color display. No graphics card or capability is required.

X*PRESS INFORMATION SERVICES
Marketed through local cable companies

List price: $19.95 suggested monthly premium, over and above cable fees and installation. No charge for hardware or software. A demonstration disk is available.

Requires: For IBM PC or compatible, 256K RAM, MS-DOS 2.0 or higher, an asynchronous port; for Apple IIc and IIe, 128K RAM; X*Press Apple Software Module; for Commodore 64, 128, and Plus 4, 64K RAM, X*Press Commodore cartridge.

PRO MONITOR
TSA Proforma Inc.
67 Mowat, Suite 239
Toronto, Ontario
Canada M6K 3E3
416-532-3356

List price: $495

Requires: IBM PC or compatible, 256K RAM, two drives, asynchronous port, one or two monitors. Charts, monitors, and accumulates X*Press data. Provides dial-up access to historical databases.

PART 3

Technical Analysis of Stocks by Computer

8

Technical Analysis Programs

What These Programs Accomplish

Technical analysis programs do four things:

1. They retrieve stock price and volume data via the telephone from commercial databases such as Dow Jones, Warner, Compuserve, and Hale.

2. They store the data in organized files on floppy or hard disks for quick recall and easy updating.

3. They use the data to draw basic stock charts on the computer's monitor screen.

4. They can process the charts in many different ways at the command of the operator. The end result is purely visual information on the screen—lines, curves, rays, bands, and points. All this information can also be presented in numerical form, but the visual display is what people buy these programs for.

Chart processing is the meat of any technical analysis program. Visualize a basic chart displayed on the screen. Its vertical axis, rising along the left-hand side of the screen, represents price. The horizontal axis represents time and is marked off in days. A typical chart might display 200 days of closing prices, initially as a scattering of dots across the screen.

At the command of the operator, the program connects the dots to create a jagged line across the screen. To smooth the line, the operator may request the application of an exponential moving average. He or she may or may not know or care how an exponential moving average is calculated. It doesn't matter. Calculation is a push-button project, the computer's job. Calculate it does, and the jagged line disappears. In its place appears a thin, smooth line that tracks through gentle curves from one side of the screen to the other. The line makes it apparent that the price of the stock has been steadily snaking upward for six months but has recently turned down. Does the downturn matter?

The operator quickly requests two more moving-average calculations. One is called a 10-day moving average and the other a 30-day moving average. The curves appear on the screen superimposed on the existing curve. The 10-day curve arcs high above the 30-day curve, turns, and dives. Near the right-hand side of the screen, the 10-day curve crosses through the 30-day curve and keeps on plunging. The operator acknowledges crossover as a commonly accepted sell signal, but he or she is unconvinced. The operator knows that often enough a stock rises from a sell signal and drops from a buy signal, and so the operator decides to try an envelope.

An envelope is created by drawing identically shaped lines, one above and one below the jagged representation of daily trading. The lines are just barely pricked by the historical upper and lower extremes of price.

The resulting figure (it appears instantly) looks rather like a fat worm arranged across the screen. As long as the stock rises and falls within the envelope (within the body of the worm), it is thought to be trading within its "normal" range. However, if an excursion in price breaks outside the envelope, something novel is evidently happening. In this example, the stock's decline is still well within the trading envelope and the sell signal can be regarded as spurious.

These are just a few of the techniques which the computer can accommodate in technical analysis. (A typical technical analysis program may have a repertoire of 100 different commands.) To support this work the computer becomes a drawing machine, driven by (otherwise laborious) calculations that are all carried out offstage, instantly. If you dislike arithmetic, you will find this process enormously appealing. All the presentations of results and manipulations of data are pictorial.

The advantages of computerized chart analysis over hand analysis of printed charts are clear. The charts are updated instantly and automatically. You need not wait for charts to be printed and mailed to your attention, nor do you have to maintain them by hand. The range of techniques you can use with the computer is not in any way limited (as it is with hand plotting) by the volume of work involved. You can evaluate a conclusion on its own merits without being unconsciously swayed by the sheer weight of your own work in achieving the results. The computer takes the burden onto itself.

You can follow more stocks and test many more techniques. You can experiment to determine which techniques are most appropriate to which stock instead of applying a single technique wholesale to every stock you track.

If you are an experienced technical analyst and trader, the advantages of computerization are probably obvious by now; if you are an investor, you may be looking closely at technical analysis for the first time. Let's back up and review the technique from an investor's point of view.

Should an Investor Try Technical Analysis?

Perhaps three of four software packages now offered for computerized investors are specifically designed to support technical analysis. Technical analysts are sometimes characterized as chartists. They collect and plot two types of data primarily, stock prices and trading volume. From patterns which can be discerned in or superimposed on the charts, the technical analyst is able to extract buy and sell signals.

Technical analysis has been almost exclusively the province of stock traders, that is, people who are interested in profiting from short-term swings in stock prices. To succeed at stock trading, you must do well enough to offset the high commission costs associated with rolling in and out of the market; in addition, in most cases you must realize trading profits large enough to offset the damaging tax consequences of taking short-term capital gains. It probably understates the case to suggest that more traders fail than succeed in meeting these high profitability requirements by trading stocks. Traders tend to gravitate into trading options contracts, where the dollar consequences of a profitable decision can be hugely magnified and the consequences of an unprofitable decision can be kept within bounds preset by the trader.

Traders will not be reading this book for a treatise on the value of technical analysis. They know all about it. The value of technical analysis to investors is less obvious. Basically, it is a method of controlling losses and timing purchases. It is practical for investors to use technical analysis because the computer has brought the subject down to earth. The computer is a marvelous teaching machine, and you will find that it makes the basics of technical analysis very easy to learn and use.

̇ining When to Cut
̇osses

̇ ̇ ̇rs, who are by definition looking for income and/or long-term capital appreciation, rarely bother with charts. They assume that the charts of "good stocks" will trend up over the long term. This fundamentally optimistic approach has certainly been sustained by the growth of the economy during the twentieth century. Within this span, of course, there have occurred some intermediate and short-term market "corrections" during which some investors lost most of their money.

Here is a brief parable about one hypothetical investor: The market started down. He did nothing. The market kept on going down. He reminded himself that he was in the market for the long pull. The market plummeted. He remarked that even if he were not in the market for the long pull, it would be too late now to do anything about the situation. The market sank into the 500s. In an effort to salvage what little value remained in his stocks, the investor sold out and took his losses. The market turned up.

Another hypothetical investor was cool enough to ride out the slump, which lasted over a year. She eventually recovered the entire value of her assets. However, there were steps she might have taken to protect their value—and to keep that value accessible in an emergency—throughout the slump.

Down markets are a dreary old story. The thing to notice anew is how very slippery the market is. At what point should you call a halt? How high is too high? How far down is too far down? Technical analysis provides numerical answers to these questions. If the XYZ Corporation is trading at $120 and takes a nosedive, you can consult your computer and prepare to sell at a price of $112.875 exactly. And do it.

I think you will fare a little better using stop-loss values generated with the help of a technical analysis program than you will with arbitrarily set stop-loss values; e.g., sell on any 15 percent decline. The reason is that most traders will make their exit at one of the technically favored sell points. Their sales put a great deal of stock on the market suddenly, and the stock price drops in consequence—better to exit with them than after them.

Timing Your Stock Purchases and Sales

Technically informed traders vote their opinions by buying and selling stocks. The value of the computer is that it lets you guess fairly accurately what most of the traders are thinking—before they start moving their money. You need not agree with the tenets of technical analysis to profit by it. It is sufficient to determine how the technical analysts, as a voting bloc, are likely to move their money.

Viewed in this light, technical analysis makes sense. It creates a frame of reference around the performance of a stock. Within this frame you can draw some lines that limit your losses and define your expected gains. The lines are not arbitrarily set. They approximate the opinion of many stockholders. These stockholders, who happen to be traders, make up what is perhaps the only large, identifiable bloc of like-minded stock market participants. Not a few of them are professional money managers, so this particular body of opinion is very well funded indeed and is therefore compelling.

Technical analysis is equally useful for timing the purchase of investments. Investors rarely try it. They more typically use the power of the computer to identify, on the basis of fundamental balance sheet strengths and apparent growth, a list of 5 or 10 companies that seem to be worth more than their stock prices suggest. (It has been remarked that an investor is a person who wishes to buy a dollar for 75 cents.) Before committing the money to purchase the stocks, however, a computerized investor may wish to display the stocks' charts.

Surprisingly often, it turns out that a fundamentally attractive stock is one which has fallen from favor and is in midpassage, headed straight down. The stock chart will not show you what the stock will do next, of course. It will show you what technically inclined traders think it is likely to do. If the stock is plummeting, you can be assured that they will not lift a finger to stop it. You might as well wait and purchase the stock as cheaply as you can. A scan of the other attractively priced stocks on your list may turn up one that has hit bottom and turned back up. This one would be a better buy, and the traders would, for technical reasons, support your fundamental choice. Chances are, your investment would get a nice launch.

As an investor, you should both buy stocks and sell stocks. The difference between an investor and a trader is one of pacing. If you buy and sell a single stock within a six-month period, you are by definition a trader. If you wait six months and a day, you become an investor. It makes sense for both investors and traders to take into consideration *all* the information available about a given stock. The computer makes it easy. Traders can run fundamental analyses to find undervalued, overvalued, and volatile stocks to play. Investors can run technical analyses to take technical opinion into account. In summary, the computer is breaking down some of the old, neat distinctions about market participants. Given a computer, anybody can do anything, and you are perfectly free to be a trader in one stock and an investor in another.

An Overview of the Top Programs

Major technical analytical packages are available from Savant, Interactive Data, Summa, Telescan, and Dow Jones, among others. Two of these programs, those from Savant and Interactive, are offered as components of integrated investment packages. Integrated packages include a portfolio manager, a technical analysis module, a fundamental analysis module, and a communications program to bring in data. If you want a complete investment system and regard technical analysis as just one aspect of your work, you may favor an integrated package. If technical analysis is your chief concern, any of these programs can be taken into consideration.

Which is best is an open question. Any ranking depends heavily on the way you happen to prefer to work. In evaluating the programs, you might start with a list of techniques and indicators you use now and then try to identify a program which offers that particular combination of indicators. I think you will find, however, that you will expand and change your range of techniques as you computerize, and so your current methodology is not a complete guide to automation.

All the programs will run the set-piece procedures of technical analysis. They all calculate and display moving averages, oscillators, volume allocation indicators, and relative strength. Speed resistance lines and trend lines tend to be handled somewhat differently by different programs, but all these programs will draw them. Differences between the major programs are pointed out in the detailed reviews in the following chapters.

What Technical Analysts Actually Do

Readers who have not been exposed to technical analysis should bear in mind a few basics about what technical analysts do.

They note the closing price of a given stock, as everyone else does, but having noted it, they have just begun their work. They hope to pin an arrow on today's number, pointing up or down, to tell them whether tomorrow's number will be higher or lower. A physicist might call this converting a scalar value, which has magnitude only, into a vector value, which has both magnitude and direction.

The direction of the price of the stock can only be guessed. Technical analysts believe the best basis for the guess will be found in the history of the price of the stock. If the stock went up today and yesterday and the day before that, chances are that it will go up again tomorrow.

Common sense suggests that this is not a bad assumption. Probability theory, however, tells us the dice have no memory. The question instantly arises: Are we playing with dice? Is the stock market indeed a random walk?

However you may choose to answer this large question, the point at hand is that technical analysis relies on the notion that what has happened before will probably happen again. This central idea leads to a search for trends and cycles in the history of the price. It is believed that "a trend will continue until it is broken," and that a cycle will, by definition, repeat itself. Any new data—meaning today's price—must be evaluated in terms of the established trend or cycle. If the latest price falls within the range which one would predict by extending the existing trend, fine. Nothing happens. But if the latest price breaks away from the established trend, perhaps a buy or sell decision will be in order.

What we are really doing here is creating a yardstick for measuring the importance of price movement. When a downward price movement exceeds a certain value, we declare that to be enough and sell. When it exceeds a certain value in an upward move, we can declare it a winner and buy. The yardstick is arbitrary, but in my opinion it is better than no yardstick at all. It gives an approximation of what other technically oriented investors and traders are seeing and thinking. This can help because they are so numerous and because they bet in accordance with their opinions.

Technical Analysis as Revealed Truth

Technical analysis is somewhat seductive. It promises a lot for a little. Price and volume data are cheap to bring into your computer. The techniques are easy to pick up and use, and it is assumed that the price of a stock is its whole identity—the last word on what people think of it. If you have studied the price, so the theory goes, you need not trouble yourself digging into a company's earnings, growth rates, balance sheet ratios, and the technology and markets of the products. All this information is already assumed, by the technical analyst, to be distilled into the price.

Price changes are thought to have predictive value. If good news is forthcoming about a stock, the price often rises before the news is widely known. When the good news is finally made formally public, the price often drops as traders take their profits or sell short.

Like most attractive theories, these ideas appeal strongly to common sense. They are, however, rather easy to puncture, and some fundamental analysts take delight in pointing out the evident absurdity of various tenets of technical analysis. In fact, some of it is truly crackpot stuff, and you should be careful not to take it too seriously.

Some of it is fine. Technical analysts smooth and plot price curves. Fundamental analysts smooth and plot earnings growth curves. At this level of useful techniques, there is little basis for condemning or favoring either approach.

It is at the level of technique that your computer operates as well. Theory is *your* department.

The Useful Happenstance

Let us now directly address the problem of making a fortune in the stock market.

The problem is usually approached in three steps: (1) Find a zigzag stock, (2) find an indicator (or set of indicators) that predicts or reliably "confirms" the zig points and zag points, and (3) bet the indicator.

When the indicator zigs and the stock zags, you lose. For this reason, most speculators use multiple indicators. This is supposed to help. I suspect that it does not.

There are quite a few widely recognized types of technical indicators and thousands of variations of them. They are like insects: many and various.

I try to be pragmatic about indicators. It seems to me that there is such a thing as a useful happenstance. If you notice that the descent of a stock happens to coincide with the descent of a raindrop on a windowpane, there is no reason not to bet the raindrop, provided that you are prepared to test the coincidence constantly. When the coincidence fails (as of course it will), you must look for another indicator. There are no good indicators or bad indicators. There are appropriate and inappropriate indicators. The descending raindrop fails when the stock turns up. A more appropriate indicator might then be an outdoor thermometer, assuming that it's spring.

Similarly, if a technical buy or sell indicator happens to work for a particular stock, you might as well use it until it fails.

Many people get into trouble with indicators because they begin to think of the two things they are watching, the indicator and the stock, as somehow mechanically linked. The linkage is largely coincidental. There are no gears and no push rods—and no destiny. Instead, there are luck, shared opinion, and the merest soupçon of fact. Luck, opinions, and facts change. You should be ready to change indicators as well.

This is not to say that trends and cycles in the prices of stocks do not exist. They do. What I am suggesting is this: The trends and cycles are so hopelessly complex that if you and your computer happen to find an indicator that truly reflects the cycle or trend of a particular stock, you should regard your discovery as the luck of the moment. There may or may not be some cause-and-effect relation that ties the movement of the indicator to the movement of the stock. It really doesn't matter as long as the two movements coincide. It's nice while it lasts, but don't expect it to last very long. Seize the moment. Keep testing the indicator. When the indicator and the stock begin to diverge, hit the silk. Liquidate your position. Hunt for another stock and another indicator.

How to Track Down the Winning Indicator

The notion of screening for an "appropriate" indicator is essentially new. It is peculiar to computerized investing or, rather, computerized speculating. Uneasiness about relying on any one indicator has led speculators to check multiple indicators and rely on the majority or consensus of readings. This complicates an already muddy picture. What you want is one indicator—the right one. It takes a computer to find an appropriate indicator. And it takes a microcomputer a long time, thinking, to come up with one—a day or two. By contrast, if you attacked the problem by means of hand calculation, you might emerge with an answer in a few years' time. The answer would be useless because the moment for your indicator would be long past.

The computer can help you identify the appropriate indicators for particular stocks and test their validity as time passes. A few programs are now available that do this. They probably represent the leading edge in the technology of computerized investing. I would not regard any of them as the last word on this subject; they are still evolving. One is an accessory program called the TechniFilter from RTR Software. It works in conjunction with the Dow Jones package or the Savant package. Another is a slightly more limited program offered as a component of the Winning on Wall Street package. These special programs are reviewed along with the other technical analysis software in the following chapters. MicroVest's Profit Optimizer (not reviewed here) may also be one to consider. It costs $495. The company is based in Macomb, Illinois.

All these programs are loosely called *optimizers*. Optimizers are difficult programs to write, and they are not hot sellers, since they appeal chiefly to people who are willing to try something novel. The programs run slowly because the problem is enormous. The usual instant gratification, video game, computer "feel" is not manifest in a program that causes your computer to simply sit and think. Demonstrations tend to be unspectacular, and sales die on the vine. Because of sheer technological difficulty and an untested market for the end product, at least one software company set aside its optimizer project without completing it. They gave up. One should be delighted to learn of this dismal state of the art.

Because the notion of an appropriate indicator is not yet widely understood or fashionable, it has a fair chance of actually working just now, emphasis on the word *chance*. Whether an optimizer will work for you depends as always on your luck. Do not bet the barn on it. Try the usual $300. See how you do. If you are sold on the concept, take a look at Swing Trader, the $1440 optimizer from Pardo Corporation in Evanston, Illinois. It appears to be the most advanced program of this type for microcomputers.

9

Savant: The Cadillac of Technical Analysis

Read This First

Savant offers the most logically organized investment package. For this reason, it is used in this chapter and Chapter 10 to illustrate the general techniques of charting as augmented by computer. Subsequent chapters show how five other major charting programs attack similar investment problems in different ways.

The Car Wars

In an early review of the Savant program in *The New York Times,* the writer remarked that it had impressed him as the Cadillac of technical analysis programs. The analogy stuck. Subsequently, a reviewer for *PC Magazine* wrote that if Savant had created the Cadillac of technical analysis, then its chief competitor at that time, Summa's Winning on Wall Street, must surely represent the Mercedes-Benz. The car metaphors have been adopted by the companies themselves. Savant ads quote the Cadillac review. Summa salespeople do not fail to declare their product's affinity to Mercedes-Benz.

The analogies to expensive automobiles help the salespeople. They suggest excellence and carry an aura of wealth. They also promise something *tangible* you might get by using the software—nuts and bolts. The software itself is a pure abstraction, a few thousand lines of code. It is as difficult to buy as it is to sell.

The way to choose among these programs is to dispense with the car analogies and try to evaluate the software in terms of what it actually does. It does not speed you down the road in comfort and style. It will draw charts, gather news and prices, and file data. If you examine these abilities, you can then judge which software you prefer. Allow some time to study the problem; the initial cost is high, and you will be using the software for years.

Commands versus Menus: What's Easiest to Use?

The supplier of an applications program should promise two things: (1) The program must do its job of accounting, word processing, or whatever, and (2) some provision must be made for teaching the buyer how to use the program. Suppliers of commodity software such as Lotus 1-2-3 and Framework can offer seminars and personal instruction in computer stores. Suppliers of investment software do not have these resources and often sell directly to geographically remote customers. They must make their programs self-explanatory. They may manage to do this with good, clear documentation and tutorial programs. Within the program itself they can provide help screens and instructive menus. Documentation and tutorials are fine. Help screens are fine. Menus raise some problems.

For a beginning user, the menu is a godsend. It shows a numbered list of everything the program can do and lets the user select from that list a number to make it do exactly what he or she wants it to do.

A computer program which displays a menu of the possible courses of action is called a *menu-driven* program.

There is another kind of program, called a *command-driven* program. It assumes that you know what you want the program to do and can direct it with verbal or mnemonic commands—DO this, DO that. The paradigm for a command-driven applications program is Ashton-Tate's dBASE III. As the program comes up, a tiny dot appears on the screen. At the dot, you are supposed to type in a command to tell the program what to do next. No hints, no encouragement, no list of various possibilities. Just the dot. To learn what to do next, refer to the manual.

Command-driven programs are actually faster and in the long run better than menu-driven programs. Menus, which are so helpful in the first few weeks of program operation, begin to get in your way after that. It takes time to display a menu. Usually one menu is not big enough to display the whole repertoire of a program, so you may expect to see main menus that direct you to second-order menus that direct you to third-order menus. For example, from the main menu you might select the communications menu, and from the communications menu you might select Dow Jones. From the Dow Jones menu, you might select news. This progression is characteristic of a nested menu program. It is typical of most software which teaches itself to the user. The patient, deliberate progression from menu to menu may eventually make you frantic. It may make you want to slap the computer.

With a command-driven program, you get where you're going right away. If you want to see a graph of a particular stock, you can have it on the screen in one quick burst of keystrokes.

For a programmer, the first design problem to face is this one: command-driven or menu-driven. The answer is usually a compromise. Savant's is an exceptionally good one. Their main menu is shown in Figure 9.1.

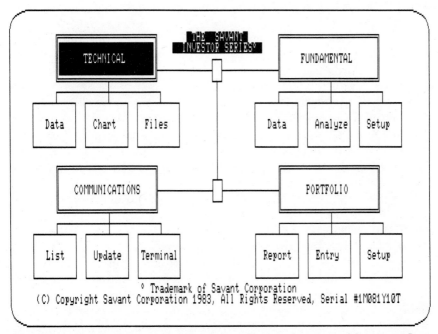

Figure 9.1. The main menu of the Savant system. The logical structure of the menu reflects the overall plan of the program and includes all four elements of a complete investment software system: technical analysis, fundamental analysis, portfolio management, and communications. Three of the four modules are finished. The portfolio manager is still being written.

Menu items are selected by directing the cursor into the appropriate block or by typing in the initials of the desired module. To activate technical charting, for example, type in TC.

What's in a Menu? Everything

Figure 9.1 suggests not only what you get with Savant's Technical Investor, but also what you might look for in any comprehensive investment software package. It is divided into quadrants, each corresponding to one of the major components you need: technical analysis, fundamental analysis, communications, and portfolio management.

There are two ways to operate the menu. The first is with a cursor. Using the cursor keys, you chase an illuminated block (indicated in the figure as black) into the box designating what you want to do. You then press Enter. The main menu disappears, and in its place will appear, for example, a portfolio, a stock chart, or a blank shopping list for retrieving current prices over the phone from Dow Jones or Warner Computer Systems. Note that the organization chart style of the menu saves you the trouble of working your way through a series of nested menus. You can squirt the cursor straight to your objective.

The second way of using the menu is even more direct. You type two-letter commands corresponding to the box designating what you want to do. If you want to draw a chart, for example, you can type in the two letters TC for "technical charting" and go straight into the charting module.

Beyond this big, gateway menu to the program's major modules there are few additional menus. If you are an experienced user, you will operate the program from this point by entering a succession of two-letter commands.

The manual contains 100 pages of two-letter commands. Some of them you may never use. Some of them you will not discover until you happen to think of a technique and look it up to see if the program can support it. More than once I have been pleasantly surprised to find that the Savant programmers anticipated my ideas and wired in commands I needed in order to try them out.

It is not necessary to learn a single command to make the program work. If you wish to see a chart on IBM, for example, you need only enter the charting module from the menu and then type the ticker symbol, i.e., IBM. The program will simply take over and draw the chart.

Savant's reviews have certainly been favorable, but they have been based in large measure on an appreciation of the automated features. Beyond these built-in charting routines, this program really begins to deliver. There is a fine-grained detailing in Savant's programs that I have not seen equaled in other investment packages. If you are trying to feel your way into computers, this program will help you. If you know computers but are trying to feel your way into technical analysis, this program (and its documentation) will help you. After a few weeks, when you have "grown up" into both the computer and the analytical techniques, you will not have outgrown the program. The command-driven features will sustain your work at a high level of professionalism.

The main menu in Figure 9.1 is conceived as a very general, open outline. Within this outline it is susceptible to great change. Command-driven programs can grow in every direction without fundamental re-writes. They are not confined by the specificities of menus. The fact that the program can freely expand is to your advantage. It means you are not locking yourself into a rigid catalog of functions and features when you buy it. When Savant first published this program and its menu, only the left half actually worked. The left half calls the programs you will get if you purchase the Technical Investor. Since then they've been adding modules. The Fundamental Investor is now complete, and the Portfolio Manager is forthcoming.

The program package is not pasted together from separate components after the fact. It has been conceived since the very beginning as an integrated system. You can purchase it as such. You can also purchase the Technical Investor or the Fundamental Investor as stand-alone programs. When sold separately, each analytical program is supplied with the necessary communications utility. In the integrated package, each uses the common communications module.

As a practical matter, integration means that you need update prices over the telephone only once. The updated price information will be accessible to all three main modules: the charting database, the portfolio database, and the fundamental database.

The Charting Machine

Let's skip to the heart of the program. If you enter the command TC at the main menu, the screen will be split into two rectangular frames, as shown in Figure 9.2. Initially the frames are blank. A prompt appears at the lower left-hand corner of the lower frame, requesting a ticker symbol. After you enter it, current charts will be drawn automatically within the frames. The upper frame is a bar chart of price data, typically based on high, low, and closing prices. The lower frame is a bar chart of volume. The frames are designated as *miniscreens*. Figure 9.2 shows two miniscreens, but you can split either or both of them and put three or four separate panels of graphic information on your screen, as shown in Figure 9.3.

The screen in Figure 9.2 can be altered and redisplayed in many different ways in order to meet your wishes. Both the horizontal and the vertical ranges can be changed so that you can scan for, and zoom in on, a time frame of particular interest and attenuate or magnify price, volume, and indicator fluctuations.

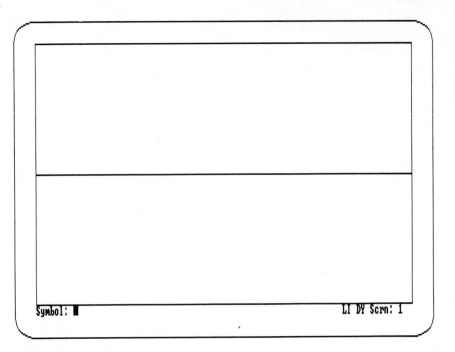

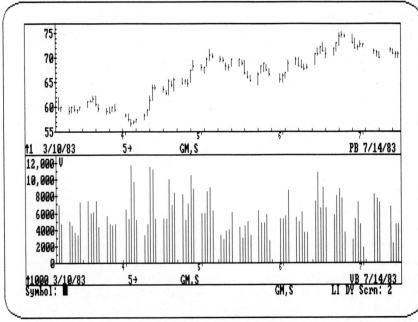

Figure 9.2 (a). The starting point. This is the computer's equivalent of a blank sheet of paper: a monitor screen divided into two blank frames. When you type in the ticker symbol of the stock you want to chart, the system will automatically plot and display price and volume charts such as those shown for General Motors in (b). Beginning and ending dates and ticker symbols label the charts. The scales are set up by the computer with numerical ranges appropriate to the stock it is charting.

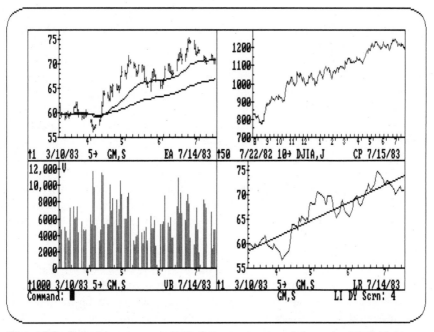

Figure 9.3. Savant's program can divide the screen into two, three, or four separate segments called miniscreens. Each miniscreen can be used for charting independently of the others, much as if it were a separate monitor. This figure shows a range of charts easily accessible to experienced users of the program. A high/low/close bar chart of price action in GM stock is shown in the upper-left miniscreen. Superimposed on it are 100-day and 30-day exponential moving-average plots. The corresponding volume bar chart appears directly below it. On the upper-right miniscreen is a smoothed chart of the Dow Jones industrial average. Below it is a smoothed chart of GM. A least-squares fit to a linear regression line is superimposed on the price swings to demonstrate the main trend of the stock. When you require it, this program is capable of a virtuoso performance.

You can regard a miniscreen as a window you might fill with several years of a stock's price history or (at the push of a function key) replace with just a few weeks of trading. If you are looking at a close-up of, say, a three-month trading interval, you can use commands to rescale the miniscreen to scan back and forth in periscope fashion. If you like, you can keep the entire history of the stock on view in a window in one part of the screen and then use another window to zoom in on a short trading period, such as the last 12 months. In this way you can examine both long-term and short-term trends and cycles simultaneously. Perhaps a particular stock appears to rise and fall in a long-term cycle that usually peaks in anticipation of Christmas retailing strength. You can keep the annual cycle in view while you examine, in another miniscreen, a short-term uptrend in a chart spanning just the late summer of the current year.

You can replot the data against a linear scale or a logarithmic scale. You can adjust the time base to include or exclude weekends and other nontrading days. Once you split the screen into three or four separate miniscreens, you can use any miniscreen for any purpose. (See Figure 9.3 for some examples.) It is as if you had an array of four separate monitors. Use them to plot comparative charts of other stocks or indexes and indicators such as oscillators. You can plot a point and figure chart adjacent to price bar and volume charts for the same stock. Charts of more than one stock can be overlaid on a single screen for comparative purposes, and a stock and an index may also be plotted together. In this way you can see how your stock is doing relative to the Dow Jones industrial average or any other index. A somewhat more informative view of a stock versus an index can be developed by plotting only the difference between the two. This process is fully automated by the program.

The initial scaling of any graph is automatic, so you don't have to worry about rescaling as you move from graphing one stock to graphing another. But you can intervene and specify a desired scale for each graph if you wish. As is typical of the program, the screen in Figure 9.2 is a fully automated production. You enter the ticker and a current 250-day graph appears. But if you prefer to do it your way, you can work through the scaling and format decisions step by step, using the program's deep repertoire of commands, and arrive at a very different looking presentation of the same stock's data.

You can store the procedures you used to specify these graphs and call them up en bloc with a function key. The next time you look at this particular stock, you will be able to graph it in exactly the same way, automatically, using your own recorded procedure. Typical procedures include not only scaling and time frame instructions but also detailed instructions calling for multiple miniscreens, smoothing techniques, volume allocations, oscillators, comparisons against indexes—whatever you want.

As you get used to the program, you will rely less on the automated default procedures and settings and more on procedures of your own devising. Automating your procedures enables you to view a stock in exactly the same light, so to speak, from day to day and week to week. An automatic charting procedure can also be used to see how well each of several stocks measures up to a common, filtering set of technical criteria.

We have considered here the most basic aspects of the charting process. I have indicated how the program responds to just three basic questions: How big is the chart? What are the scales? What information is to be included?

The astonishing catalog of diverse answers to these three simple questions shows the depth of the program. An impressive effort has been made to anticipate the needs of every investor who might ever use the Technical Investor. Everyone who uses it is, at the outset, a beginner. The program provides robots to take care of beginners. As you gain experience with the Savant program, you will be able to use it to devise robots of your own.

The program has two tiers. One is utterly automatic and is informed at decision points by a standard set of default values. It autoscales and plots price and volume movements over the most recent 250 days for the XYZ Corporation. Presto.

The loftier tier of the Technical Investor is command-driven and requires your intervention and judgment at decision points. You must tell it how many days you want to plot, against what scales, and from when to when. You must tell it which technical analytical techniques you wish to use and precisely how you want them carried out. These complex and very individual instructions can be recorded and triggered by one or more function keys. Presto again.

Moving Averages: the Essential Tools

If you pick up a book on technical analysis, chances are that you will find within it some charts depicting price movements as lithe and smoothly curving lines. The lines have been created by an artist using a soft-nib pen. If you look at an unretouched stock price chart on which no lines have been drawn, you may notice that it looks more like a used machine gun target, perhaps reflecting the accuracy of a gunner with the hiccoughs. The data points are peppered along a path, but the path (if your eye can detect one) is wide and ill defined. How do you get from this scattershot pattern to a neat textbook-style line so that you can see which way the stock is going?

There are several ways to pilot a line among and over the points, a line that represents something like a consensus for the population of points. The process is called *smoothing*. There are many methods for accomplishing it, including regression analysis, Fourier transformation, and the calculation of moving averages. These techniques are widely applied in science and business. Among investors, the favorite smoothing technique is probably the moving average. The calculation of a moving-average line is the first step for many analysts in examining a chart. It is also one of those simple but tiresome tasks that computers do supremely well.

A moving-average value is recalculated for each day that it is to be plotted on the stock chart. Here's how to calculate a five-day moving average by hand. On Monday morning, add up the closing prices for the past five days of trading and divide the sum by 5. Plot the resulting average price as a point on the graph.

On Tuesday morning, repeat the averaging procedure. In this recalculation, the sum will include Monday's closing price, but the week-ago Monday's closing price will be dropped from consideration. Plot the result. On Wednesday, repeat the calculation and plot this result. Each day, a fresh closing price is added into the sum and a week-old closing price is dropped from the sum. After you have performed the daily recalculation for a few weeks, use a soft pencil to connect the points you have plotted. You will find that they are easy to connect with a smooth line.

When a computer is instructed to construct a moving average for a particular stock, it first takes up a starting position deep in the archival record of that stock's prices, for example, 400 trading days ago. It then begins working its way forward to the present day, pausing at each intervening day to recalculate the moving average, note the result, and position and plot the moving average on your screen.

You can watch the process in action. When the skeletal stock chart first appears on the screen, it may consist of two scaled axes and a peppering of points. When you request a moving average of, say, five days' closing prices, a line sprouts from a point at the left of the screen and speedily grows, threading its way across the screen among the points until it is complete. A 30-day moving average superimposed on a high/low/close bar chart is shown in Figure 9.4. Note that in this illustration the full screen is used for the price chart. To add a volume chart, you can subdivide the screen into two miniscreens, as was done in Figure 9.2, and then enter appropriate commands to select a volume chart.

Now let's consider some of the extreme types of moving averages. The shortest plausible interval for the calculation is one day. In this case, the "average" consists of yesterday's close divided by 1. If you request a one-day moving average of your computer, it will simply connect the dots marking each day's close. The resulting line will be jagged and rather kinetic, as if it were tracing the path of a pinball. At the other extreme is a 500-day moving average. This one will be a nice, smooth line, so smooth in fact that it may deviate only very slightly in response to a sudden vertical shift (up or down) in the price of the underlying stock. We use a moving average to smooth the price moves of the stock, but when the line becomes so smooth that it is virtually undeviating, it only vaguely hints which way the price is trending. It is said to be *insensitive*.

Moving averages, as tools in your shop, are ranked and racked in

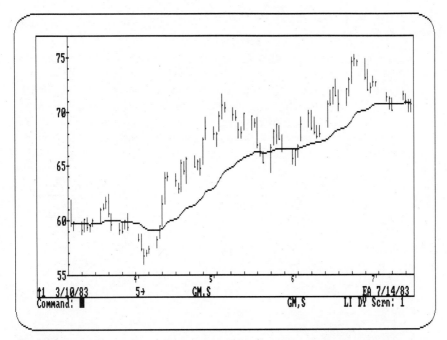

Figure 9.4. A full-screen plot of high, low, and closing prices for GM. Superimposed on it is a 30-day moving average. The moving average is perhaps the most basic tool of technical analysis. It smooths spurious price swings to make the overall price trend more apparent.

order of their sensitivity. A two-day moving average is too sensitive. It ricochets back and forth almost as freely and widely as the stock price itself. In contrast, a 500-day moving average is too insensitive. You might as well use a straightedge. Moving averages taken over a short period (typically 5, 6, or 10 days) are considered sensitive and quick to respond to underlying price movement. Moving averages taken over longer periods (30, 100, and 200 days) are progressively less sensitive. It takes a sustained and major deviation in the price of the stock to put a kink in a 200-day moving average.

Somewhere on the scale of sensitivity is a moving average which reflects more faithfully than any other moving average the true path (note the spiritual undertone) of the stock. Your computer can tell you exactly which one (see the chapter on Summa's Winning on Wall Street and Strategy Command and the chapter on RTR's TechniFilter). At this point, suffice it to say that most people rely on one or more moving averages to smooth the data, mainly to make the data legible, and to generate buy and sell signals. Dual moving averages (one long, one short) are commonly used to generate buy and sell signals.

Reading Buy and Sell Signals from Moving Averages

A strategy using two moving averages might typically stipulate that you will buy the stock whenever the 10-day moving average crosses up through the 30-day moving average and that you will sell when the 10-day moving average falls back through the slower-moving 30-day moving average. Buy and sell signals produced in this way are shown in Figure 9.5. Sometimes they work. I regard moving-average lines simply as artificial barriers. When a price breaks through one, it should make a little

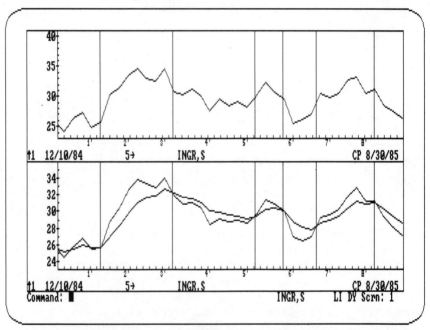

Figure 9.5. This illustrates how buy and sell signals can be produced using moving averages. The upper chart is a plot of closing prices for Intergraph, a fairly volatile technology issue which is traded on the NASDAQ national market. In the lower miniscreen are superimposed two curves. One is a 30-day moving average of Intergraph prices; the other is a 10-day moving average of Intergraph prices. A trader's rule of thumb suggests that one should buy when the 10-day average crosses up through the 30-day moving average and sell when it crosses it again, headed down. In this chart, the crossovers, or buy and sell signals, are marked with vertical lines. The first vertical line, in mid-January, is a buy signal. The second, in mid-March, is a profitable sell signal. The next two trades are not profitable, but the final two are profitable. This is a good illustration of the problems and the promise of the technique. It can be "tuned" to a particular stock, using optimization programs such as the TechniFilter, to produce trading strategies with historically excellent predictive value and thus presumably good profitability.

silent crash in your mind. You may buy or sell or not, but you know it is time to pay attention.

Types of Moving Averages

To draw a moving average with the Savant program, you type in a command of the form MA;n, where *n* represents the number of days over which the average is to be taken. For a 10-day moving average, type MA;10. The program will then calculate and superimpose a simple moving-average line on the price chart.

There are two other types of moving average, the weighted moving average and the exponential moving average. Both emphasize the most recently included data; consequently, they respond more sensitively (turn quicker) than simple moving averages taken over the same period. Exponential moving averages are more readily calculated by hand than weighted moving averages, but since the computer is doing the calculating, there seems little basis for choice between the two methods. I would use either one in preference to a simple moving average in most applications. To spot recent trends, sometimes it is helpful to compare simple with weighted moving averages taken over identical periods.

The Savant Technical Investor will draw any of these three major types of moving averages, as will almost any other technical analysis program. Savant's program will superimpose these averages on one price chart, another requisite feature common to most programs. This is one area where color programs can be clearly superior to monochrome programs. Color helps the eye keep all the lines sorted out. The Savant program as run on a computer with IBM's standard 640 × 200 graphics does use color, but in a decorative way only. It does not use color functionally to help you distinguish between interwoven lines on a graph. If you have the IBM enhanced graphics adapter, the Savant program will use color functionally. Dow Jones's Market Analyzer uses color functionally with standard IBM graphics. Interactive's Active Investor does too, and supremely well.

Among the many fields where the concept of moving-average smoothing is applied, investment analysis has one quirk. Formally, a moving average should be plotted about its centerpoint. Investment analysts almost invariably tack the moving-average line to the most current day. This offsets the whole line to the right. The Savant program will plot a moving-average line either way—centered or offset—at the option of the analyst. If you use the offset, you'll be seeing the version of the chart most technical analysts probably favor.

Your Stock Takes Off. Is It a Blip or a Trend?

A trading band is shown in Figure 9.6. Every time one of your stocks makes a price excursion, you must guess whether it is just a blip or the beginning of a new and major uptrend or downtrend. If the price swings within "allowable limits," you can safely ignore it. If it exceeds these limits, you may have to act. To help define (not discover) what the limits might be, you can chart a trading band. The bands are formed using the technique for plotting moving averages, but the moving-average curves are replicated both above and below the actual moving average. By drawing and redrawing these upper and lower boundaries, one can hope to construct an envelope which the price penetrates only in advance of a major move.

The Technical Investor will draw these tandem moving-average lines using any of the three major modes of calculation: simple, weighted, or exponential. The envelope need not be symmetrical about the actual moving average. You can, for example, set the upper boundary of the

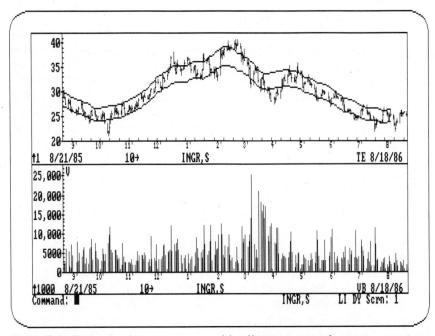

Figure 9.6. Trading bands are sometimes useful in filtering out insignificant price excursions and seeing subtle trends. Savant provides a command to plot and position these bands. Note the "whiskers" rising from the early upper slopes of an uptrending band and poking down out of the downtrending band. These can be used as buy and sell indicators.

band 5 percent above the moving average and set the lower boundary 7 percent below it.

Bands are time-consuming to construct. You must have the computer draw one on the screen to see how you like its fit. If the fit is not just right, you must erase and redraw the band. It would be higher-tech if one could project a tentative band onto the screen and then expand or contract it at will or adjust both boundaries up and down in synchronous fashion as if the band were a single unit. Alas, one cannot. Left-right mobility for each boundary would also help. The band is an arbitrary construction, and a less rigidly defined method for drawing it might make it a bit more useful.

How to Draw Straight Lines on the Screen

Technical analysts need the computerized equivalent of a straightedge to draw various lines of definition and demarcation on the screen. These are trend lines, support and resistance lines, speed resistance lines, and various rays and barriers that can be used in customized analytical techniques.

To draw a straight line on the screen, the first step is to establish its position. This is done with cursor controls. When the Savant program is put in its drawing mode with the two-letter mnemonic command DM, a point appears on the screen marked with cross hairs. This cursor can be moved up, down, right, and left using the keyboard cursor control keys. The keys are appropriately marked with arrows. The cursor can also be moved on the screen along any of the four diagonals radiating from its initial position by using the Home, PgUp, End, and PgDn keys. These keys are set at the four corners of the cursor control pad, and their effect is clear to the operator from their respective positions.

Suppose we wished to draw a horizontal line, perhaps to mark a price resistance level. To put the cursor on the screen, we would enter the drawing mode command. In response the cursor would make its appearance in the middle of the screen. We would "fly" the cross-haired cursor to the highest peak on the price chart and then press the letter H on the keyboard to request a horizontal line. The system draws it automatically, beginning at the vertical axis and extending all the way across the chart. The cross-hair cursor is shown in the upper-left miniscreen in Figure 9.7. The line created through the cursor is shown in the upper-right miniscreen.

Similarly, if we wished to draw a vertical line (perhaps to mark the day when we bought the stock), we would first position the cursor and

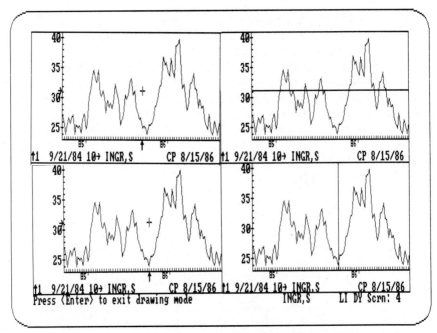

Figure 9.7. This is how the program is used to draw horizontal and vertical lines on the screen. The two miniscreens on the left show the positioning of a graphic device resembling a cross hair. This can be moved freely about the screen using the Up, Down, Right, and Left cursor control keys. When it is in position (marking a stock's historic high or low, for example), a line can be drawn through it with the commands H for "horizontal" or V for "vertical." Horizontal lines are helpful in marking price support and resistance levels. Vertical lines help define coincidence between stock highs and lows and other indicators on lower miniscreens, most typically volume.

then press the letter V for "vertical." The moment the V is pressed, the vertical line skewers the cursor and spans the graph from top to bottom, as in the lower miniscreens of Figure 9.7. As an aid to exact cursor positioning, tiny arrowheads track the cursor along both the horizontal and the vertical scales so that you can read its position in both time and dollars.

Normally the cursor moves in tiny increments, for precision's sake, and this means it moves very slowly indeed. You can make it race to the general area of interest by holding down the shift key as you operate the cursor controls. When you need the precision of slow motion, you simply release the shift key.

Here is another example of the attention to detail inherent in this program. You can reverse the role of the shift key so that the cursor normally speeds along and the shift key retards it instead of accelerating. To toggle the function of the shift key, you use Num Lok. This feature seems almost fussy—a pure embellishment—until you actually start drawing lines. It is in fact a great convenience.

Both horizontal and vertical lines can be drawn directly, without the cursor, using commands which provide numerical positioning information. For example, if you want to draw a horizontal line at the $5 level, you can just type in HL;5 and watch the line appear. It is not necessary to formally enter the drawing mode to sketch such lines on a graph; you can do it any time.

If you use point and figure charts in addition to or instead of time-based charts, you will be pleased to find that in its drawing mode the program provides special one-letter commands specifically intended for point and figure chartists. The letter U will cause the program to draw a line extending northeast from a point defined by the cursor's cross hairs. The letter D will send a line from the cursor to the southeast. The lines are of the form $x = y$ so that you can use them to create bearish and bullish support and resistance lines on point and figure charts.

If you don't like the look of a particular line, the command UP for "unplot" will erase it and you can try again in a new position. Unplot, incidentally, has universal application in operating the program. You can use it to reverse the effects of almost any misstep.

Trend Lines Help You Notice When a Stock Turns

For most of the straight lines analysts use, which are neither horizontal nor vertical, the drawing mode entails a slightly different procedure. The cursor is used to pinpoint two positions; a line is then drawn automatically from one point through the other and on to the border of the miniscreen. Cursor positioning is exactly as described above. When the first point is reached, however, it is marked by depressing the space bar. The mark puts a little box on the screen. You can now move the cursor out from behind this box—a process resembling molting—and on to any second point. When the letter L is entered, a line will be drawn from the mark through the cursor. The most common practical application of this procedure is probably in creating trend lines. For a bearish resistance trend line, as shown in the left miniscreen of Figure 9.8, you would mark an early high, move the cursor to a subsequent lower high, and press L to create the trend line. When a trend line is broken, as it is in this illustration, you can declare that a trend has been broken.

In my experience, a stock or index usually does take an opposite tack after breaking through a trend line. A bullish (ascending) support trend line has been drawn in the right miniscreen by connecting points marking

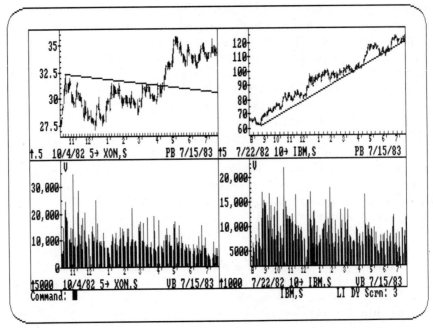

Figure 9.8. Trend lines can be drawn to connect a series of highs or lows. The left mini-screen shows a bearish resistance trend line drawn for Exxon. The idea is that when the stock price penetrates the line at last, a new trend will be established—up. Some traders buy on a price move that carries the stock above its bearish resistance line. A bullish support line is shown for IBM in the right miniscreen. When the stock breaks below this line (as it subsequently did), the uptrend is considered broken. A trader would probably take profits at that point. The program draws trend lines from point to point, and the points are positioned with cursor controls. Trend line drawing is thus a trial-and-error procedure. With Interactive's Active Investor, one can scoot whole lines about the screen.

price lows. When this trend line is broken, it is considered a sign that the stock will begin a new trend—down.

Line-drawing procedures represent a point of distinction among the various technical analysis programs. The Savant solution is not ideal, nor are any of the others. An ideal program would give us a portable line and let us scoot it around the screen and rotate it freely to achieve a satisfying fit to the data. This is what you would do with a ruler if you were working on a chart by hand, but the technique has not yet been carried over literally to computerized technical analysis. In most cases one must draw a line, erase it, and then try another and keep trying until the fit is good. The Interactive Active Investor program has "scoot-able" lines, but point-to-point, horizontal, and vertical lines must be positioned by eye rather than by means of precise coordinates. Some programs automate the process of drawing parallel lines; some do not.

Some position lines at statistically significant intervals, e.g., at plus and minus some fraction or multiple of one standard deviation from a linear regression line.

When you examine technical analysis programs, make it a point to exercise every one of their line-drawing capabilities. You will be drawing lines frequently with the program you finally select.

10

Savant's Automated Techniques and Indicators

Linear Regression Reveals
a Straight-Line Trend
Underlying the Zigs and Zags

It is virtually impossible to draw a single straight line through a collection of closing-price points that will exactly skewer each of the points. This is because three successive closing prices will almost never lie along a perfectly straight line. By playing around with a straightedge, you can usually find a line that "splits the distance" between most of the points, but the process is intuitive and therefore hard to repeat in a consistent manner from graph to graph.

The least-squares-fit procedure defines a "good-fitting" line automatically by stipulating that the squares of the distances from the points to the line should be kept to a minimum. Such a line, representing price, is shown in Figure 10.1. You elicit the line by entering the letters LR at the keyboard. If you use it a lot, you can store the command to a function key and then just push the button whenever you want to display a linear regression line on the screen.

A linear regression line is formally called a least-squares fit to a linear

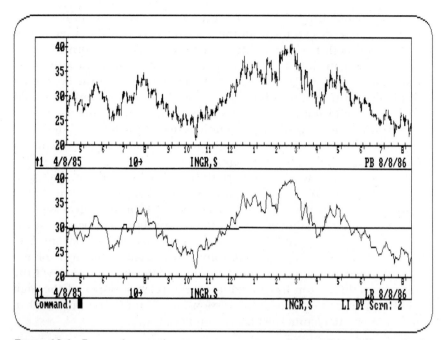

Figure 10.1. From a glance at the zigzag price excursions of this stock, it is not immediately apparent what its net movement has been, up or down. The linear regression line, which you can put on the screen by typing the two letters LR, shows a mathematically consistent determination of the trend. In this case, it is slightly up. Note that in the lower miniscreen the price curve has been smoothed for clarity.

regression. It is a useful mathematical solution to a common practical problem. The purpose of squaring the distances is to eliminate all negative numbers prior to calculation. The computer, of course, does the squaring, summing, and minimum seeking for you. It also writes the equation of the line and uses it to create the display on the screen. You can get the same quick solution from a good scientific or financial calculator, but not the display.

In practice, if an investor is confronted with a scattering of points representing price or volume and wonders which way the trends are going, he or she will call for a linear regression line. When the investor sees how steeply the line slopes up or down, he or she has learned something. This is particularly useful in a stock that oscillates within a rather narrow trading range. To see how it has trended over a longer term, the linear regression line is very helpful.

To draw a linear regression line with the Savant program, set up a graph and display price or volume points. Then simply type the mnemonic command **LR**. The linear regression line will instantly appear. The line will be drawn to fit all the data you have on the screen. You can use it on both price and volume data. If you want to draw it from a certain point in time to another point in time, you must adjust the horizontal scale or range so that the selected points lie at the beginning and the end of the graph's horizontal axis. This is a nuisance. It would be easier to point out the desired range of points with cursors. Useful as this function is for assessing, from the slope of the line, the steepness of change in price and volume, it cannot be applied to any calculated values or indicators with this program.

Linear regression is a much more fully realized tool in Summa's program, Winning on Wall Street. A discussion on that program is included in the following chapter. The time span over which the regression line is calculated can be adjusted easily. Regression lines can be drawn for any set of points, not just for volume and price data as with Savant. You can use linear regression to determine and visually compare, for example, the relative slopes of a long and a short moving average over the most recent three months of trading or the relative slopes of the high and low price curves. Linear regression lines can also be projected in parallel to create channels with the Summa program.

Speed Resistance Lines: A Helpful Test for Market Tops and Bottoms

Speed resistance lines are fun to draw, and some traders have great faith in them. The Savant program draws one-third and two-thirds speed resistance lines. See Figure 10.2 for an example of a chart of an uptrending stock with these lines superimposed. To construct this pattern of rays, the program first picks out a past major low and a recent major high. It then notes the price difference between the two points and divides it into thirds. The two-thirds speed resistance line is then drawn. It extends from the low point through another point, directly below the high, which is two-thirds of the distance from low to high. A one-third speed resistance line is drawn from the low to a point, directly below the high, which is one-third of the distance between low and high.

The whole business is, of course, quite arbitrary. You could set up resistance lines at the seven-eighths and one-fifth levels. However, there is a body of lore (consensus) that sustains the one-third and two-thirds cleavages. If the stock which has been rising steadily should fall back through the two-thirds speed resistance line, you can start worrying

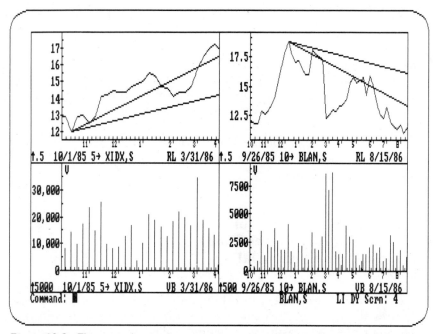

Figure 10.2. This uptrending stock passes the test imposed by speed resistance lines. Although it experienced a sharp retreat and briefly fell through the upper line, it did not drop to the second line. This suggests that it has probably not reached a top and may continue climbing. A trader relying on this technique would have held on to the stock despite the sharp but short retreat. The right-hand miniscreen shows the same technique applied to a stock which is trending down and has not bottomed. A trader would not purchase the stock. Note that there is no predictive or magical power in these lines. They are simply tools to help the trader or investor define his or her buying and selling intentions.

about it. If it breaks the one-third speed resistance line, decide whether to sell it. It may be quite a long time before the stock recovers to this level.

The idea of a stepwise progression from watchfulness to action is good. It is reminiscent of the weather service's responsible method of alerting us to the possibility of a tornado. First comes the tornado watch and then, when danger is imminent, comes the tornado warning. Whether you actually head for the storm cellar is, of course, up to you.

Speed resistance is used in reverse to help alert you that a stock has bottomed. In this case (right miniscreen) the lines originate at the high and project through points at the one-third and two-thirds levels above a recent major low. By convention, the two-thirds line is taken to be the lower one and represents a resistance level. If the stock breaks through it, you can have hopes for it. If it breaks up through the one-third line, you may wish to buy the stock.

In both uptrends and downtrends the program must pick out a recent major high and a recent major low in order to draw the pattern of speed resistance lines. It begins by planting the cursor on the highest high and the lowest low that happen to be displayed on the screen. If you agree with the selected high and low points, you can approve them by pressing Enter. If not, you can shift the cursor with the cursor controls to mark the points you consider the "real" major high and low. If the high and low are off-screen to the left or right, you may have to rescale or pan the display to mark them.

Relative Strength: Is Your Stock Doing Any Better Than the Dow Jones Industrial Average?

There are really two different techniques called *relative strength*. One measures the price performance of a stock against its own historical performance. This measure is sometimes called Welles Wilder relative strength. The command RI elicits a plot of Welles Wilder relative strength.

The more common sense of the term is as a measure of how your stock is doing relative to an index such as the Dow Jones industrial average. You may also wish to evaluate a stock against a broader market measure, such as the S&P 500, or against one or several other stocks in its group. You might, for example, measure the performance of IBM against that of Data General.

The Savant command for relative strength display is the mnemonic RS. It was used to create the graph in Figure 10.3, which plots the performance of three different OTC stocks against that of Genentech. You can compare more than three issues or indexes, but it becomes difficult to distinguish among them unless you have color and an enhanced graphics card. If you like to pick stocks that consistently outperform the market, you will find the relative strength command very useful.

A modified version of this command displays a plot of the relative performance of a $100 investment in each of several stocks. This is sometimes called normalized relative strength. In such charts, the zero line represents $100, and curves above and below it show percentage appreciation and declines from that original value.

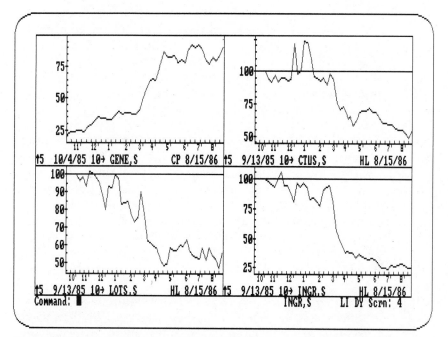

Figure 10.3. This plot shows how three different OTC stocks have performed relative to Genentech, a market leader in the period shown. Genentech's closing price chart appears in the upper-left miniscreen. Relative strength charts for Lotus Development (LOTS), Intergraph (INGR), and Cetus (CTUS) are presented in the other three miniscreens. In each relative strength chart, the horizontal line drawn at the 100 percent level indicates the performance the stock would have to maintain in order to precisely match the performance of Genentech.

The technique of charting the relative strength of issues and indexes can be helpful in showing how your stock is doing relative to other stocks in the same industry group and relative to the market as a whole.

Allocations of Volume: What Your Computer Thinks Joe Granville Is Thinking

To this point we have been concentrating on the graphic analysis of price data. Volume data can be examined using many of the same techniques, such as moving-average smoothing and linear regression. In addition, the Technical Investor provides five calculated indicators which are unique to volume analysis. The indicators are not Savant's creations; they have been around for a while, and each has developed a following among technical analysts.

They are all based on the idea that volume can be allocated after the fact into up-volume and down-volume components. The prototype for this type of volume indicator is the *on-balance–volume indicator*. The idea is credited to Joe Granville. To calculate it by hand, begin by noting the volume on day 1 of your analysis. Then note the volume on the following day. If the price has gone up, add the volume on day 2 to that recorded for day 1. If the price has dropped, subtract the volume for day 2 from that recorded for day 1. If the price has not changed, there will be no change in the value of the indicator.

The exact interpretation of the indicator has never been entirely clear to me, but it is apparent from the calculation that volume weights price. A rising price on large trading volume will send the indicator up fairly dramatically. A rising price on small volume will send the indicator up, but not much. Conversely, a massive institutional sell-off will make the indicator sink, but an ebbing price on a small volume will have little effect. The principle squares with common sense, but it is hardly universal. It is quite common for a stock's price to erode on small volume and for traders to stand off to one side watching it fall, muttering, "But there's not much volume in it." I have done this; you probably have too. It is expensive.

It is also commonplace for a stock to go sneaking up into a nice rally on light volume. It may be that in these cases the buyers and/or sellers know more than the market at large knows. Anticipation of large demand can raise a price quite readily, long before the demand actually materializes and trading escalates to large volume levels.

Several other volume indicators are basically elaborations of the on-balance–volume concept. One is called the price-volume-trend indicator. It is a cumulative indicator, like the on-balance–volume indicator. However, instead of designating the whole day's trading volume as up-volume or down-volume in accordance with the closing price change, the price-volume-trend indicator accumulates just a part of each day's volume in accordance with the size and direction of the price change. If the price goes up 10 percent, 10 percent of the day's volume will be added to the indicator. If the price goes down 10 percent, 10 percent of the day's volume will be subtracted from the indicator.

A third volume indicator, the daily volume indicator, also represents an attempt to accumulate each day something more indicative than the whole-day volume figure. The closing price of the stock is compared with the midpoint between the day's high and low prices. Volume is allocated in proportion to the distance and direction of the closing price from the midpoint price.

The positive-volume indicator changes only on days when the volume has increased over the previous day's trading volume. Quantum increases in volume are considered suggestive of panic buying or panic selling. Short of an actual stampede, increases in volume suggest the general drift of the herd. The positive-volume indicator increases proportionately as the price changes from one day to the next. If the price rises on rising volume, so does the indicator. If it falls on rising volume, so does the indicator. But whatever the price may do on days when volume decreases is simply ignored, and the indicator value is left unchanged.

As an index to the mood of the majority, you can read the indicator either way you choose. If you believe the majority is always wrong (a common, not to say majority, view of the marketplace), assume that the market will go down when the positive-volume indicator is getting peaky. If you believe volume predicts price, you may consider this index bullish.

The positive-volume indicator has a mirror image: the negative-volume indicator. This is supposed to reflect the buying and selling sentiments of people who are not moving their money in accordance with the herd. If you accept as axiomatic the view that the majority is always wrong about the market, it follows that the minority must always be right. As a device to track the minority view, the negative-volume indicator ignores (remains flat on) those days when volume has increased. It tracks only days when volume has decreased from the previous day's trading. The change in the indicator is a function of the magnitude and direction of the price change. A negative-volume indicator is shown in Figure 10.4.

Each of the five volume indicators can be plotted without smoothing. Exponential moving averages of the indicators may also be plotted (with a couple of extra keystrokes to specify the term of the average) and displayed alone or superimposed.

It is precisely here, with volume analysis, that the literature of technical analysis can sometimes veer off in the direction of pseudoscientific gibberish. The assumptions behind volume allocations vary, but they are all enormous and groping assumptions. When we smooth prices, we make no assumptions. When we declare allowable limits to price movement, we are making a declaration of our intentions, not of some revealed principle.

But when we allocate volume, we are necessarily assuming that a hard, hidden, machined clockwork makes the market tick. Nonsense. There's probably some sort of clockwork in there, but the gears and ratchets are machined from Silly Putty.

It does not follow, however, that volume allocation indicators are worthless. They sometimes happen to work. They faithfully indicate the sentiments of the faithful and must therefore be taken into account. *Everything* that influences the price of a stock and can be known should be known, profound or silly as this may sound. After all, some responsible assumptions (e.g., earnings lead price) don't quite work. Some dicey assumptions (volume leads price) often do. What we are after is an

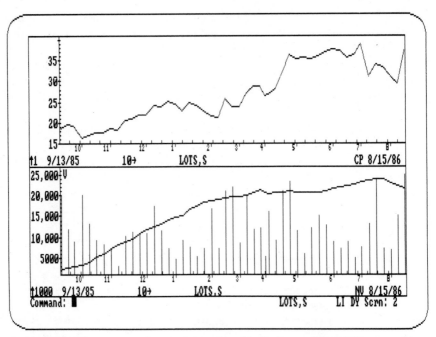

Figure 10.4. The negative-volume indicator plotted in the lower miniscreen is supposed to suggest the sentiment of buyers and sellers of stock on low-volume trading days. One interpretation suggests that since price and volume are supposed to rise in unison, this indicator should "normally" trend down. The alternative and opposite interpretation suggests that since large-volume moves represent herd sentiment, the negative-volume indicator hints at the transactions of especially sophisticated investors, who get in or out before the grand stampedes. This negative-volume indicator is one of a full complement of five different volume indicators plotted by the Savant program. Most charting packages provide these capabilities.

assumption—any sort of assumption—that happens to work for a particular stock for the duration of the period in which we happen to have our money invested in that stock. The useful happenstance: Whatever works, works. You don't have to buy a market ideology in order to use its pet indicator now and then.

The Oscillator Function and How It Anticipates Price Moves

In Figure 10.5 the upper miniscreen shows the price action of Lotus Development Corporation over the span of a year's trading. Below it is plotted one type of oscillator. Vertical lines drawn on the two charts

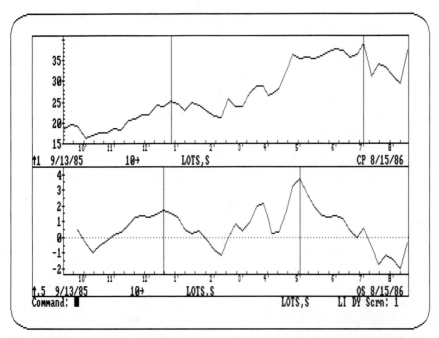

Figure 10.5. A demonstration of how one type of oscillator, called a momentum oscillator, can anticipate price moves. The oscillator is plotted in the lower miniscreen. The vertical lines in the lower miniscreen mark sell signals. On the upper miniscreen, where the actual closing prices of the stock are plotted, the vertical lines mark price peaks. The sell signals do precede the price peaks slightly, and this is obviously a highly desirable quality. This oscillator curve was selected as the best from a family of curves drawn on the screen by the computer program. This process of discovering an oscillator with good past predictive performance for a particular stock is amenable to automation. No commercial program yet exists for it, however. The Savant program helps you work it out by a process of successive experimentation.

indicate the times when the respective curves reached peak values. Note that peaks of the oscillator curve anticipate the peaks of the price curve by one to three weeks. Given such advance notice of sell points, one could have traded the stock quite effectively.

The attraction of oscillators follows from their power to anticipate price moves. They are, unfortunately, among the most skittish of indicators, and they notoriously produce false buy and sell signals. Some traders believe that indicators can be "tuned in" on the cycles and trends of a particular stock or index. The idea is quite attractive if you can get the computer to do the tuning for you. Many people have worked on this problem, and we may expect to see commercial software in this area. At this point, oscillators must be developed and tested by hand.

An oscillator, as the term is used by investment analysts, is any index that swings back and forth through zero. An infinite number of oscillator functions can be constructed, and hundreds of favorites are followed by different analysts.

The oscillator in Figure 10.5 is actually a plot of the rate of change of the price curve. This is a common technique, and you may see it called a *momentum curve*. You might also regard it as a plot of the slope, the tangent, or the first derivative of the smoothed price curve.

Rate of change in price is measured by asking how much change in the price accompanies an incremental change in time, say two days. If the price curve is bottoming, the change may be zero. If the price curve is peaking, the change may be zero. Between these extremes, the rate of change will achieve its maximum value as the stock climbs steeply toward its new high.

As the price approaches the high, however, its rate of growth slows markedly and finally stalls. At this motionless stall point, the oscillator plot touches zero. If the price curve is what a mathematician might call a "nicely behaved" curve, the oscillator will peak before the price peaks, producing a useful sell signal. In real life, there are few nicely behaved price curves. Consequently, the oscillator may produce sell signals before, coincidentally with, or after the price peak. Moreover, within the span of a long uptrend, the rate of change of price may speed up and slow down many times without ever signaling an actual price peak.

For this oscillator to be really useful, the stock should move in approximately sinusoidal fashion; that is, it should draw a nice regular hump on the chart. If instead it draws a staircase pattern, the oscillator will generate one false sell signal after another. It helps to smooth the staircase into an approximation of a hump, and the program can do this.

Buy signals, which have the same sorts of problems, are generated when the stock is tending to bottom and the oscillator turns up. Some traders like to use one oscillator for buy signals and another for sell signals. The oscillator in Figure 10.5 is based on a horizontal measuring increment of two days, and the rate of change is averaged over a period of five days. The curve was selected from a family of curves generated by changing the increment within the range of one to nine days.

The handiest way to invoke the oscillator command in the Savant program is as part of an automated string of commands consigned to a single function key. After each curve is displayed, the string can be edited slightly to progressively change the increment and/or the period of the moving average. The curves appear superimposed on the screen. You can pick out which curve in the family of curves has most faithfully anticipated past price peaks. I do not believe that this method can be reproduced using any of the other programs reviewed here.

To produce another common type of oscillator, the price curve is successively smoothed with two different moving averages: one short, one long. The algebraic difference between the two moving averages is then plotted as an oscillator function. We know that moving-average crossovers are regarded as buy and sell points. The oscillator forewarns us that the averages are tending toward a crossover and helps the eye gauge its coming. An oscillator based on the difference (i.e., the vertical distance) between 30-day and 100-day moving averages is shown in Figure 10.6. You may also wish to refer to Figure 21.5 in the chapter on the Telescan program. This general type of oscillator can be constructed from a menu item in Telescan's analyzer, and the display more clearly illustrates the concept.

In writing a computer program to support technical analysis, the programmer must allow for the construction of all sorts of oscillators. Accordingly, the purchaser usually gets an erector set of commands and

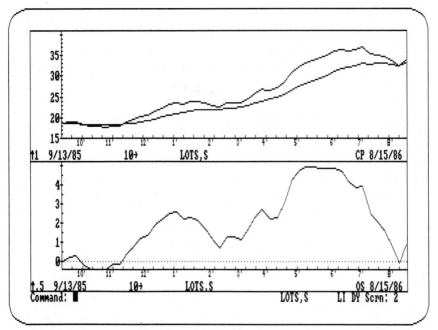

Figure 10.6. The plots in the upper miniscreen are 30-day and 100-day moving averages of closing prices for Lotus Development's stock. The oscillator in the lower miniscreen graph swings up and down with the difference between the two moving averages. This type of oscillator makes it easy to notice when the two averages are converging toward a crossover, indicating a buy or sell point. When the two averages cross, the oscillator curve passes through zero. Note that the oscillator curve bottoms well before the buy signal is actually reached. This can be helpful in anticipating buy and sell signals. It is particularly handy in tracking jaggedly shifting price charts, where the approach of a crossover is not apparent from direct inspection of the moving-average curves.

functions to create his or her own oscillators rather than one or two simple mnemonic commands that display specific oscillators on the screen.

Programmers evidently assume that anyone who wants to use an oscillator is sophisticated enough to construct a command to elicit it. I doubt this reasoning, but it seems to prevail. To create an oscillator, you need what is essentially a midget programming language. You use it to write a procedure the computer must memorize, i.e., a macro command. The generalized form for an oscillator, $f(x) = A - B$, is so very general that it requires quite a bit of experience and imagination to plug in useful and realistic values and functions. Savant simplifies the notation and complicates your life by dropping the invariant minus sign from its command notation. The command is supposed to be assembled like a string of beads—rather similarly shaped and colored beads—that absolutely must be strung in the right order. The procedure makes your eyes jump.

The command structure easily accommodates any sort of oscillator in common use. This is its strength. The trade-off for this flexibility of application is learning difficulty: It is tedious. Prompts appear to help you fill in the blanks if you have left something out of a command structure (a bead, so to speak), but you need to understand the structure fully before the prompts can be of any real help.

The whole oscillator question can be reduced to one menu item, as follows: "To find an oscillator with the best predictive record for the stock of the XYZ Corporation, punch number 9." This is the actual approach taken in one type of strategy optimization program. It is still under development. From a discussion with its author, I estimate a running time, from the moment the command is entered, of three or four days on a PC and a bit more than half that long on an 8086 machine. Processor and clock speeds do matter when you run strategy tests.

As an intermediate and practical solution, perhaps the two garden variety oscillators, which plot slopes and moving-average differences, respectively, could be elicited with menu items or (at least) more self-evident command structures. Some programs handle the problem this way, and it simplifies things.

Point and Figure: A Useful Tool Rescued from Antiquity

This technique for following stocks was devised late in the nineteenth century. A typical chart is shown in Figure 10.7. Computerized plotting may give the technique a renewed vogue, since hand plotting is the most troublesome aspect of it. The plot is quite different from a conventional

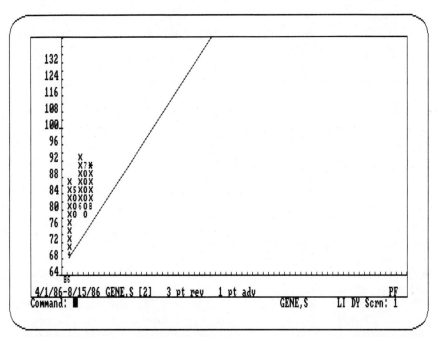

Figure 10.7. A point and figure chart plotted by the Savant program for Genentech, using the three-point reversal technique. Computerized plotting is a great relief in this type of analysis, which is rather tedious to work out by hand. Note that the program produces support and resistance lines on command. A bullish support line is shown here. A rising stock is supposed to stay above this line. A drop below it might trigger its sale by some traders.

Cartesian plot of price or volume against time. There is no time axis, and the chart worms and turns and grows, according to a proponent of the technique, "under the aspect of eternity." You can figure out by scrutinizing a chart roughly when a price turn occurred, but it is not as easy as with a conventional price chart. Point and figure is basically a smoothing technique. In its quaint, elegant way, it accomplishes the same thing you might try to achieve with a moving average or a fast Fourier transformation. The goal in every case is to identify a clear price trend and to ignore minor or spurious excursions in the price of the stock away from this trend.

In point and figure, smoothing is accomplished by defining as threshold values the dimensions of the units on the chart. For a stock priced between $20 and $100, for example, a unit is defined as corresponding to $1. If a stock moves up decisively from $23 to $24, you mark the change by putting an X in the box corresponding to 24 units. If it advances another full dollar to $25, add another X atop the first. But suppose the stock just fiddles above $24, making moves to $24⅛, to $24½, to $24¾—and then back to $24⅛. These little moves are considered spurious. Since they don't touch or exceed the threshold value of $1, they don't merit putting a mark on the chart. This cleans up the data so that only fairly significant moves appear on the chart.

An ascending stack of Xs represents an uptrend. It takes a three-unit change in price to declare a downtrend. When this happens, the event is marked by shifting over one column to the right of the column of Xs and then down one unit (just one, not three). Here you put an O. So long as the downtrend continues, you add an O for each full unit (dollar) of price decline. The three-point reversal applies once again to the change from downtrend to uptrend. By requiring a full three-point change before a trend reversal can be declared, the point and figure technique further screens out trivial or spurious price changes. Three-point reversals are used in this explanation, but one can alter the smoothing effect by using, for example, two-point or half-point reversals. The program accommodates such changes.

There is a private (cabalistic) language associated with the interpretation of this technique, and it is worth delving into its literature for this alone. No other analytical technique brings you "the Bearish Catapult," "the Bullish Triangle," and "the Triple Top." If you like Nabokov ("a trip with the tip of the tongue"), you'll get a kick out of point and figure terminology. As to its value in market analysis, it is probably about on a par with other smoothing techniques. For some trading patterns, these charts are a lot easier to read at a glance. You can quickly spot patterns of progressively higher highs interspersed with progressively higher lows: an uptrend. Conversely, you can readily observe a stock that keeps making lower highs and lower lows: a downtrend. This trend-at-a-glance feature is the forte of the point and figure technique.

A damped sine wave on a conventional chart of price versus time is instantly apparent on a point and figure chart as a triangular clump of Xs and Os. According to the lore, triangles often precede breakouts in one direction or the other. You are supposed to be able to determine which way a price will go by studying such formations, but I think this is overinterpreting the data.

Scaling can be a problem. Savant provides a means of rescaling point and figure charts to make them fit on the screen, but the company is quick to point out that changing the scale compromises the meaning of the chart. Instead of reducing a big chart, you should probably scan it.

Savant provides automatic line drawing in the drawing mode to help you create bullish and bearish support and resistance lines. The chart itself is drawn automatically. Because point and figure charts require decision making at each plotting step, the approach is more susceptible to error than conventional plotting. If you try it by hand, you'll find that mistakes take a lot of undoing. The computer eliminates the possibility of error.

It would not be surprising if the popularity of point and figure analyses continued rising with that of computerized investing. Note, however, that most of the tools for analysis provided by the Savant program and other programs are specifically designed for conventional price charts and have no application to point and figure charts. Most technical analysis programs do create point and figure charts, but it is a rather vestigial feature, as is the technique itself. When this technique was in its heyday, Bernard Baruch was in his, and the stock market was essentially a place to exchange railroads.

It will be interesting to see what can be done with point and figure charting now that the plotting part is so nicely computerized. I suspect that point and figure charts are more susceptible to pattern recognition algorithms than Cartesian charts. Tests of the predictive value of point and figure chart formations (such as the marvelous Bullish Catapult) have been run in the past using mainframes. The printed results of past studies, however, are far less helpful than the power to run a fresh study every Saturday morning on your PC. Ideally, an indicator must be tested constantly; when the indicator and the stock go their separate ways, you can quietly withdraw your bet. Oscillators and moving averages have received the most attention in this area (strategy optimization), but little has been done commercially with point and figure.

User Procedures Automate Your Favorite Techniques

We have already remarked on this program's seeming ability to grow with the user. Menus, prompts, and standard defaults are provided for beginners. Advanced users can take advantage of the 100-page command dictionary in the manual. All the commands are mnemonic. In response to the command MA, a moving average will be displayed.

The commands make up a programming language. After you have become familiar with the individual commands through using them, you will want to string them together into little programs. Suppose you want to draw a chart of IBM's closing prices, connect the dots, and then superimpose plots of 10-day and 30-day moving averages. A sequence of commands to make this chart appear on the screen could be entered as follows:

NS; 1; ES; IBM; CP; 1; MA; 10; MA; 30

If you check the same chart every day, you may wish to have the computer memorize this longish string of commands. To do so, you precede the string with the command EP ("enter procedure") and the symbol *. The whole entry will look like this:

EP;*;NS;1;ES;IBM;CP;1;MA;10;MA;30

Forever after, you can draw the IBM chart in exactly this way by simply punching function key F8. Savant provides for a total of 38 such "user procedures," each of which can be executed with a single keystroke. If you have a favorite charting method you use with stock after stock, this is the best way to use it. If you use different procedures for different stocks, this is a good way to store them and reuse them in a consistent manner. In effect, the user-procedure feature enables you to write your own personalized menu.

A number of useful standard procedures are written into the program. You can use them right out of the box and get a feel for how much can be accomplished on the screen by poking a single key. It is rather as if you had become an artist-magician and could create a complete landscape with a single brushstroke.

Convenience Features

The most evident convenience is the power to cut the screen into one, two, three, or four separate panels so that you can plot and compare different stocks and different indicators. The ability to plot anything directly above anything else, on a common-time base, is paramount in comparative evaluations. The feature also can be used to simultaneously display four different and disparate charts. You might plot, for example, price bars, a volume indicator, performance relative to the Dow Jones industrial average, and a point and figure chart—all on the same screen. Additional plots can be superimposed on each miniscreen. You can store up to 10 miniscreens for quick recall, complete with elaborations such as moving averages and trend lines. Storage space is found on the program disk, so you can keep the stored miniscreens accessible for later comparison even if you need to change the database disk. (The quadruple-miniscreen approach used to be a unique feature of the Savant program, but it is now offered on the Dow Jones technical analysis package as well.)

A seemingly minor convenience feature but one that is in constant use might be called the number extractor (Figure 10.8). Once drawn, a chart can easily be scanned for patterns and trends, but it is not easy to read from it the *exact* coordinates of any one point. With a paper chart

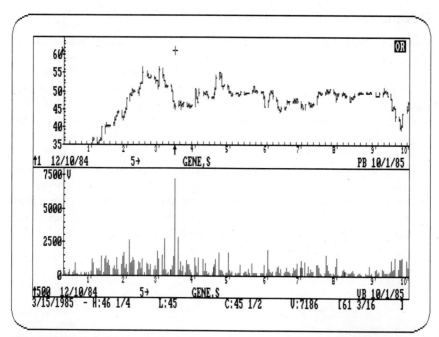

Figure 10.8. Note the cross-hair cursor above the sharp descent in price corresponding to the volume peak in the lower miniscreen. The cursor is positioned at this point in order to read out, in the panel below the lower miniscreen, exactly what happened on that day. From this panel the user learns that the specific date was March 15 and that the stock's high, low, close, and volume were $46.25, $45, $45.5, and 718,600, respectively. By moving the cross hairs left and right with the cursor controls, one can read out the trading data for any day. This is especially useful in quantifying price peaks.

you might use a straightedge, pull lines to each axis, and then read the price and date values from their respective axes. This procedure is more difficult on a computer than on paper. You can pull lines automatically from cursor positions, but the axes are scaled in fairly wide increments, and the date axis in particular is difficult to read. Savant's simple solution is elicited with the two-letter command VW, for "view data." It puts a cursor on the screen. As you reposition the cursor, its price and time coordinates are displayed below the axes in numbers you can read directly. If you want to know the day and price associated with a price peak, simply position the cursor on the peak and then read the price and date as displayed below the axis. The view data technique is particularly helpful if you need to rescale the graph or prepare to draw a line from point to point. The command is not mnemonic, so I learned it as the Volkswagen command to lock "VW" into my own memory.

Documentation and Help

There are no detailed help screens. You can gain access to an on-screen command menu at any time by typing ??. This is a scroll-through list of commands, however, not a comprehensive explanation of what they do. You can also scroll through an alphabetical list of the ticker symbols of the stocks stored on the database disk. This shows you which stocks are available for charting. No sublistings (e.g., individual portfolios) can be displayed in this manner. In using the program I prefer to work from a printed-out paper list of stocks in various portfolios.

The program is fully supported by Savant. You can call the company any time for help. The call is on you, and I think this is fair enough.

The manual is excellent. It is thick, well organized, well written, and clearly illustrated. You will notice clarity of thought, thoroughness, and intellectual maturity in its presentation of both the program and the technical analysis techniques it automates.

11
Winning on Wall Street

This program from Summa is recognized as one of the best technical analysis programs. The basic techniques of technical analysis have been covered in some detail in the last two chapters, and you may wish to refer to them for discussions of specific methods. Winning on Wall Street accomplishes all the basic techniques, and in much the same manner as the other high-level technical analysis programs. A summary of the program's overall capabilities and limitations is included in Chapter 15. The discussion which follows is focused on unique features of the Winning on Wall Street program, features you cannot find in other programs. Some of them are quite remarkable.

A Comparison of the Summa and Savant Programs

For some time, Winning on Wall Street by Summa Technologies, Inc., and Savant's Technical Investor were widely regarded as the two heavyweights for technical analysis. Things are not this simple anymore, but if you are making a selection of software for stock market analysis, you should certainly compare these two powerful, very different, yet rather evenly matched contenders. An understanding of their features should be helpful to you in weighing these programs against alternative programs as well.

Each has quite a distinctive "feel" in actual operation, though both accomplish all the basic technical analysis techniques. The prices of the programs are about $100 apart. Winning on Wall Street costs $495 and includes a portfolio manager; the Technical Investor costs $395 and does not. Both include communications programs.

Savant's program is more convenient to use and faster in action overall because it is command-driven. Summa's program must be operated at a more deliberate pace because it is menu-driven, but it would be easy for a beginning user to run it right out of the box. Summa has more features. Savant lets you do a bit more with the many features it has.

Winning on Wall Street is a disk-intensive program, which makes it sluggish if you are using a standard PC with a pair of floppy drives. A hard disk probably would pick up the cadence of the program smartly. With or without a hard disk, the interactive graphing component of the program, which operates out of the computer's memory rather than its disks, runs very fast indeed once it is loaded.

While you are actually working with graphs, Winning on Wall Street seems quicker than the Technical Investor. This is because it draws graphs on the screen much faster. Subsequent processing for material already on the screen (drawing lines and averages, for example) proceeds at comparable speeds for the two programs. Summa's higher charting speed is purchased at the cost of some operating restrictions. You cannot freely change time scales on any graph or from graph to graph, and you are restricted to analyzing groups of 10 stocks at a time. However, it is pleasant to snick from graph to graph at a single keystroke and to fill the screen in moments.

Winning on Wall Street has six features I consider reasonably significant that are not included (or at least not explicit) in Savant's package. These are (1) adaptive filtering, which is a smoothing technique, (2) a superior application of the least-squares-fit technique, (3) a charting facility that directly compares price and volume on the same axis against a common scale, (4) a matrix evaluation program which uses purely statistical means to forecast a stock's most likely next high and low, (5) an optimization program, and (6) a tool kit for the creation of the user's own formulas.

Judge the importance of these features in terms of your own style of analysis. Each feature will be treated in turn below.

Adaptive Filtering

Adaptive filtering is a more sophisticated smoothing technique than the moving average (Figure 11.1). The upper plot is a result of adaptive filtering applied over a period of 24 days. The lower plot in the figure

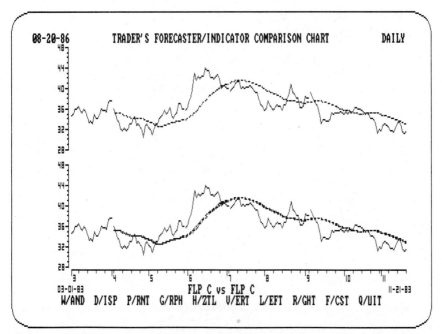

Figure 11.1. A comparison of smoothing by adaptive filtering and by the moving-average technique. The term *adaptive filtering* was originally applied to a method for filtering noise out of telephone transmissions. The idea is similarly applied in stock market analysis. We hope to emphasize a signal containing information and to suppress the excursions from that signal as background noise. The upper plot shows smoothing by adaptive filtering for Floating Point Systems stock. The lower plot is identical, but superimposed on it is a 24-day simple moving average. The moving-average and adaptive filtering curves are so similar that superimposing them simply creates a slightly fattened line. The adaptive filtering concept is mathematically more ambitious, however. Mathematical excellence is characteristic of the program.

is a 24-day simple moving average plotted right on top of the line produced by the 24-day adaptive filtering technique. The lower plot suggests how similar the results are. In general, I found that if I plotted a smoothed stock price curve with adaptive filtering and then smoothed the same curve a second time using a simple moving average, the two smoothed curves were snuggled within a line width of each other, as they are in Figure 11.1. One reason to run a moving average is to create a chart that looks just like the charts being created by other traders so that you can guess at the consensus on the stock of interest. If you use adaptive filtering instead of a moving average, you'll get a curve that's a micronudge away from everyone else's and will have the satisfaction of having used a superior smoothing technique. I doubt it matters much in terms of the bottom line.

Least Squares Made
More Useful

Here is a feature with obvious practical value. Winning on Wall Street does a better job than Savant with one standard tool: the linear regression line. With the Summa program you can draw a linear regression line within any selected time frame, from a few days to 190 days, without replotting the chart. Savant's linear regression calculation uses all the points on the screen, so the only way to vary the term of the regression line is to change the scale of the graph. A shorter-term linear regression is helpful in drawing and defining the slope of short-term trend lines in a consistent way.

Figure 11.2 shows what can be done with Summa's flexible linear regression utility. The stock is Tektronix, Inc. Two linear regression lines are calculated, using points ranging from the vertical bar positioned

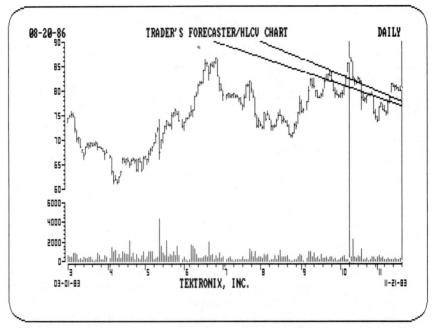

Figure 11.2. Linear regression is applied to the price movements of Tektronix during the period from early October until the end of the year. The upper line shows the trend of the daily highs, and the lower line shows the trend of the daily lows. The convergence and the downtrends can be read as caution signals for buyers.

Linear regression analysis, as provided by the Winning on Wall Street programmers, is a superior feature, largely because the time frame over which the regression line is to be drawn can be easily marked off with movable vertical bars. With most programs, one must redefine the horizontal axis to define a time frame of interest, since linear regression is applied whole-sale to all the points on the screen.

at the price peak of October 10 to the vertical line marking the year's end. The upper line represents the trend of daily highs; the lower line represents the trend of daily lows. The technique makes it easy to notice that the two lines are converging as the downtrend progresses. You can freely position vertical bars anywhere on the time scale and thus define any time frame for this calculation.

Summa also uses linear regression techniques to create midchannel support and resistance lines. The lines appear at specified distances above and below the least-squares fit to the midpoint prices. You can specify the spacing between the hypothetical midpoint line and the support and resistance lines by keying in an allowable fraction or multiple of standard deviation between 0.5 and 3.0.

Application of the linear regression technique is not restricted to price and volume data. You can apply it to calculated indicators such as moving averages. This isn't push-button easy, but it can be accomplished. You employ the user-formula feature of the program to create a plot of the selected indicator and then apply the linear regression technique to that plot. You can get some useful information this way, such as an estimate of the slope of the 30-day moving average. The technique is illustrated in the upper plot of Figure 11.7.

Direct Price-Volume Comparison

Here is a fascinating utility that seizes the price-volume correlation problem by the throat and displays the two variables on the same axis in normalized form so that you can actually see—for a given stock within the given time frame—the exact relation between volume and price. A plot of this type is shown for Tektronix, Inc., in Figure 11.3. The dotted line is price, and the more or less solid line is volume. The two stocks are normalized and are pinned on to the axis on the fortieth day. The vertical scale is read as a percentage deviation from the value of the variable on the fortieth day. The range of the chart is fixed at 40 days. You can shift this time frame, but you cannot expand or contract it.

I love this utility. It seems to confirm what I have always suspected: A useful general relation between price and volume has never been divined. At first the plot on the screen looked utterly chaotic for every stock I examined. After a while I began to notice certain patterns. Mirages, no doubt.

One way to use this feature is as a stock preselector. If you like volume allocation indicators [such as price-volume trend (PVT), on-balance volume, daily volume, and negative-volume or positive-volume trend], you can use this utility to discover a stock that actually works as price-volume

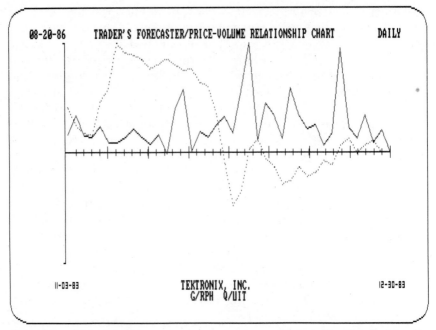

Figure 11.3. This chart shows what price versus volume really looks like. The two key variables are normalized and are pinned to the same axis. It is clear that the relation between price and volume, for this stock at least, is not clear. The dotted line is price; the solid line is volume. This charting utility is unique to the program and is the only direct price-volume comparison machine I have seen.

ideology suggests. Technical analysis is emphatically not a science. If the data don't fit your hypothesis, you are perfectly free to go find different data (i.e., a different stock) that make the hypothesis look prettier. You can then put money on the hypothesis, until the stock wanders off unaccountably in the wrong direction. The trick is to keep testing the correlation between the stock and the hypothetical trend indicator so that when it begins to fail, you will notice it quickly. One way to test it is with an optimization program.

Matrix Evaluation Predicts Next High, Low

It is possible to make predictions, based on statistical analysis of past price data, of the future high and low for a stock. A program to accomplish this is provided as a menu item by Summa. The company clearly declares that it is what it is, a purely statistical mechanism and not an oracle. They suggest that the program be used as an aid in setting objectives. Presumably this means stop-loss and target price levels. This seems a reasonable application for the technique, provided that it is used (as Summa urges) in conjunction with other techniques. It is certainly a more informed approach than setting arbitrary growth or stop-loss levels.

Optimizer Pinpoints the Most Profitable Indicator

The optimization feature is a Summa exclusive and a substantial technological step in the right direction. Many traders base their buy and sell decisions on moving-average crossovers. A typical strategic rule of thumb, for example, might stipulate that you buy a stock when its closing price rises sufficiently to break through its 24-day moving average. Similarly, you might plan to sell a stock if its closing price plunged back through its 24-day moving average. The question is, which moving averages should you use: 10-day, 24-day, or 50-day? Something in between? The answer must come from an optimization program.

An optimizer is a program that evaluates the past predictive performance of a whole series of indicators and tells you which one has been working best for a particular stock.

Summa calls its optimizer the Strategy Command. It reports in tabular form the actual dollar and percentage results you would have obtained in the past using each of 100 possible buy and sell strategies. The strategies are dictated by price crossovers of moving averages. The averages are calculated over periods ranging from 1 day to 100 days. The optimizer is a basic one, since we are talking about a closing price penetrating an average price rather than one moving average crossing over another. But it is a beginning, and a Summa spokesperson told me they are working on a more highly developed program as well.

To get an optimizer for the Savant program, you must purchase one from another supplier, RTR. RTR's optimization program, the TechniFilter, is Savant-compatible and costs about $300. It is a superior optimizer in that it tests various dual moving-average crossover, or "shadow," strategies. It does not test oscillators.

User Formulas

Savant does provide, with its difficult oscillator command, a format which can accommodate many custom formulas, but it does not explicitly provide a system, or language, for writing formulas. Summa's formula set is first rate. Winning on Wall Street provides arithmetic operators (add,

subtract, etc.), statistical operators (average), and some algebraic operators. It includes standard trigonometric functions and a very useful
inverse trig function, the arc tangent. Exponential functions can be managed directly or through the use of natural logarithms, which are also
provided. For the most part, you would not need any of this stuff, but
if you are hard bitten, it's there. A casual user might need it from time
to time to create, for example, moving averages of volume data, which
are not available via the menu.

Other Differences

Winning on Wall Street provides a traveling vertical bar called a wand
instead of a conventional cursor. The wand is excellent for defining the
timing differences between two plots on the upper and lower parts of
the screen. In Figure 11.4 the technique is used to correlate price and
volume.

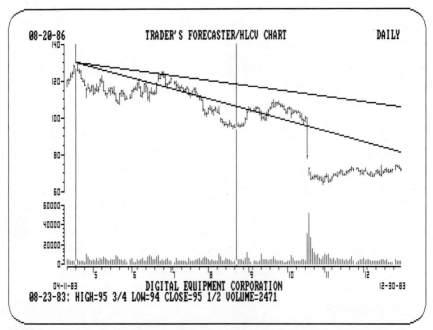

Figure 11.4. Here the vertical wand is used as a number extractor by positioning it on an
intermediate low. The high, low, and closing prices for that day, along with the date and the
volume, appear below the chart. Speed resistance lines were calculated and drawn by the
program automatically, using this date as a low point. An investor relying on this technique
probably would not have bought into DEC in the months preceding the precipitous October
drop.

In Savant's program vertical lines can be drawn easily enough, but they cannot be moved and do not span the screen from top to bottom or extend from one plot into another. Establishing coincidence lines from an upper to a lower miniscreen requires drawing two lines, and each is a position-and-try project. This is one area in which Savant gives away points on convenience to Summa.

Winning on Wall Street is not just menu-driven, it is perhaps the most relentlessly menu-driven program I have encountered. It takes 2 minutes and 45 seconds from the time the program boots to the moment the first graph appears on the screen. It takes this long to work through the menus and wait out the spinnings of the disks. As an experiment, I loaded the program into a RAM disk. This cut the wait to 1 minute and 55 seconds, and much of this time was allocated to spinning the remaining mechanical disk drive, which held the sample data on 10 stocks.

When you finally break through to the charting module, the pace accelerates dramatically. The charts are essentially predrawn in groups of 10 in the computer's memory. When you request a chart, it pops up on the screen right away, and you can jump from chart to chart with great speed and facility. In consequence, the program "shows well" in seminars and controlled selling situations. This is the part of the program that really counts—graphing—and Winning on Wall Street excels at it. Any change in the configuration of the graph, however, requires a trek back into the menus. This bogs down the analytical process.

Split Screens, Split Data: A Pesky Problem

It is sometimes helpful to try to reconstruct some of the basic decisions of the program designers. These are decisions you must live with every time you use the program. Savant and Summa differ markedly in their approaches to the fundamental problem of allocating space on the screen.

A prototypical single-screen chart includes two graphs plotted one above the other. They have one axis in common: time. The upper plot shows prices, and the lower plot shows volume. If you request a moving average of "the data," the program must determine which data you're talking about, price or volume. The programmer may prompt you with an on-screen request to specify the upper or lower half of the screen or simply assume that you want one or the other and proceed accordingly. But the basic problem comes up with every screen you operate on and is thus never quite laid to rest.

Savant's programmers had a truly happy inspiration when they elected to cleave the screen of the Technical Investor into four separate miniscreens. The program always regards each miniscreen as a separate entity. Summa's Winning on Wall Street and other one-screen programs do not have the advantage of this built-in logical device, the miniscreen, for distinguishing clearly between the several types of data that can be plotted anywhere on the screen.

Here is the practical payoff. With Savant's program you can apply any function to any price or volume data, any time and anywhere on the screen. Each type of data has a miniscreen to itself. If you specify a 10-day moving average of the data in miniscreen 3, you'll get it. It won't matter whether the data happen to be price or volume. You need only specify the miniscreen where you want the smoothing function applied.

With Summa's program and other programs, where the relation between data type and screen section (upper or lower) is never firmly resolved, you bump into split-screen specification problems. Some functions work on the upper screen, some functions work on the lower screen, and some functions work on either screen—sometimes but not always. Sometimes prompts appear suddenly to ask you if you want to operate on the lower screen or the upper screen. Sometimes you wish they would appear, but they do not.

Savant does not really have the last word, however, because the problem becomes even thornier. Suppose you want to apply a linear regression line to a moving-average curve. We are now once removed from the original data, but still on the same miniscreen. Specifying upper versus lower will not suffice to distinguish between the three available types of data (price, volume, and average), and here Savant's blanket solution comes undone. Savant worked around the problem with its Oscillator command—you can apply smoothing functions to a momentum curve, for example—but it is a tactical and not a strategic solution to the problem. A special solution to smoothing volume data was worked out. It's a neat trick but a trick nevertheless. How should you tell the computer you want to operate on data once removed from price or volume, such as averages or oscillators? Nobody has shown the way yet.

How Summa Splits the Screen

Summa attacked the split-screen problem by anticipating and allowing for three different types of split-screen charts. Each type of split screen is offered as a menu item. The concept leads us to a rather ambivalent interpretation of the word *indicator*. We usually take the term to mean some function which moves in anticipation or confirmation of price. In the context of this program, *indicator* can be taken to mean any data at all: high, low, close, volume, a moving average, a volume indicator—you name it. For all practical purposes, *indicator* means the same thing as an algebraic *x*.

The three split-screen displays are as follows:

1. *The HLCV chart.* This consists of high, low, and close price bars plotted above volume. This is the familiar standard chart. See Figure 11.5.

2. *The indicator versus volume chart.* This is any single indicator (high, low, close, volume, a moving average, or any calculated value you wish to define) plotted above volume bars. You might use this screen format to plot a 30-day moving average above a volume bar chart, for example. See Figure 11.6.

3. *The indicator versus indicator chart.* Any pair of indicators may be plotted one above the other using this format. You can plot one stock's prices above those of another company. You can plot any two kinds of data for the same stock, using the upper chart for one indicator (perhaps closing prices) and the lower plot for another (perhaps an oscillator of complex design). See Figure 11.7.

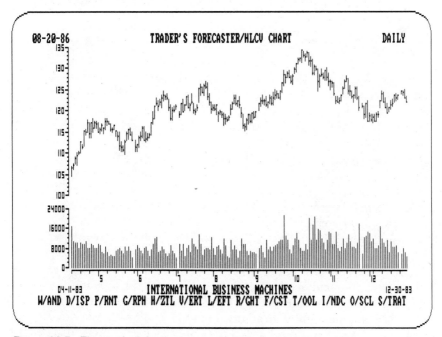

Figure 11.5. The standard, familiar price and volume bar charts as presented on the screen by the Winning on Wall Street program.

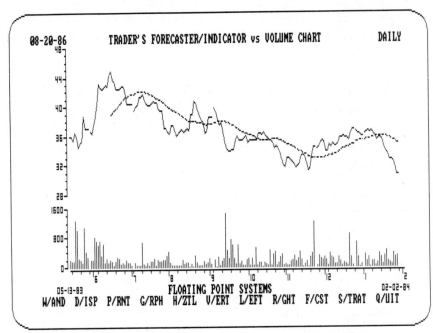

Figure 11.6. A plot of an "indicator" versus volume. The term *indicator* is very broadly defined in the program documentation. You can use this screen format to plot as indicators the high, low, close, or volume points or any of the calculated curves more commonly designated as indicators, such as moving-average indicators and volume trend indicators.

In practice, most of what the forecasting program does is accessible from the standard HLCV chart. One is shown for IBM in Figure 11.5. It is not strictly a price-volume chart. You can replace the volume data with an oscillator plot (per menu item O/SCL) or with a plot of a volume trend indicator (per menu item I/NDC).

Moving averages and linear regression functions are accessible under menu item F/CAST. Speed resistance lines, trading bands, and mid-channel support and resistance lines are applied via the T/OOL menu option. Selection of each of these menu items will result in the display of an appropriate submenu. The W/AND option displays the vertical bar wand, which can be moved back and forth on the screen with cursor control keys. L/EFT and R/IGHT are used to mark the wand's position when you use it to define brackets around a time frame, as you would in a regression analysis. H/ZLT and V/ERT are for drawing horizontal and vertical lines, respectively. D/ISP will display, beneath the screen, the price, volume, and date at any point marked by the wand. G/RAPH prints out the graph, and P/RNT prints out the numerical data that were used to create the graph. S/TRAT evokes the strategy command

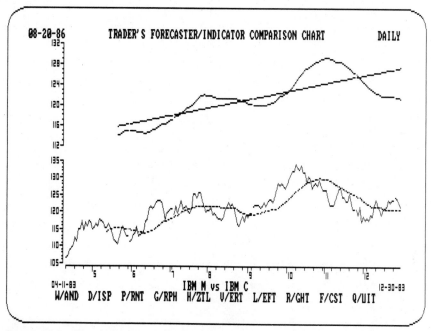

Figure 11.7. This is an indicator versus indicator plot. It is useful in comparing two stocks, a stock and an index such as the S&P 500, or any two curves pertaining to one stock, such as a price curve and an oscillator curve.

for the stock on the screen and will replace the graph with a tabular report of the outcome of strategy tests for this stock.

The indicator versus volume chart shown in Figure 11.6 is perhaps the least useful of the three formats, but you can do quite a bit with it. You can plot neat line (as opposed to bar) graphs of the high, the low, or the closing prices, all versus volume. In effect you can extract these individual variables from the bar chart that comprises all of them. Having isolated a plot of the highs, for example, you can smooth it or apply other functions to it alone. In the figure, the daily high prices have been plotted, connected, and smoothed with a moving average.

You can also plot any nonprice indicator, such as volume, on the upper half of the screen. If you want to smooth volume data, this is one place you can do it, using the moving averages available under the F/CAST menu item. Note that menu items for most analytical techniques (oscillators, volume trend indicators, speed resistance lines, channels, and bands) are not accessible from this screen.

The indicator versus indicator chart is a particularly useful format. Figure 11.7 shows two price-based plots, both for IBM. The close is

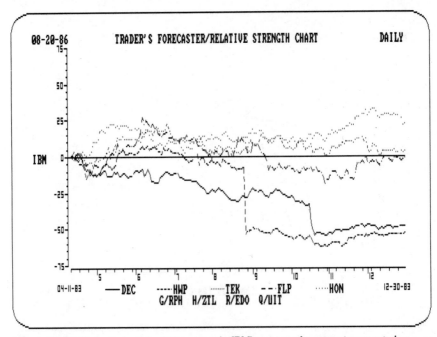

Figure 11.8. One way to plot relative strength. IBM's price performance is presented as a straight baseline at zero, and other technology stocks are shown varying around this line. Any stock or index can be selected as the baseline for the comparison. Note that five different stocks are plotted. Graphic devices (e.g., dotted and solid and dashed lines) are used to help the viewer distinguish between the several lines on the screen. Color provides the best solution to this common difficulty, but few investment programs support color, and none support the new very high resolution color monitors. Winning is strictly a monochrome program at this writing.

plotted on the lower half of the screen and smoothed with a 30-day simple moving average. Then, when you write and apply a user formula for the 30-day moving average, the average alone is replotted on the upper half of the screen. The linear regression line was drawn using the F/CAST menu item. If you wish to compare any two stocks, use this screen. If you want to create a chart of closing prices above a smoothed volume indicator, you can do it on this screen, again by writing and applying user formulas. This screen is the system's answer to any "Can it do?" question you might ask. The answer is almost invariably yes, but you probably will have to become adroit with user formulas to put your technique on the screen.

On the other hand, the indicator versus indicator screen is more than a cachepot for miscellaneous standard technical analytical techniques. It is a means for you to try your own ideas. There is no question the program will support some pretty complex Sunday afternoon stock market musings. I don't know of another program with this much flexibility of application.

Summa versus Savant: the Bottom Line

Savant's technical module is just that, a module. The complete program does both fundamental and technical analysis. If you want to do both, Savant is clearly your best choice. Summa's Winning on Wall Street is strictly a technical analysis program, and it is packaged with an excellent portfolio manager specially attuned to the needs of traders. Winning is sluggish and cumbersome and seems to have grown by accretion; there is no instantly apparent master plan in its design. But you can make it do anything once you become familiar with it. With Savant's program, you are restricted to the generous but finite list of standard techniques the program provides.

Probably neither program should be regarded as finished. As an owner of either one, you will presumably be given opportunities to upgrade the system as new code is written. Savant seems eminently expandable, because its design is as logical and natural as a tree. It needs expanding. The linear regression function is not fully exploited. With no user formula set, you cannot stretch its performance beyond its built-in command set. For problems which are not exotic, that is to say, most everyday technical analysis problems, Savant's is by far the easier and more efficient program to run.

Thanks to the user-formula feature, Winning on Wall Street can indeed be stretched beyond the limitations imposed by its menus and its somewhat convoluted basic design. You may have to write a few user formulas to make the program do some of the things Savant covers with built-in commands. The program is top-heavy with features, and you will have to learn its quirks to get it to do what you want in everyday applications. Mathematically, however, it is a tour de force, and it does bend over backward to help beginning users exploit its power.

12

Interactive's Charting Program

This excellent program is one component in an integrated software package called the Active Investor. It is currently offered by Interactive Data, a Chase Econometrics subsidiary in Boston. Altogether, the package includes a fundamental screening program (essentially Value Line's original Value/Screen package), a communications program, a portfolio manager, and the charting package.

The charting and portfolio programs rank among the very best. Both were created by Ed Gillott, who originally marketed the charting program and a rudimentary version of the portfolio manager as the Anidata Market Analyst. Interactive bought the program, and it is no longer available from any other source. The complete package costs $495; it is discussed further in the chapters on portfolio management and integrated software. The package is evidently priced as a loss leader, since Interactive sells data. If you do not buy a great deal of data, i.e., if you just want to follow a small selection of stocks, this is a bargain package.

The technical component, which is considered here, is a powerful program and holds a number of clear competitive advantages over the better publicized programs. In terms of sheer pizzazz, there is nothing else like it. It virtually makes a video game from the standard techniques of technical analysis. The Active Investor package is not being vigorously marketed by Interactive. It is not unlikely that the marketing will be passed to a third party, perhaps a discount brokerage. In any event, an interactive spokeswoman says the company will continue to support it with data, so if you are interested in the program, call Interactive and ask about it.

Split Screens and Menus: The Old Bugaboo

Let's reexamine briefly the basic problem produced by splitting the screen into upper and lower half screens. Consider an analogy.

Suppose the programmer had drawn on the screen an animated graphic representation of a hammer and two nails. Suppose the screen is split by a line into upper and lower halves. One nail appears in the upper half of the screen, and the other appears in the lower half. The hammer can move about freely in response to commands. A menu appears across the very bottom line of the screen, saying, "Designate nail to hit: (U)pper screen nail, (L)ower screen nail." If you enter U, the little cartoon hammer will migrate to the upper screen and start hammering at the upper nail. Conversely, if you enter L, the little hammer will drop to the lower screen and start hammering at the lower nail. So far, so good.

Imagine a third nail appearing somewhere on the upper screen. Simply specifying (U)pper versus (L)ower will no long enable the hammer to distinguish between the nails. You require a more elaborate menu, specifying perhaps Upper (A), Upper (B), and (L)ower. Or you need a pointing device, a mouse. Or you might have the hammer work counterclockwise through (A)ll the nails.

In technical analysis we don't have a hammer and nails. We may have instead a smoothing function, such as an exponential moving average, and a pair of plots. If there is a volume plot in the lower screen and a price plot in the upper screen, it is simple enough to selectively smooth the price plot with a moving-average function by specifying the (U)pper half of the screen.

Perhaps in the lower plot we will apply a different hammer, the function which draws the on-balance–volume (OBV) indicator. But having done so, we are confronted with four plots, two in the upper screen and two more in the lower screen. We cannot distinguish among them with a simple (U)pper versus (L)ower screen specification. If we try to draw a linear regression line against the OBV indicator, it may instead be drawn against the volume bars. If we try to create a trend line against a moving average of price instead of against unsmoothed price data, we may again be frustrated.

In a good technical analysis program, we have in our tool kit at least

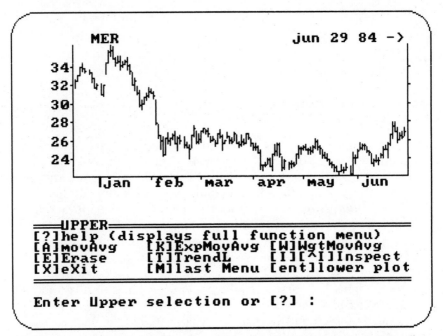

Figure 12.1. Interactive has clearly understood the critical problem created by splitting a stock chart in the traditional way, with price data plotted on an upper panel and volume data plotted on a lower panel. The problem for both the programmer and the user of the program is this: How do you determine which commands apply to which half of a split screen? Given two different charts, how do you "aim" your commands at the chart on which you wish to operate?

Interactive attacks the problem by dealing with the upper and lower half screens one at a time. In this figure, the upper half of the screen is, as usual, used to plot prices. The lower half, however, is dedicated to a menu of commands that apply to the price chart on display. In Figure 12.2, the relationship is flipped. The lower, volume data chart is displayed along with a menu of commands that apply to it.

four different hammers (the smoothing and linear regression functions) that we may wish to use against any type of nail, or plot. On the screen we begin with two nails only—price and volume—but the nails, or plots, tend to multiply as we work. It would not be uncommon to see six different plots on the screen. Six nails, four hammers: 24 possible combinations. Application of the proper hammer to the selected nail now calls for a full-screen menu. This will not do. The screen is already full of charts.

The situation can be simplified somewhat with logical assumptions. Moving averages are most frequently applied to price. Hence, in a limited program the moving average functions can be confined to the upper screen as a field of operation. This is a small-computer/small-program solution and not really an acceptable one.

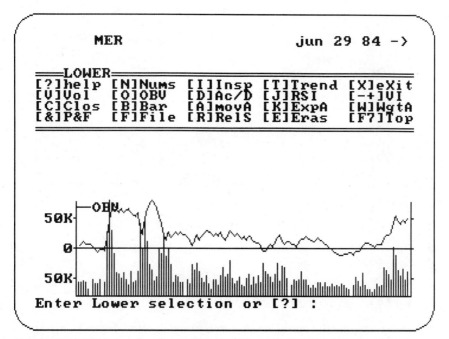

```
         MER                        jun 29 84 ->

    ===LOWER:========================================
    [?]help   [N]Nums  [I]Insp  [T]Trend  [X]eXit
    [V]Vol    [O]OBV   [D]Ac/D  [J]RSI    [-+]VI
    [C]Clos   [B]Bar   [A]movA  [K]ExpA   [W]WgtA
    [&]P&F    [F]File   [R]RelS  [E]Eras   [F7]Top
    =================================================



         ┌─OBV
    50K │
        │
      0 │
        │
    50K │

    Enter Lower selection or [?] :
```

Figure 12.2. When the price chart in Figure 12.1 has been completed, the user can elicit this volume chart, along with the menu which applies to it. When both charts are finished, they can be put together to form a typical price-volume display. The principle is sound but doesn't work very well in practice.

The split-screen problem is not well solved by any of the programs reviewed, although Interactive seems to understand it most clearly. It is perhaps the underlying reason for the multiple screen formats in the Winning on Wall Street program and for the multiple miniscreens in the Savant program. In general, command-driven programs seem to provide better solutions to the problem than menu-driven programs. This is because a command can include a letter or a number code that directs it to operate at a particular place on the display screen. However, what is needed is an address, or a pointer, that aims a command at a specific curve. No program offers such a feature, but Interactive has the next best approach, the "last-plotted" specifier.

There are no excellent answers. Interactive's Market Analyst makes a brave beginning, and its logical approach may be helpful as you begin to use the program (Figures 12.1 and 12.2). The two figures appear side by side to show the logic of the screens. The price half chart in Figure 12.1 appears above a menu. The menu fills the area normally reserved for the volume half chart, i.e., the lower half of the screen. In Figure 12.2 the arrangement is reversed. The volume half screen appears where you would expect to find it, on the lower half of the screen, but the upper half of the screen is expropriated by a menu. Each menu applies to the half screen with which it appears.

The simplification is clear. In a more typical program we would find one tiny menu that applied to *both* half screens, and we'd have the built-

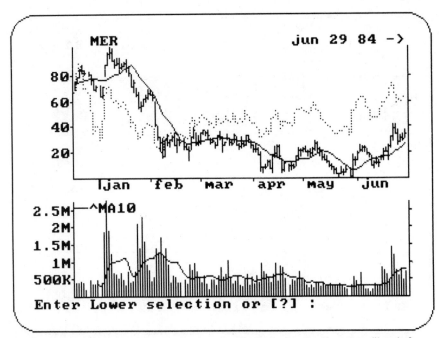

Figure 12.3. This chart shows what can be accomplished using the "last-plotted" trick. In this figure the last-plotted smoothing command was invoked immediately after the volume bars were plotted. The result is the smoothed curve representing a 10-day moving average of volume.

The upper screen displays a bar chart of high, low, and closing prices; a 12-day simple moving average of closing prices; and a 14-day moving average of the relative strength as characterized by J. Welles Wilder. Note the clear graphic definition of the various lines. The lines are even more sharply distinguished in color. The program's use of color is functional and superb.

in problem of "aiming" the menu's functions at one half screen or the other. In Figures 12.1 and 12.2 upper or lower screen specification is not necessary because each half screen has a half menu pegged to it.

When you're finished using the price menu to build the price chart, you bring up the volume menu and a volume chart. Finally, you synthesize the two finished half charts into a single, familiar, and conventional price and volume chart such as the one shown in Figure 12.3.

But Forget the Half Menus

The separate half-menu–half-chart concept sounds logical in principle, and it represents a frontal attack on the split-screen problem. In practice it doesn't work out very well.

As you finish one graph, you may inadvertently but very easily blot it out of existence with the menu for the next. About half the time the menu which appears below the price plot will be the one which applies not to the price plot but to the volume plot that is yet to be drawn. Items on both minimenus are appropriate to either half screen, and only a tiny portion of the program's truly impressive command repertoire appears on either of the little menus.

There are three keys to running the program successfully: (1) Abandon immediately the attractive notion of half-screen, half-menu correspondence, (2) memorize and then abandon the half menus, and (3) forever after, toggle between upper and lower charts with the function keys F7 and F9. Use the function keys as your screen specifiers. Any time you would like to examine a full-screen menu of commands, you can use a simple ? to put a comprehensive command dictionary on the screen. When you've had a look, you can return to an intact charting screen; nothing will have been blotted out.

I think the half menus may help account for the program's lack of recognition in the computer press. The first menu to come up after the program is booted will suggest to a casual observer that the program can do only 10 things, one of which is exit. Before long, the menus *really* get in your way. As you free yourself by learning the commands, you'll discover that the command repertoire of the program is astonishingly powerful. All the half menus have shown you is the tip of the tip of the iceberg.

But how, in its full-screen, command-driven mode, does Interactive solve the problem of specifying which nail is to be hit with which hammer? How do you aim a given command at the data on which you want it to operate?

The Last-Plotted Specifier

For upper and lower screen specification, the choice is made with the function key specifiers F7 and F9. These are the two most southwesterly keys on the board, and your left hand can find them in the dark. One of these two keys will put you in the neighborhood of the data on which you wish to operate. In most applications the keys will select between price and volume charts.

The smoothing functions will usually operate only on price data. If you are working in either half screen and request a moving average with the command A, for example, the smoothing function will be applied to price data and a moving average of prices will be drawn on the active chart.

Even if you are working in the lower half screen and request a moving average, the smoothing function will be applied to price points. To smooth volume, as shown in Figure 12.3, you need to use a trick, as follows.

The last plot drawn is always accessible to any function. To use a smoothing function against any "last-plotted" set of points, such as volume points, you would hold down the Control key while activating a smoothing function command. The command Control-A, for example, will draw a moving average of the most recently plotted function in either half screen. In Figure 12.3, the Control-A command was invoked just after the volume bars were plotted. The system prompts for the term of the average, which is 10 days in this case. Note that the term of the volume-smoothing plot appears as a legend on the lower screen.

For data once removed from the basic set of price and volume points, such as an on-balance–volume plot calculated using both price and volume points, you can request smoothing by doing so immediately after the on-balance–volume plot has been drawn. You can run a 10-day moving average on the OBV, for example, or run a least-squares-fit line against it. Least-squares-fit lines are always run against the last-plotted data.

Because of this last-plot trick for picking out particular plots on which to operate, the Interactive Market Analyst can do more with the data than most programs, without any full-blown apparatus for singling out the data on which it operates. This is a brilliant improvisation rather than a universal solution, but it takes Interactive's program a step beyond Savant and Summa in terms of analytical range.

With Savant, you can apply any function to any miniscreen, with the proviso that only one set of points is resident in the miniscreen: price points or volume points. A special command is provided to smooth oscillator plots. Each of the five volume trend indicators is plotted unsmoothed as a special case of an exponential moving average (the one-day moving average, which is no average at all). To smooth a volume trend indicator, you simply enter a desired number of days after the two-letter command. You cannot apply linear regression to these second-order plots with Savant, however.

With Summa's program, you can run moving averages of calculated or volume data by resorting to user formulas and/or the indicator charts. This is a bit of a production, but second-order plots are susceptible to linear regression and other functions.

With Interactive's last-plot specifying device, you can pretty much do whatever you want at the moment it occurs to you, without resorting to special screens or commands or writing formulas.

You do have to keep in mind the sequence in which you have applied various functions or at least remember which one you did last. Suppose you have plotted volume bars on the lower screen and then superimposed upon them an on-balance–volume plot. If you now apply a last-plot smoothing function, such as a 10-day moving average, it will smooth the OBV curve. If you want to smooth raw volume instead, it will be necessary to replot the original volume data. This does nothing to change the information on the screen; it simply sets up the volume points for a subsequent last-plot smoothing operation.

Distinguishing between Plots

Because Interactive can paint so much varied information on the screen, it is most spectacular in color. By drawing different plots in different colors, the program helps the eye distinguish between the original price data, one or more moving averages, and calculated indicators. Note that monochrome users are also given an aid to distinguishing among different curves. Bar, solid, and dotted-line formats are used in the price chart in Figure 12.3 to distinguish between price data, moving-average data, and a 14-day Welles Wilder index of relative strength.

Coincidence between Graphs

As shown in Figure 12.4, Interactive uses a movable vertical line, or wand, to show coincidence between price and volume data and to extract date, volume, high, low, and close numbers at any point on the charts. Note that the wand spans both charts. The wand is positioned with the cursor control keys. It moves slowly at first but accelerates as a function of the length of time the key is held down. If you simply press and hold, you can send it speeding across the screen. For fine positioning, use a quick, repetitive, press-and-release keying technique. This clicks the wand from one point to the next and keeps it from getting up to racing speed.

Contrast this wand with Summa's. In Winning on Wall Street, the wand is used to mark positions as well as extract numbers. Speed is constant, though it bogs down when the number extractor is used. In the Interactive program, the wand is used strictly to show coincidence and to extract numbers. The program has no facility for marking points, apparently because it is not necessary to mark points in order to draw lines. Trend lines are movable, and speed resistance lines are positioned by first maneuvering a trend line to link the selected major high with the major low.

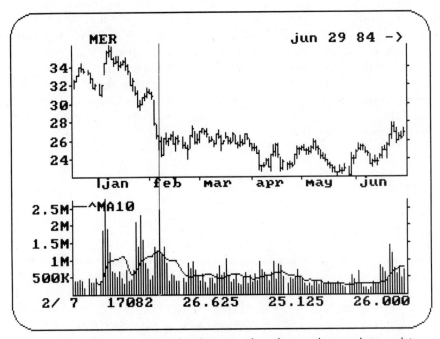

Figure 12.4. A vertical wand is used to show coincidence between lower and upper plots and to extract numbers. The date, volume, high, low, and close are shown below the chart for the day marked by the wand. The wand responds to the cursor keys. It moves slowly initially but accelerates rapidly if the key is held down. This is simpler and handier than specifying its speed, as one would with other programs.

Note the legend displayed for the smoothed volume curve. MA10 stands for a moving average taken over 10 days. The label is passive but in some future version of the program might make a good target for a pointer. This would be a way to direct specific commands to the curves on which one wished to operate.

Lines You Can Scoot

To put the system into its drawing mode, enter the command D. A horizontal line will appear, spanning whichever half screen is in use. The line has a pulsatile appearance, rather like the baseline on an oscilloscope, that tells you it is "live." You can move it anywhere you want. You can raise it, lower it, and rotate it with cursor controls. The Left/ Right cursor keys indicate the direction of rotation. Once it has been rotated, the Up/Down keys will propel it in the directions normal to (i.e., at right angles to) its length. This sounds complicated, but in practice it isn't. It is precisely the control set you would wish for to maneuver a trend line. You scoot the line into an approximately correct position and then nudge it into place exactly.

For trend lines, Interactive is unbeatable. With Savant's point-to-point trend lines, you must try, erase, and try again. Winning on Wall Street uses linear regression lines to establish trend lines. This is laudable for its consistency of method, but there is no other method provided. The Summa program will not draw lines from point to point. With Interactive's system you can use free-form trend lines or base them on a linear regression template. There is unfortunately no way to define the time frame for the linear regression other than by rescaling.

In the price chart for Apple in Figure 12.5, the two trend lines were each positioned and then saved to memory. Once a line has been saved (by entering an S), its appearance becomes solid; the pulsatile, mobile

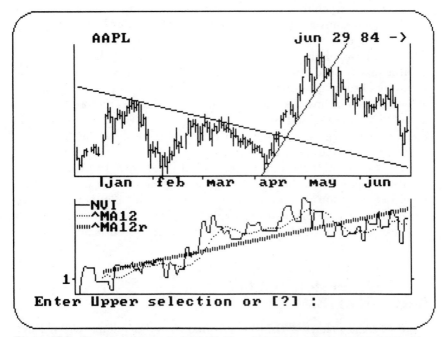

Figure 12.5. Trend line drawing is delightful. The whole line can be scooted and turned to obtain a satisfactory fit to the data. This is easier to accomplish than with point-to-point line drawing, which requires many repeated trials and erasures. The feature is unique to the program. Winning on Wall Street has a less intuitive and more consistent method which involves aligning trend lines in parallel with linear regression lines. One can also accomplish this with the Interactive program, but it takes some doing.

The lower plot was created by first drawing a negative-volume indicator. This indicator was then smoothed with a 12-day moving average. The last-plotted technique was used to make sure the negative-volume indicator, rather than the price bars, was smoothed. Finally, a linear regression line was drawn against the 12-day moving average of the negative-volume indicator. The linear regression line was restricted to the moving-average points by the last-plotted technique. This is a tour de force. No other program I have seen has this ability to single out a curve and apply any desired charting function to it.

line can be moved out from behind this fixed line and maneuvered away to draw another trend line.

This chart is a reasonably good example of a trend line buy signal. The original trend is bearish, as indicated by the trend line declining to the right. The trend is sharply broken by ascending prices in mid-April. The uptrend lasts until mid-May, as indicated by the bullish trend line ascending to the right. The trend is considered broken when the price breaks down through the ascending trend line. There is a six-point difference separating the buy signal from the sell signal, or about a 23 percent profit before commissions for a trader who has played this one-month trend. I like trend lines. The technique is simple, direct, and easy to read.

On the lower chart in Figure 12.5 is a far more complex exercise involving a negative-volume indicator. One can probably read some signals into or out of this indicator, but it is presented here chiefly as a demonstration of the program's unending ability to draw things. No volume points were drawn on this chart. The command for the negative-volume indicator is (appropriately) the minus sign key. The indicator is shown as a solid line resembling a city skyline. Superimposed on it is a last-plot 12-day moving average of the negative-volume indicator. Finally, a linear regression line was drawn for the points that constituted the 12-day moving average.

Note the useful legend in the upper left-hand corner of the graph. It names the plots and shows the graphic devices used to present them. No other program reviewed here can produce this plot with just three keystrokes. It is a virtuoso performance. If it were drawn on a color monitor, the lines would be differentiated by different colors.

Channels, Scales, and the Best Part of IBM

Figure 12.6 is a chart of IBM's performance in the bull market of 1982–83. It is a fairly classic illustration of using a technical analysis technique to alert one to the end of a trend. After IBM made its major ascent from below $60 to above $130, the show was essentially over. A trader relying on trend line breakdown or 100-day moving-average penetration would probably have exited IBM between $120 and $125, shortly before or shortly after the price peak.

There are three things to notice about these charts: their scale, the channel trend lines, and the plotting of price data on the lower screen.

The appearance of a price plot where one would normally expect a volume chart demonstrates the program's power to apply any function

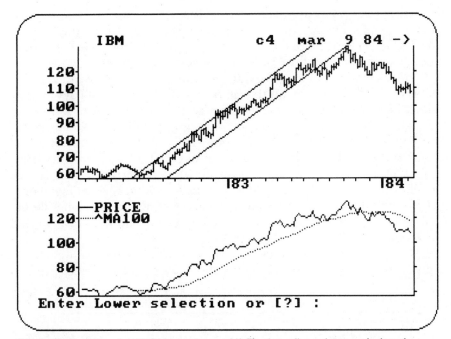

Figure 12.6. When should IBM have been sold? The first sell signal occurred when the stock broke down out of the trading channel shown in the upper half of the screen. A trader using this technique would have missed the subsequent price peak. A trader using a 100-day moving-average crossover to generate a sell signal would have stayed in the stock until after the peak had passed. It was clear by the end of November, from either method, that the long-steady uptrend was over.

The program has no difficulty drawing price data on both the upper and the lower halves of the split screen. Also note the expansion of the horizontal scale to include two years' trading. The program expands and compresses the time scale in response to push-button commands. You can "zoom out" for a long view without keying in new ranges for the horizontal scale. Specific rescaling instructions are required by other programs.

against any half screen. The lower screen was selected with the function key F9. Closing prices are plotted here (elicited with a C), but the system could as easily have plotted price bars. It was not necessary to use the last-plot feature to draw the 100-day moving average on the lower half screen. The command A produces a smoothed price curve wherever it is applied.

The scale of the chart should be compared with that indicated in the other figures. The other charts cover seven months; this one covers about two years. Interactive provides three commands for modifying the time axis of the chart: Scroll, Zoom, and Compress/Expand.

Scrolling is accomplished with a Control-S command. It initially prompts you for the number of days you wish to shift the time frame.

You may wish, for example, to examine a chart as it would have appeared 100 days ago. Enter −100 and the chart will be drawn on the screen. This is a "periscope" scan of the time axis and does not change the total number of points on display in any frame.

To back out for a wider view, you can enter the command Z for "zoom." This enables you to expand the chart from 70 days to 140 days to 280 days. To pack still more data onto the screen, you can use the Compress/Expand feature, which is accessible through function keys F8 and F10, respectively. One push of the Compress key will pack two days of price data into a single data point. This will in effect turn a 7-month chart into a 14-month chart. Four strikes of the F8 key transforms the original daily data into weekly data points and displays a chart spanning about three years. If you start with weekly data, the same compression will put an 11-year price history on the screen. The Expand key, F10, works precisely opposite to the Compress key.

The nice thing about these rescaling features is their automation. There is no need to figure out specific dates to enter; simply push a

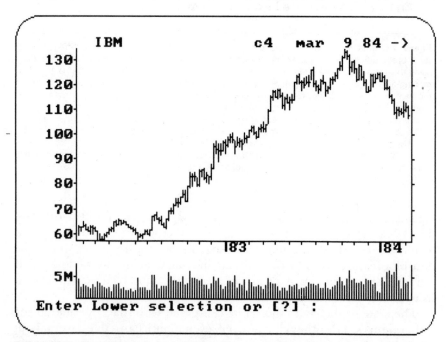

Figure 12.7. The proportioning of available space on the screen can be changed. On this screen, over 80 percent of the space has been allotted to the price. The volume chart contracts to make room for it.

button repeatedly to magnify or shrink the time frame. You can do this so rapidly that it is possible to watch trivial trends drop into perspective and major trends surface into full view. The process is rather like animating a cartoon.

Interactive provides another means of expanding and contracting charts; this one operates in the vertical dimension. If you are deep in a technical study of price action and want to take a better look at it, you can balloon the price chart to fill the screen, as shown in Figure 12.7. The command to accomplish this is Control-Y, and it prompts you to enter a percentage figure corresponding to the amount of screen space you wish to allot to the upper chart. If you entered 100 percent, the vestigial volume chart in Figure 12.7 would be squashed out of existence and the price chart alone would fill the screen. Conversely, you can allot less than 50 percent of the space to the upper chart. The lower chart will expand vertically as the upper chart shrinks.

A fixed y-axis can also be altered in scale, with a simple Y command, to change the presentation of data without changing the size of the chart. Unfortunately, and unlike competitive programs, the command operates on the next chart to appear; the currently displayed chart is not automatically redrawn to accommodate the new y-axis scale.

The Magnifying Glass

Figure 12.8 shows a delightful plaything called the Inspection command. It has practical value in a program capable of drawing and distinguishing between so many different kinds of lines. The lightly outlined square superimposed on the price chart defines an image to be magnified. The magnified image appears in the heavily outlined square on the lower chart. The heavy block is in effect a window opened through the lower chart onto some nether region, and it has no effect on the volume data it temporarily blanks out. When you press the Esc key, both blocks disappear and the underlying charts will be seen to be intact.

The purpose of the magnifying glass is to help you inspect the price chart, particularly in areas where many lines converge and cross. It is in precisely such congested areas that buy and sell signals are usually found. The Apple chart in Figure 12.8 is typical. It magnifies three crossovers, each of which could be regarded as a buy signal or a confirmation of a buy signal. The closing prices are represented by the solid, blocky line. The 10-day simple moving-average curve is the dotted line. The thick line composed of paired vertical strands is the 30-day moving

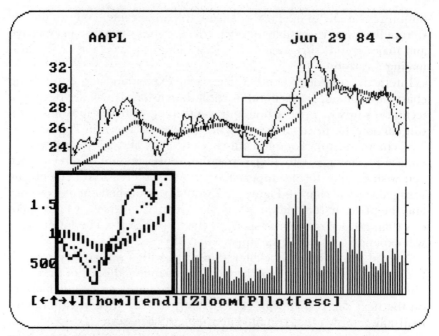

Figure 12.8. The inspection box on the price chart can be moved freely about the screen with cursor controls. Anything within the box appears, much magnified, in the thickly bordered magnifying window at the lower left-hand corner of the chart.

The magnifying window displays three distinct buy signals for Apple stock. The stock's subsequent steep rise suggests they were good, profitable signals. Buy and sell signals often appear in crowded, complicated sections of a chart. The magnifying window helps you to see them clearly. It is unique to the Interactive program.

average. The crossover points mark buy signals. Note that all three signals anticipate the trend line breakthrough indicated in Figure 12.5.

A momentum oscillator would have produced an even earlier buy signal. It is a common trading strategy to buy when the momentum oscillator signal is "confirmed" by the price crossing its 10-day moving average curve. By betting this earlier signal rather than the presumably safer trend line signal, a trader could have enhanced his or her one-month profit by 5 percentage points for a total gain of about 28 percent on the original investment. Now that options are traded on several rather volatile OTC issues, the profit potential in a short-term uptrend like this one has become far more dramatic.

The lightly outlined square that captures the image to be magnified can be piloted freely about the screen with the cursor controls. It can also be expanded vertically into a tall rectangle.

Auto-Analyze and the
User-Formula Set

The Interactive program provides an automatic plotting and printout feature similar to that offered by other programs. A single charting procedure is followed for every stock to be displayed and/or printed out. A pause between charts is automatic. When you have finished scrutinizing a chart on the screen, you can activate the automatic plotting sequence for the next stock by entering a command to resume the procedure. The auto-analyze procedure is global; it charts every stock on your disk. If you want to control the time and paper supply consumed by this process, it would be well to keep smallish groups of stocks on separate disks. On the other hand, the auto-analyze procedure has been adapted in an ingenious way as a technical filtering program.

Here is how this works. Before starting the auto-analyze procedure, you can set up certain conditions you want a stock to meet. Only those stocks which meet these preset conditions will be displayed. This is a good way to speed through your database of stocks, skimming off for display only those which are technically interesting. The conditions are set using the user-formula set and special conditional operators.

You might stipulate that only those stocks which have appreciated by 20 percent in the past two months will be displayed. You might require that a positive-going 10-day, 30-day moving average crossover must have occurred. Anything for which you can construct a formula can be used as a conditional screening (i.e., filtering) criterion. To set up more than one criterion, however, you will have to make more than one pass with the auto-analyze procedure.

The user-formula set is not as extensive as Summa's in terms of mathematical operators. There are no trigonometric functions, for example, but in their place Interactive provides the Boolean operators you use in the filtering process. These operators evaluate to true or false. They are easy to use if you follow the illustrative examples in the program manual closely.

Technical stock-screening capability is included by Interactive almost parenthetically, but it is a costly accessory to other programs, not a standard feature. An unadorned Interactive program will run stock-screening procedures that would require the RTR TechniFilter as an accessory to the Savant or Dow Jones technical analysis programs. Interactive does not offer an optimizer, which is a major feature of TechniFilter. Interactive's documentation of the filtering feature is sketchy (2 pages are devoted to screening in Interactive's manual, versus 48 pages in that of TechniFilter). But as a bargain stock-screening tool, Interactive's auto-analyze feature is well and cleverly exploited.

Cycle Fitting and the
Fantastic Stochastic

A cycle fitter is provided. This is a series of vertical bars you can superimpose on a price chart like the bars of a jail. By expanding and contracting on command the spacing between the bars, it is sometimes possible to mark repetitive price patterns such as peaks and valleys. Telescan's program has a similar feature but actually uses a variable-period sine wave instead of simple bars. This seems to be a very literal interpretation of the cycle-fitting concept, and Interactive's approach may be a bit more realistic in terms of its expectations of the data.

Still, you make some pretty clumsy assumptions in using a utility like this, assumptions that are not apparent as you push the buttons that make it go. In my opinion, cycle hunting should be accomplished with a utility program designed to do nothing but that. I have not seen such a program for commercial distribution, unfortunately.

Another feature for technical studies is the Stochastic. Partisans of this technique will find it helpful. Only one of the other programs reviewed here, MetaStock, offers this feature.

Oscillators, period shifting for moving averages, and several other functions are provided in the user-formula section. These formulas are already written in. You can also write your own additional formulas using the functions provided.

A DIF file utility is included in the original Anidata version of the program. It enables you to move price and volume data to and from other programs such as Lotus 1-2-3 and other spreadsheets that recognize the DIF format. Savant and Summa offer similar utilities, but as extra-cost options. You can use this feature to upload, for subsequent charting, DIF files of prices accumulated with an FM radio modem or from a TV cable. Interactive's Active Investor version of the program does not retain this feature, unfortunately, nor will it access by telephone any database other than Interactive's. The restriction to a single source of data is, in my opinion, the program's major weakness, as it will make you a captive customer.

13

The Dow Jones Market Analyzer Plus

Dow Jones pioneered the field of technical analysis for microcomputers, and the Apple versions of the Market Analyzer are in widespread use. The new Market Analyzer Plus was created for Dow Jones by RTR software. RTR wrote the original, and the company also writes and markets under its own name the excellent TechniFilter program.

This Dow Jones program is among the more recent major technical analysis packages to appear. It will run files created under the earlier Market Analyzer, and it is grounded on the long experience of the company in this field. As a new program, it reflects the current level of technology pretty well: It offers multiple miniscreens, an easily graded staircase of capability the new owner can ascend at his or her own pace, and a powerful command-driven system that will click briskly through any conventional analytical study.

We were given an opportunity to review a prerelease copy of this program, which was still in its final stages of development as this book was being written. There may be a few subtle differences between the finished version and our review copy, but it is unlikely that there will be any major alterations. The outstanding features of the program are as follows:

- Eight miniscreens.

- An automatic chart display and/or printout feature which can treat each stock differently.

- Functional use of color.

- A unique menu of statistical analytical procedures that helps put the day's price changes into perspective. Any truly strange behavior will stick out. Changes within an acceptable range can be clearly understood as such. You don't have to know anything about statistics to run these programs, incidentally.

- A neat solution to the on-screen menu problem: menus in windows.

- A highly developed formula set which can be semiautomated to create families of curves.

- Clever and functional application of windows throughout the program.

- Full compatibility with the RTR TechniFilter stock-screening, strategy-testing, and optimization program. The two programs have in common RTR's user-formula kit and the procedures for using it.

- The program does more with the J. Welles Wilder concept of relative strength than any of the others reviewed here.

- The unique ability to analyze stock groups and create and chart indexes of group performance.

- Point and figure charting for indicators other than price.

- A "midnight update" feature which enables you to update your files during the off hours, when on-line rates are low.

- A chart-stacking printout feature which enables you to align a great many indicators directly below the chart of a particular stock on a printout.

In my opinion, the two most imposing features among those listed here are the power to create and plot group indexes, and the statistical evaluation of new data immediately upon downloading—right after the market closes if you wish. You cannot accomplish these things directly with any other program, and they are powerful tools.

A limitation of the program is its exclusive reliance on the Dow Jones database for on-line data. For some types of data, other sources are considerably less costly. The program does provide a DIF file upload, so perhaps you could bring in data from Lotus files of data accumulated from FM radio or TV cable sources via this back door to the program.

The Main Menu

The program occupies three separate disks, one each for charting, communications, and reporting. In addition, one or more disks are used for storing stock data. No matter which program disk is in your default drive, the comprehensive menu shown in Figure 13.1 will appear. If you select a menu item which calls a program on one of the other disks, you will be prompted to insert that disk. If you have a hard disk, the whole system will fit on it.

The main menu gives a nice overview of what the Plus can accomplish. A few of the menu items give access to major subsystems. The item U under the heading "Charting," for example, will let you in on a huge

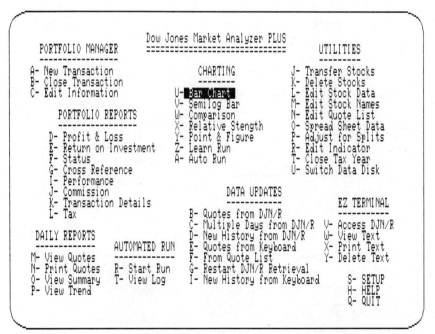

Figure 13.1. The main menu will come on-screen with any of the three program diskettes you choose, though it applies to all of them. This is chiefly a reference menu, a directory of what the program can do. You return to it rarely.

subset of commands and formulas, and most of what the program does in the way of technical analysis follows from the selection of this one item. One can use it every day. Other items on the menu, such as the item P, which adjusts for stock splits, may be used only once or twice per quarter. Because it suggests no logical hierarchy of functions, this menu is more in the nature of a help screen than a working menu; it saves the experienced operator the trouble of referring to the manual. In short, don't be overwhelmed by the dense detailing of the menu. The program is simple to run.

Eight Miniscreens

Figure 13.2 suggests how much information the Plus can pack onto a monochrome screen. The figure shows four separate dual charts, or the equivalent of eight miniscreens. If one includes the possibilities for superimposed plots, it becomes clear that Dow Jones can put a great deal of information on view all at once.

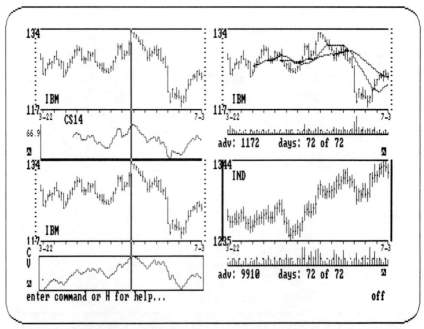

Figure 13.2. The question is not how many charts you can fit onto a monitor screen but how many charts you can stack one above the other. Stacking makes it possible to observe timing coincidence. The Plus puts two stacks of four charts each on the screen. One chart remains active, but the rest cannot be operated on.

The most meaningful question in regard to conventional (i.e., time-based) stock charts is not how many can be put on a monitor screen but how many can be stacked. Stacked charts illustrate coincidences between indicator formations and price formations. The Plus provides a special printout feature that enables you to stack a number of indicator charts below a single price chart. The concept is excellent. It would be nice if someone exploited the idea on a monitor screen, perhaps by scrolling several indicator charts in a window below a price chart.

Multiple miniscreen charts displayed on the monitor must be constructed one at a time. Once a quadrant chart is complete and you have moved on to another chart, you cannot go back to change the first chart without redrawing it. In other words, the miniscreens cannot be separately addressed, as they are in the Savant program. MetaStock, which can put up to 72 tiny charts on the screen, suffers from the same problem.

It is possible to store drawing commands in a buffer memory with the Plus, enabling you to recreate a whole chart at a keystroke. This is the technique to use in swapping charts, or putting one aside for subsequent full-screen charting. I found it helpful in some applications to use a screen configured like the one in Figure 13.10. In this figure, a stock index of semiconductor stocks is displayed full-screen. Superimposed on it in the lower left-hand corner is a chart of one of the stocks that was used to make up the index. The semiconductor index can be left on display while stock charts in the "window" are successively scrutinized. This superimposed format can be replicated with MetaStock, but MetaStock has no inherent macro capability and thus cannot recreate a chart at a keystroke. (You can add a macro program to MetaStock at extra cost.)

The Basic Chart

Figure 13.3 illustrates the familiar price-volume chart as presented by the Dow Jones Market Analyzer Plus. Two-thirds of the space is allocated to price charting, and one-third to the volume bars. We happened to have 72 days of data on IBM, but the time scale will default to as many days as you have stored. ADV stands for average daily volume; it is indicated by a dotted line superimposed on the volume bar chart.

Note that Dow Jones sells daily data in multiples of 12 days. The program does not handle weekly data directly. You must download daily data and then compress the data to display a weekly chart. A compression command is provided. The restriction to daily data is an important limitation, as it significantly raises the operating cost of the program. Data-

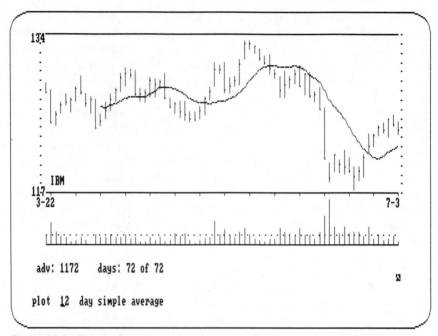

Figure 13.3. The standard price and volume charts. The treatment of the volume chart is exceptional. Only the tops of the bars are shown, since variation is apparent only here. The rest of the bars, from below the lowest volume reading to the baseline, are simply dispensed with. It saves space on the screen. The "ADV" label stands for average daily volume. The dotted line crossing the volume bars marks the level of average daily volume. Any sharp daily surge in volume will send the volume bar well above this line. The screen is well thought out.

bases other than Dow Jones, such as Warner Computer Systems, sell weekly data, and the other analytical programs are set up to accommodate these data. It might be possible to work around this problem with the Plus by exploiting its built-in ability to import and export DIF files. DIF files can be created using data from any source.

Vertical scaling is automatic and typically produces offbeat numbers such as the $134 shown at the top of this scale. I routinely convert the vertical scales to multiples of $5 or $10 when I want to examine a chart closely. A vertical command to change the scale enables one to do this easily. Grid lines can be superimposed on the chart on command, and more informative vertical axis labels appear along with the grid. Some incremental date markers also appear on the horizontal axis when a grid is requested.

If the chart becomes busy with too many lines, you can selectively erase the grid, but the helpful scaling numbers stay put. You need them because no pointer is provided to extract numbers from the chart. A mov-

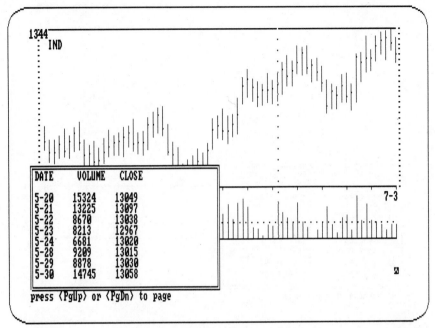

Figure 13.4. Instead of extracting numbers associated with a particular point on the chart, you can display in a window the data from which the chart was plotted. You must determine by eye from the graph what date you are looking for. Then scroll through the price and volume data in the window to learn what happened that day.

able vertical wand is available, but it only establishes coincidence and does not read out data points.

Figure 13.4 shows how numerical data are recovered for viewing. The data points displayed in the window can be scrolled to the date of interest, assuming you can estimate from the chart what that date might be. This is not as useful as a pointer-type number extractor, but it illustrates how neatly the program makes use of the windowing technique.

Help in the Window

Figure 13.5 shows much of the command menu for the program, windowed in the lower left-hand corner of a chart. It is called by touching the letter H. A second page of the menu is displayed when you touch any key. Another touch and the menu disappears, and material on the chart which has been obscured by the menu is instantly restored. This is the most attractive solution to the on-screen menu problem. Both the

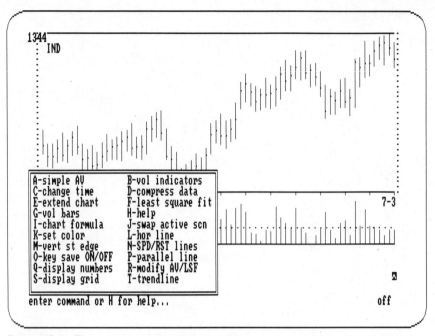

Figure 13.5. The on-screen command menu appears in a window when you request it. You can then scroll through the commands. The menu does not completely obscure the chart. Thus, you can keep the charting problem in view while you hunt through the commands for a specific keystroke to solve it. The window and the menu within it disappear instantly when you have entered the selected command.

Plus and MetaStock use this approach. The menu is there when you want it and gone when you don't. With the Plus, the chart remains pretty much in view as you scan the menu for a command to operate on the chart.

The screen is rigidly formatted in that the price chart is almost invariably the upper chart. The lower chart is either volume data or an "indicator" chart. The term *indicator* is interpreted here, as in the Summa program, to mean anything at all: price, volume, volume indicators, or other calculated values.

The command J is provided ostensibly to toggle back and forth between upper and lower screens. When you start to chart a stock, the upper screen is the active one. Certain commands will automatically send you to the lower screen (such as B, which plots volume indicators). In practice you use J to get back to the upper screen. The smoothing and line-drawing functions can be applied to either the upper or the lower screen, whichever is active, provided that you are working with price or calculated volume data, respectively. The basic volume bar chart is inviolable. You cannot smooth it or superimpose any lines on it. If you want to smooth volume data, you must first replot the data using a user formula (the letter V) and then apply one of the averaging commands.

Volume indicators and user formulas are normally plotted on the lower screen and thus blot out the volume bar chart. You can erase such plots and restore the original volume bars plot with the command G.

If you have used the lower half of the screen to plot one indicator—perhaps on-balance volume—and would like to plot another, coincident indicator, use the command Y. This elevates the lower plot to the upper screen and frees the lower screen for a new plot. This is a nice feature and illustrates the writers' consciousness of the importance of stacking charts.

At this level of operations, where we are primarily entering commands from an on-screen menu, the program is somewhat limited by the scope of the menu. However, the menu provides the beginning user with a ramp up into the program, and as a teaching device for commands it is excellent.

And Beyond the Menu . . .

The menu command I, which per the menu enables you to "chart formulas," effectively clicks the program into a command mode, and one is tempted to call the "formulas" commands. If you type in a letter C, for example, the program will plot closing prices. The letter V plots volume, and H and L plot highs and lows, respectively. Formula building is similar to Savant's process for command building. To average closing prices over 12 days, for example, you enter CA12 and the plot appears. There is no waiting for calculation, no disk spinning. The system responds to formulas as it does to direct commands—instantly. These are not user formulas in the conventional sense. They are an extension (and sometimes a replication) of the command set provided on the menu.

Figure 13.6 shows a plot of the Dow Jones industrial average. It illustrates the use of the program's standard formula CS14 to create a plot of J. Welles Wilder relative strength. Formulas are always plotted on the lower chart at the outset. The upper chart has been operated on with a least-squares-fit procedure. The dotted lines paralleling the least-squares-fit line are spaced by the program at standard deviation intervals. From the upper chart, one could conclude that the average has stayed pretty consistently within plus or minus two standard deviations of the least-squares-fit line. On swings outside the second channel, one could begin to get uneasy about the market or anticipate a snapback.

The lower plot of Welles Wilder relative strength is presented here

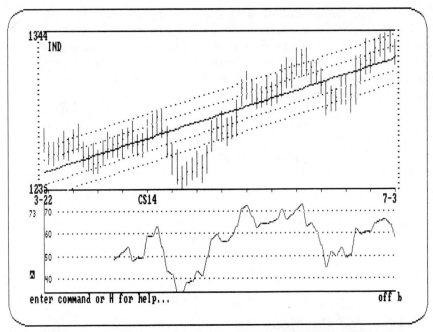

Figure 13.6. The program often seems to reflect the thinking of J. Welles Wilder, whose concept of relative strength is illustrated here. The upper plot shows the Dow Jones industrial average. The lower plot is the relative strength indicator. The theory suggests that if the indicator exceeds 70 or drops below 30, the stock or index will then tend to fall or rise, respectively, until the relative strength index returns to its normal range of 30 to 70.

Linear regression was used to draw the solid line on the upper chart. The dotted lines suggest trading band boundaries stationed one and two standard deviations above and below the linear regression line. Most of the swings of the index fall within three standard deviations of the centerline.

because the concepts of J. Welles Wilder are pervasive in the program. They are not restrictive; the program will also do the other standard technical studies. The attractive thing about the Welles Wilder relative strength index is that it points very directly to abnormal, or extreme, stock prices. If the plotted index in this chart were over 70 or under 30, one would be able to read it as a signal that the Dow had gone too high or too low. Indeed, this chart bears out the notion, since excursions above 70 and below 30 were soon corrected by the market. The linear regression channels point to the same exceptional swings.

We have commented at length on the validity of indicators in earlier chapters and refer you to those chapters for the essential caveats. The Welles Wilder index has looked pretty good to me lately, though the 70/ 30 brackets seem a bit too tight. If you use it to attract your own attention rather than as revealed truth, you may find it quite valuable. You can set your own brackets to suit a particular stock you want to follow.

Labeled scales are not provided, incidentally, on indicator plots. The horizontal scaling lines on this one were drawn in one at a time using the horizontal line command, L. The highest value on an indicator plot is called out to the left of the vertical axis, however.

The Extension: A Probe into the Next Two Weeks

Figure 13.7 shows another, similar plot of the Dow Jones industrial average. Note the extreme right side of the price chart. Although the chart was drawn on July 3, the scale extends two weeks beyond this date.

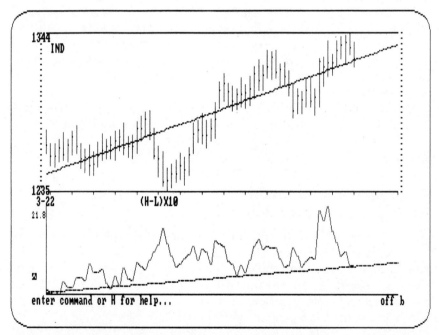

Figure 13.7. Although this chart was drawn on July 3, the horizontal scale projects into the future two weeks beyond this date. July 3 is the date at which the price bars stop. The two-week extension of the graph enables you to see where a trend line or linear regression line would take the market, assuming no changes of trend in the meantime.

The lower chart illustrates a plot of a user formula, (H-L)X10. The formula is a request for a 10-day exponential moving average (the X10) of the difference between the high (H) and the low (L).

If the least-squares-fit line can be accepted as a projection of the future course of the Dow, the point at which the least-squares line touches the vertical axis forecasts the approximate level of the Dow (or whatever stock you happened to be charting) two weeks into the future. This assumes, of course, that the present trend will continue unaltered. Since you are projecting only two weeks ahead, this is not an untenable assumption.

The lower chart illustrates the projection of a simple trend line. Trend lines are drawn from point to point, using cursors. The cursor's jump, and thus its rate of progress, can be varied by pressing a number key (1 through 9) simultaneously with the selected cursor key. In the version of the program I tested the cursor control response was a bit skittish in practice, but a variable-rate speed control is a great idea.

The formula in the chart, which is displayed above the plot, is (H-L)X10. In the notation of the program this calls for a 10-day exponential moving average (X10) of the difference between the high and the low (H-L). Formulas of this type can be used to construct moving averages, oscillators of both major types (momentum and moving-average difference), oscillators of your own devising, and a variety of volume indicators. After using the program for a while, you may find that you prefer to use the formula set (or command set, however you think of it) in preference to the menu commands.

The formula notation is essentially the same as that used in the RTR TechniFilter, which is a chart-sorting and strategy optimization program.

Programmable Automatic
Chart Display and Printout

As you key in a set of instructions to draw a given plot, you can save the instructions in sequence in a buffer memory. The sequence can be stored in association with the stock and recalled for use in an automatic plotting procedure. In this way you can program the system to automatically display and/or print out stock charts which are individualized for each stock. Other programs offer automatic plotting, but this generally entails the blanket application of a single set of charting instructions.

Charting with different instructions for different stocks is unique to the Dow Jones Market Analyzer Plus. This may sound like a luxury item, but it is not. It helps to plot each stock in the same way every time you update the data. It assures consistency in decision making. If you're *consistently* wrong about a stock, you will be in a much better position to correct your technique than will someone who is wrong willy-nilly.

Moreover, indicators can be custom-tailored to specific stocks. This is the whole point of using an optimizer and is one of the things you can do with a computer that you can't do very well without one. As such, it constitutes a competitive advantage. Automatic, programmable charting can help you determine which indicator works best with which stock.

More Power to You: The Group Indexes

Here is a simple feature which in my opinion justifies the price of admission. It is the power to create and plot indexes of stock groups. Figure 13.8 illustrates the technique. In the left-hand plot the performance of a group of biotechnology stocks is charted from March to July. In the

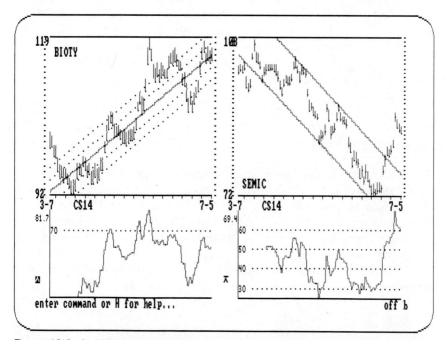

Figure 13.8. In 1985, between March 7 and July 5, the stock market, as measured by the Dow Jones industrial average, trended up in an unremarkable way. In this same period, the biotechnology group soared and the semiconductor group plunged. Narrowly defined group indexes tell you much more about the trend of a particular stock than the DJIA. Even the widely accepted industry group indexes are too broadly defined. The Plus enables you to define and closely track your own group indexes. You can create and follow any sort of group you like. In addition to industry groups, for example, you might wish to track groups of institutional favorites, low-PSR stocks, or high-beta stocks.
    The Welles Wilder relative strength indexes are displayed below the group indexes. The "normal" range is between index values of 30 and 70, and these values may be regarded as lower and upper limits, i.e., buy and sell signals.

right-hand plot the performance of a group of semiconductor stocks is charted over the same period. Each is shown in conjunction with J. Welles Wilder relative strength indexes. Figure 13.8 suggests how pointless it is to formulate grand generalizations such as "the market is up" and "the market is down." In this rather unremarkable period for the broad market, biotechnology stocks surged and semiconductor stocks plunged.

Group indexes tell you a great deal about what is really going on in the market. As this is being written, newspaper business pages are still running major essays on the decline and fall of the American semiconductor industry. The newspapers reflect a prevailing point of view, and it may even be a valid one.

However, it is evident from the chart that the semiconductor stocks turned up two weeks before the last-plotted date, broke out of their well-established downtrend, and even touched the maximum allowable relative strength. There was some news to sustain this little rally, mostly pertaining to the vigorously accelerating development of the 1-megabyte RAM chip. The news appeared in the electronic industry trade publications but had not yet filtered out to the business press at large. An analyst might look for the semiconductor group to make a second and major bottom and then consider buying into it. By that time, however, another group may look still more attractive, or a majority of stock groups may signal a major sell-off. The power to dissect the market into industry groups is a tremendously valuable one. The Telescan program retrieves group indexes, but it does not make it easy for you to construct your own.

You can also use group indexes to evaluate the performance of individual stocks against that of other stocks in a group. In Figure 13.9 the stock of Hybridtech (HYBR) is plotted against the group index for biotechnology stocks. The dotted line just above the baseline at the 100 level represents the Dow Jones industrial average. This chart was created using the conventional relative strength feature of the program. It illustrates how the stock and the index performed relative to the Dow Jones industrial average over the period of interest. Hybridtech outperformed both the Dow and the biotechnology index. As it turned out, it was an acquisition target.

The indexes are not store-bought items. You must construct them yourself by identifying the stocks you wish to include in each group and then downloading the pertinent data. At the outset this is costly, as you may download a year or more of data for 10 or 20 stocks. The biotechnology index shown in Figure 13.9, for example, cost about $20 to create. I did it on a Saturday, so the downloading cost was lower than it would have been during weekday trading hours. The cost of the Dow Jones industrial average, which is already compiled into an index and sold as

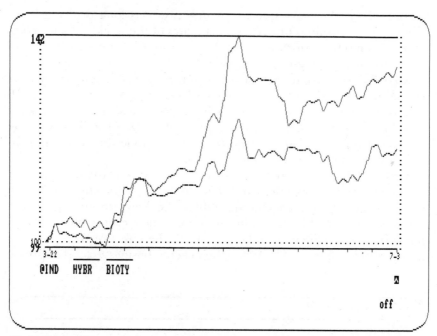

Figure 13.9. Hybridtech outperformed the rest of the biotechnology group fairly dramatically, as shown by this chart of conventional (rather than Welles Wilder) relative strength. The chart shows how a hypothetical $100 investment in Hybridtech has done relative to a $100 investment parsed out across all the stocks in the biotechnology group. Once you create a group index, the program treats it just as if it were another stock. All smoothing, line drawing, and statistical analysis and other features can be freely applied to the group index.

such, was no more than the cost of a single stock. After you set up an index, the cost of keeping it up to date is not significant. Its value to you in judging the performance and prospects of your own stocks certainly makes it worthwhile.

Group indexing technique is an important beginning, but it is not fully realized as a technique in the Dow Jones Market Analyzer Plus. Each stock is accorded the same weighting in any index the program constructs. This means you cannot adjust the index to attach special importance to large or small companies, for example. You can weight the index with your selection of stocks, however. If you want the index to attach more importance to the performance of large companies, include more large companies than small companies.

I try to design indexes that turn early. To do this, you can rely on the built-in early reactions of weighted or exponential moving averages, but there is a more direct fundamental approach. In the semiconductor industry, for example, smallish suppliers of specialized equipment and services "feel" the move into major new products long before it is reflected in the earnings or earnings estimates of the semiconductor companies themselves. In downturns, their revenues reflect early cuts in their customers' spending budgets.

Accordingly, I like to include a few of these supplier-level companies in the groups' index, just for their early-warning value. Figure 13.10 illustrates the performance of an early-warning stock, Tylan, as an inset chart on the plot of semiconductor industry stocks. As indicated by the moving averages, Tylan turns quite decisively while the group, in contrast, meanders in the direction of its trend.

This trick works for other types of stocks. If you follow consumer packaged goods companies, for example, you can sometimes chart an early-warning effect by including publicly held advertising agencies in the index. When there is optimism among their clients, their billings take off. Because they are relatively small, the effect of fresh revenue becomes noticeable quickly. When their clients' businesses level off, these

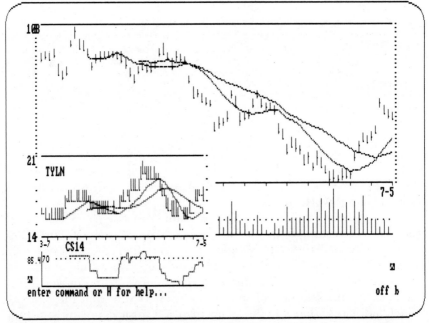

Figure 13.10. A stock chart can be contrasted with an index chart by using a window. In this window the performance of an early-warning stock, Tylan, is plotted. The semiconductor group appears in the background. From the moving averages it is apparent that the group moves much less decisively than the stock, as one would expect. Note that the inset chart is a complete one, with both upper and lower panels. The program lets you use the inset window as if it were a separate monitor.

agencies may suffer quantum drops in revenues. Their stocks naturally react to these changes, often before they are apparent at their clients' bottom lines.

How the Day Went . . .

Figure 13.11 shows tabulation produced by the Dow Jones Market Analyzer Plus after downloading of the closing prices for the day's trading. The actual change and the percentage change in the price of each stock are reported in the first two columns. The headings "c/adc" and "v/adv" stand for two useful ratios: close/average daily close and volume/average daily volume. The averages are compiled over 12 days. Instead of comparing today's close with yesterday's, you can use the c/adc number to

| date: 08-21-1986 | | 1 day change | | 12 day average | | 14 day volatility | | |
stock	close	change	% ch	c/adc	v/adv	vlty	posn	rstr
HYBR	25.25	0.25	1.00	1.03	0.92	2.19	89	72
IND	1326.40	-7.60	-0.57	1.00	0.87	0.14	65	65
CNTO	18.25	0.00	0.00	1.11	0.46	4.50	89	65
BIOAD	32.00	2.00	6.67	1.25	0.92	1.12	88	62
BIOTY	115.03	0.46	0.40	1.03	0.92	2.55	74	62
XICO	8.13	-0.25	-2.98	1.09	0.49	5.91	70	61
INTC	26.75	0.25	0.94	1.06	0.47	2.47	94	61
SEMIC	86.42	-0.48	-0.55	1.05	0.36	3.21	76	61
BGENF	7.38	0.00	0.00	1.00	0.50	3.15	50	59
TYLN	17.00	-0.50	-2.86	1.05	0.08	5.36	67	55
DRAM	8.50	-0.13	-1.51	1.04	0.22	5.36	68	55
SEMAD	-32.50	0.00	0.00	0.85	0.36	1.26	79	54
IBM	123.75	-0.63	-0.51	1.01	0.56	1.44	80	54
AMD	26.25	0.25	0.96	1.02	0.22	4.32	77	51
DJ	46.75	0.25	0.54	0.98	0.47	1.74	17	51
GENE	46.25	1.25	2.78	0.99	1.67	1.81	50	48

⟨PgDn⟩   ⟨P⟩ Print All   ⟨G⟩ Graph   ⟨Esc⟩ Menu

Figure 13.11. At the end of the trading day you can download fresh price and volume data and then display this tabulation. The actual change and percentage change in stock prices are shown in the first two columns. The other column puts the day's price and volume changes into perspective by relating them to short-term moving averages and relative strength (per Welles Wilder). Volatility is recalculated to take into account the day's new data.

You can sort the tabulation per any of the headings in ascending or descending order. This tabulation is sorted in order of descending relative strength. You might re-sort it in order of the day's percentage change in price. This would put the day's largest gainers on top of the list and its biggest losers on the bottom.

see how today's close relates to the 12-day trend of the stock's closing price. Similarly, you can compare today's volume with the 12-day volume trend. These values help keep the day's results in perspective.

The last three columns report volatility, position, and relative strength. The values are compiled over 14 days. Volatility suggests how freely the stock's price swings. A high-volatility stock may bounce like a Superball. A low-volatility stock may just sit there. Position is a measure of where the stock lies within its trend. A 100 percent value means it is at the top of its range of recent prices; a zero means it closed at its low. Relative strength is the J. Welles Wilder value, and one could quickly check to see whether this number was within the "safe" range from 30 to 70.

This tabulation does not support any heavy analysis; rather, it provides a quick look at how the day went and helps you spot problem areas fast.

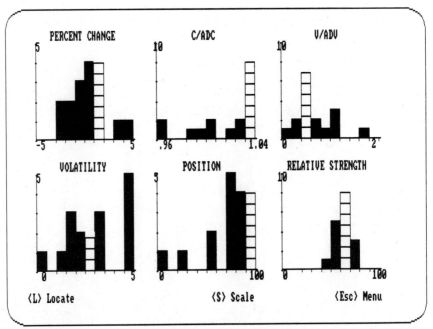

Figure 13.12. This is how the program graphs the daily trading report tabulated in Figure 13.11. In your mind's eye, superimpose a bell-shaped curve over the bar charts. The top of the curve—the tallest bar—tells you what most of your stocks did today. In this display, for example, most of the stocks did not shift far from yesterday's prices. The percentage change bars are tallest at the zero level.

The C/ADC chart shows you the close versus the average daily close for the past 12 days. Most of these stocks closed nicely above their moving averages. Some bars look like ladders. This is how the program responded to my request to find the bars which contained the performance data for Intel. From the position chart I can note that Intel, like most of the other stocks, is trading today near the top of its recent price range.

The table can be sorted on any variable. This presentation is sorted on the relative strength values so that the stock with the highest relative strength appears first. You could re-sort the list for the highest percentage change or the highest v/adv. The sorting process is almost instantaneous.

The data presented in Figure 13.11 can be presented in graphic form, as in Figure 13.12. A statistically well-behaved assortment of stocks would let you draw, above each collection of chart bars, a smooth bell-shaped curve. It might be centered over a tall central bar or heavily skewed to the right or the left. The percentage change chart, for example, shows that most of the companies were unchanged or down slightly for the day. The bars with the appearance of ladders were singled out by the program in response to my request to highlight the bars containing the data produced by Intel. We can see from this highlighting that Intel's c/adc was up, along with that of most companies in the group. Its position in range was on the high extreme of the scale, but most companies' stock prices were also at the high end of their ranges. Intel's relative strength was at the middle of the group, as was its v/adv.

The Plus produces another tabular and graphic daily summary called the Trend Report. It strongly reflects the thinking of J. Welles Wilder on evaluating relative strength indexes. You will find this particular approach to technical analysis useful. The numerical data are presented without the benefit of algebraic signs, however, so you must study the tabulation a moment to determine the direction of the trends it measures and ranks.

In summary, the charting capability of the program is rather typical, but the command language cum user-formula set advances it a notch in terms of speed and convenience. The statistical utilities and the power to create and follow group indexes add real value to the Plus. Group analysis can show you the inner workings of the market in action, and I think you will notice the difference this makes in your performance.

14

Moderately Priced Charting Programs

Two moderately priced charting programs are considered here: Meta-Stock, from Computer Asset Management, and Trendline II, from Standard & Poor's. MetaStock nominally costs $195, and Trendline II costs $275. When you consider the actual cost of getting these programs up and running on your computer, they are priced within $50 of each other, so it seems reasonable to regard them as similarly priced.

What Must You Give Up to Get the Lower Price?

A "fully priced" technical analysis program like those reviewed in the preceding chapters will typically cost about $100 to $200 more than these new, moderately priced programs. The established programs are under price pressure from the newer programs and are commonly discounted, but if you pay a lower price, you will still get a lesser program. One can reasonably ask what capabilities have been left out of MetaStock and Trendline II to achieve the lower prices.

Recall that three of the "big" programs are moving toward the goal of completely integrated, four-component investment systems, including technical analysis, portfolio management, fundamental analysis, and communications. Only one of them (Interactive) offers all four in a box, but the others are at the point of offering three, typically technical analysis, communications, and a portfolio manager. Savant has technical analysis plus communications, with fundamental analysis as an add-on module. Dow Jones has technical analysis, communications, and a portfolio manager and offers fundamental analysis in an unintegrated separate program. Winning on Wall Street has technical analysis, communications, and a portfolio manager specially tailored for traders.

The lower-priced programs are less ambitious. MetaStock will do just one thing, technical analysis. Trendline II will do technical analysis plus one more thing—communications—and this in part accounts for the price difference between the two programs. In order to make MetaStock download price histories so that you can chart them, you will have to purchase a separate communications program. It is an option you cannot realistically expect to do without.

MetaStock's Wide Compatibility with Databases

Different vendors offer different communication software to link up with MetaStock. The programs range down in price from $139. MetaStock's authors offer a communications program called the Downloader to link MetaStock to the Warner database. The Downloader is list priced at $50, but if you buy it along with the MetaStock program, the pair costs $224. There is actually an advantage to the purchaser in the functional separation of the charting and communications packages. You can choose from among seven different databases as your source for price-volume data. In addition to Warner, they are Compuserve, Commodity Systems Inc., Hale Systems, IDC (Interactive Data), I.P. Sharp, and Nite Line.

FM and Cable Links

Standard utilities supplied with MetaStock will import DIF files from Lotus or other DIF-compatible programs. This means you can set up a MetaStock receiving file in a spreadsheet and use it to accumulate quotes brought in by Lotus's Signal FM system, the Telemet America FM system, and the FNN cable TV feed from Data Broadcasting Corp. If you have Borland's Sidekick to capture screens and some programming ingenuity, you may be able to dispense with the spreadsheet buffer and create files directly from X*Press, the McGraw-Hill cable TV quote and news wire service. Moreover, Steve Achelis, who is the president of Computer Asset Management, has had talks with X*Press about directly linking Meta-Stock to X*Press. This is an exciting possibility. As things now stand, MetaStock probably provides the widest choice of databases, but you should be aware that the link-up with whichever one you select is a problem that can be solved only by purchasing additional software. The $195 base price, in other words, is not going to get you started.

On Backing Away from Brilliance: An Opinion

Here is a brief digression.

There are certain human endeavors for which the reward system must be understood as a bell-shaped curve. Wherever this is true, median-level performance earns a better reward than low-level performance, as one would expect, but median-level performance also earns a better reward than *top*-level performance. I think this concept will square with many adults' experience of the world. Dullards and geniuses alike tend to turn out empty pockets. The race is not always to the swift. The optimum beats the maximum.

It seems to me that technical analysis is one of those fields in which it simply does not pay to hone one's skills beyond a certain point. You can become transfixed by charts. You can begin to read importance into indicators and aspects of indicators that are so subtle—such light brush-strokes—that only you can actually perceive them, let alone guess their significance. You can devote more and more of your time and energy to ever more intricate chart analyses as, oddly enough, more and more of your money goes racing down the drain.

Technical analysis punishes its experts. It rewards people who are about as good at it as most other traders. This makes sense. Charts predict the behavior of the chartists. It follows that if you draw charts that look pretty much like everybody else's, you can anticipate everybody else's trades. If you grow beyond this point intellectually—study harder, write more elegant equations, create more exotic indicators—you will lose touch with the mob of ordinary traders and lose your sense of which way that mob (and the market) is moving.

It is not possible to unlearn something or to shed sophistication once you acquire it. What you can do, however, is record in the memory of the computer as you go along those techniques you use as an amateur, those you use as a young pro, and those you favor in your prime. Precisely then, it's time to stop. You can play back your prime from then on by pushing the appropriate function keys. Your personal progression from zero to the zenith shouldn't take more than a few months. You will know that you have grown too clever at technical analysis when suddenly nothing works anymore. To recover your beginner's luck, you can fish your former, less sophisticated, more profitable charting techniques out of the computer's memory. From that day on, rely on the automated good judgment of your former self. A year hence, when you've cooled off on the subject and feel a bit rusty, you can reinterest yourself and maybe rewrite your act to reflect the current fashions. Work your way back up the learning curve, but no farther than the apex.

For the same reasons, it probably would not be a good idea to spend $1500 on the most expensive and sophisticated charting package available for your microcomputer. Beyond a certain point, the return on technical sophistication diminishes steeply. Which puts us back where we started, with a discussion of moderately priced charting programs.

Macros and Auto-Run Capability

Macro keys "remember" a series of charting commands. Once the necessary instructions have been stored to a specific key—the F9 key, for example—you can apply a whole series of charting techniques by pressing that key. Typically it will call up and display a selection of moving averages, an oscillator or two, and one or more volume indicators on the chart of a particular stock. You can assign one key to each stock in your portfolio if you wish and in this way assure that each stock's chart will be redrawn in a consistent fashion from week to week. Whole sets of macros can be stored in disk files. If you run out of function keys to assign to stocks, you can reassign some or all 10 keys by loading a fresh macro file from the disk.

An auto-run capability reduces the whole charting process to a preprogrammed procedure. Working from a list of stocks, the computer will successively chart each stock and apply all analytical techniques (moving averages, etc.) specified in advance. The charts may be displayed on screen one by one or printed out in rapid succession.

The macros and auto-run capabilities can be used to preserve in amber your beginner's luck, as outlined in the preceding paragraphs, but you need hardly agree with or rely on that philosophical approach to make good use of macros. They are an integral feature of all the "big" charting packages and an almost indispensable tool.

MetaStock does not include macro or auto-run capabilities. Trendline II does. To add macro capability to MetaStock (and you'll want it), you should run it in conjunction with a commercial macro program such as SuperKey, SmartKey, or ProKey. There are several others on the market; the cost ranges down from $120. I bought Superkey for about $60, discounted.

Possibly MetaStock did the right thing. Macro programs are virtually commodity products. Their pricing and technology are highly competitive. If you buy a program that does nothing but keyboard macros, you will almost certainly get a more lavish macro capability than that which is coded into most charting software. Macro capability embedded in charting programs cannot be applied to other applications software. But if you buy, say, SuperKey, you can probably use it with every other program you own. On the other hand, you may not need $60 to $120 worth of macro capability just to help chart stocks. Moreover, the full-scale macro programs are resident in memory full time, and they eat it; 50K or 60K may go for this application. Our 640K PC slows perceptibly when the macro program is resident.

Again, the message here is that at $195, MetaStock will not do everything the big guys do. You have to option it out to achieve comparable capabilities. The freedom to select these options, however, is worth quite a bit. You'll wind up with the database of your choice and with a superior macro capability you can use with any program.

The Windows

Figure 14.1 illustrates the capability that made MetaStock famous. The program wallpapers the screen with big charts, little charts, tall charts, short charts—charts of every description. If this were a live screen instead of an illustration, you could *move* one of the charts, using the cursor controls to steer it to any desired position on the screen. You could also magnify the size of this active chart to fill the entire screen, thus blotting out the view of all the other charts. Or, having done so, you could shrink it back to the size of a credit card, restoring in the process your view of all the other charts. This special power to freely shift and manipulate whole charts is unique to MetaStock. Other programs can resize or reproportion charts, but only MetaStock lets you slide them around on the screen.

Why is this good? What problem does it solve?

Evidently, the idea is to display lots of charts simultaneously. Several programs let you store charts one behind the other, in memory, like so many cards in a deck, but MetaStock lets you view all the cards at once, face up on the table. The ability to move them around (one of them, anyway) helps you align them so that you can compare individually

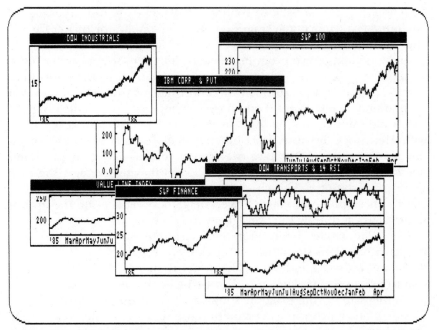

Figure 14.1. MetaStock virtually wallpapers the screen with charts. The one active chart is mobile and can be moved about freely on the screen using cursor controls. This facilitates direct comparison with other charts.

The program requires the simultaneous display of multiple charts because it cannot superimpose dissimilar indicators on a single chart. This was a sensible trade-off in program design. By isolating each indicator on a chart unto itself, MetaStock can apply to that chart the complete repertoire of technical analysis tools. The problem of singling out a specific plot to operate on—a problem which bedevils most technical analysis programs—never arises. You will notice in using the program, however, that it cannot superimpose dissimilar indicators.

plotted indicators with a common time base. The power to freely change a chart's size enables you to view the more important indicators more clearly and at higher resolution while at the same time keeping the less critical indicators on display. From the standpoint of program design, it is a new way to break out of the familiar trap (for programmers) of the single rigidly defined chart horizontally split between price and volume or between price and a calculated indicator.

MetaStock treats indicators one at a time. You cannot superimpose the plot of one indicator atop the plot of another. You could not, for example, plot the positive-volume indicator and the negative-volume indicator on the same screen. You could plot them on separate charts, shrink them, and stack them up to align their time axes. This works out satisfactorily. You cannot illustrate the crossovers of dissimilar indicators such as price and on-balance volume (OBV), but you can superimpose any number of moving averages on any single indicator (price, for example), so these more important crossovers are easy to show.

The more expensive programs have trouble with second-order plots. Suppose you have used one of those programs to draw three different volume allocation indicators on the lower half of your screen and you want to smooth just one of them. It may be impossible to tell the program which indicator curve you want to smooth. The difficulty never arises with MetaStock, because you cannot plot more than one indicator on the active screen. If you have two screens in view—typically price and one calculated indicator—and you call for a moving average, the program will prompt you to choose between the price and the indicator charts. In response to your choice, MetaStock will activate the appropriate chart and draw the average on it.

The isolation of each indicator on a chart unto itself is the key concept in MetaStock. This simplification gives the program its great versatility in dealing with each indicator. The power to move a chart around on a multichart display (as shown in Figure 14.1) can be regarded as a tool to compensate for the program's inability to superimpose dissimilar indicator plots. Since you can't superimpose them, you must try to view their charts in close proximity. Hence, the chart-scooting facilities. It is a very sensible trade-off in program design.

The program does not directly operate on the volume bar chart, although it displays many calculated indicators based on volume. Volume bars are displayed below the price bars, in the usual spot, but they are not accessible to smoothing, trend lines, or other functions. To get at the volume data, you draw a line representation of the data in the indicator panel on the upper half of the screen. This can then be smoothed, regressed, or marked for trend lines. Rate of change and moving-average difference oscillators for volume are menu items.

In moving-average charts, where lines are readily superimposed, plots can be distinguished from one another graphically through the use of solid or dotted lines. The program supports color but does not use it functionally to distinguish between superimposed lines. Since the lines are solid or dotted, functional color isn't really necessary.

The sequence of work with this program goes something like this. First, you select and plot an indicator on a full-screen chart. Second, you smooth it and draw lines on it for analytical purposes. Third, you shrink it and store it in a corner of the screen. Fourth, you repeat the first three steps for another indicator and store it directly below the first little chart. Now you can compare the two against a common time axis.

Gradually, as you fill the storage screen with little charts, you can compare more and more indicators. Evidently it is possible to store up to 36 double-paneled charts on a single screen. At their smallest size, resolution is poor, but you can redraw a chart of interest at magnified size easily. The business of sliding each finished chart into place on the storage screen is pleasurable in the sense that pasting stamps into an album is fun to do.

In opting for a freely defined desktop-type display, the MetaStock program abandons any sort of formally defined screen space, e.g., four quadrants, eight octants, etc. Having lost the definition of the screen's geography, the program cannot aim functions at different parts of the screen. It can't send the cursor back to the upper left-hand quadrant and have it redefine a trend line. It can't selectively blank part of the screen and redraw a chart. Once a finished chart has been scooted into position and left there, it goes dead. If you have the maximum of 72 charts on display, 71 of them will be dead. Only one of them can be changed. Within that active chart, however, you retain perfect control. The Dow Jones Market Analyzer Plus has the same problem with multiple charts on display: Only one works at a time. Savant displays just four charts at once, but they are all addressable and are therefore "live."

Windowing is used very effectively for presenting menus. The program provides a choice between command mode and menu-driven operation. You can pop open a window with a menu listing the commands in it any time. As you learn the commands, you will do this less frequently. The commands are one letter or one letter plus a command key. Some of the function keys are used for commands, and so you will have to be careful in reassigning them with a macro program.

The Pointer

This feature is excellent (Figure 14.2). The menu of pointer commands appears in the window. When you select a command and enter it, the menu disappears. The pointer is a cursor in the shape of an arrowhead. You use it, as in several other programs, to define the two endpoints of trend lines. Once you've drawn a trend line, you can extend it to the border of the chart in both directions by pressing X.

You use the cursor to make permanent arrowheads on the chart. The Leave Arrow command will "print" the cursor onto the chart. When you move the cursor away, an identical arrowhead will be revealed beneath it, fixed in place. Use it to mark significant buy and sell signals.

The program draws linear regression lines to the arrowhead. The point of origin is requested in a prompt, which asks how many days prior to the day marked by the arrow should be used in the calculation. You have to guess at a number. There is no easy way to read one out. In other words, the program will let you vary the term over which the linear regression is applied, but it is difficult to do so exactly. Point-to-

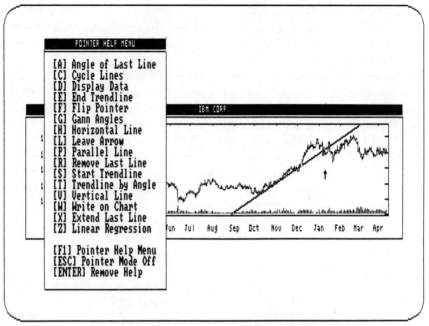

Figure 14.2. Note the use of a window to present a menu. This menu lists things you can do with the on-screen pointer. The menu vanishes once you select a command. The pointer is an excellent feature of the MetaStock program. It can "carry" the linear regression function from chart to chart, and so you can use it to identify which plot you want to regress. An imprint of the pointer can be made on the screen and left behind as the active point moves on to another task. Arrows left behind can be used to mark buy and sell points. The pointer can also be flipped to point up or down.

point linear regression with both endpoints defined by cursors or markers would have been better.

Parallel lines are automatically drawn at the command P and are positioned relative to the last line drawn. You can extend them. You can also extend the whole chart any number of days into the future and thus project trend lines into the next month or beyond.

The pointer has two features which should be declared industry standards. Both apply when you have two charts on-screen, one above the other, typically a price chart and an indicator chart. (1) When you request a vertical line, the line skewers both charts simultaneously. This enables you to define coincidence perfectly between the two panels without taking time to painstakingly work out the coordinates. (2) The pointer will "carry" a function such as linear regression from one panel to the other. If the cursor is in the lower panel and you request a linear regression, it will be applied to price. If you want to apply linear regression to the indicator, you first pilot the cursor upscreen into the indicator chart. When you request a linear regression, it will be applied to the indicator.

This currently works only for linear regression and trend lines but could perhaps be applied to smoothing and other functions one day. The feature is included almost parenthetically in MetaStock, but it could be developed by a skillful program designer as the cornerstone concept for an ideal technical analysis program. In such a program the pointer would "carry" the whole menu of functions and would be used to distinguish between superimposed indicators and variables plotted on a single chart.

Indicators

MetaStock runs four common volume allocation indicators, including on-balance volume, price and volume trend, positive volume, and negative volume. In addition, it runs several other volume-based indicators, including a volume rate-of-change oscillator, a volume difference-of-averages oscillator, a volume accumulation-distribution line, and the Chaikin accumulation-distribution oscillator. It will also draw a simple volume line chart.

Moving averages are simple, weighted, or exponential and can be used to create channels. They can be applied to price or to any indicator, and several can be superimposed on a single chart.

Oscillators include price difference of averages, momentum (price rate of change), the Stochastic, and J. Welles Wilder's relative strength.

The system will draw charts to show the relative strength of one stock against another, one stock against an index, or an index against another index. It cannot display relative strength using more than two plots, so you can't compare three stocks or compare two stocks against an index.

User formulas are provided, so you can add or create indicators as you wish. In addition to conventional time-based price and volume charts, MetaStock will also plot point and figure charts.

Trendline II

As noted above, Trendline II is a stand-alone program. It is ready to run when you buy it. It includes an integral communications program to download price and volume data from Warner. It also includes a built-in macro and auto-run facility. You can use it to create and store seven auto-run sequences, each consisting of up to 50 keystrokes. The program responds to one-letter commands, so this should suffice.

This program is more conventional in concept than MetaStock and thus takes a bit less explaining. It also does less than MetaStock, although it has several attractive features which are unique.

One is speed. Trendline II is the fastest program I have run, bar none, since we abandoned our minicomputer in favor of microcomputers. It really clicks along. This is particularly impressive when you scroll a chart across a long time base. You can scan back and forth with the cursor keys, in periscope fashion, through four years of history on a stock or index. In four keystrokes (the 1, 2, 3, and 4 keys) you can zoom in and out from "close-up" of just six weeks of trading to a long view of the whole four-year price-volume history. Only one other program reviewed here, Interactive's Active Investor, offers this kind of easy mobility in framing time, and it isn't quite as fast as Trendline II. With the other programs you typically have to fiddle around with a formal rescaling of the horizontal axis.

The program will freely superimpose price and other indicators on a single chart. This is where it differs structurally from MetaStock and where the consequences of the different programming approaches can be seen most clearly. If you are hunting for divergence between the plots of price and some indicator—OBV, for instance—it certainly helps to draw them one atop the other on a single chart.

Trendline II does this very nicely. MetaStock cannot do it at all. Trendline II even provides some features to make the picture more clear. You can raise or lower the whole indicator plot to achieve a better fit or, if the price bars are right on top of it, to simply bring it into view. You can draw a one-day moving average of price (a price line) and then erase the price bars altogether to clean the screen. The bars can be restored at a keystroke.

These are all nice conveniences, but they must be understood as just that. Having drawn OBV on top of a price curve, Trendline II is finished. It cannot operate on the indicator curve by smoothing it, drawing channel lines to flank it, skewering it with trend lines, regressing it, or any such thing. With MetaStock you can operate on any indicator with all the analytical tools in the kit. For this reason MetaStock is a superior program for the more advanced analyst. It gives up one basic tool— superimposition of dissimilar indicators—in exchange for a whole kitful of other tools.

Trendline II has a formal method for defining trend lines. You use a wand rather than a cursor to mark the beginning and ending days you wish to connect with a line. When you have selected a beginning or ending day, you will be prompted to specify the high, low, close, or median price. The price point you select defines the endpoint of the trend line. If you are in an uptrend, you connect the lows. If you are in a downtrend, you connect the highs. There is value in discipline. If you use the Trendline II approach rather than that of a program that permits free-form trend line drawing, you will be consistent in your method from chart to chart. You will never have to wonder whether you are optimistically "bending" the trend lines to put the best possible construction on the consequences of your earlier decisions. Trendline II is rigorous in this respect.

Parallel lines can be created by pressing P after a trend line is in place. This feature is used to draw trading channels. There is no linear regression function.

Indicators and Oscillators

Trendline II enables you to superimpose comparative charts of two or more stocks or indicators. It displays absolute comparisons, relative strength, or the outcome of a $100 initial investment in each of several stocks or indexes. It does not display relative strength in the Welles Wilder sense.

Moving averages are simple, weighted, and exponential. They may be applied to price data only and may be offset or centered. Trading envelopes based on moving averages can be created on command. The width of the channel is set, in response to prompts, as plus or minus a percentage of a moving average.

The oscillator created from the menu by means of a series of prompts is of the difference-of-averages type. The oscillator display is "filled in" (Figure 14.3) and easy to read.

The volume-based indicators include on-balance volume, price-volume trend, the positive-volume indicator, the negative-volume indicator, a daily-volume indicator, and a line plot of volume.

Conclusion

At essentially equivalent prices, MetaStock is a better program for intermediate and advanced analysts. It is, as a matter of fact, one of the best programs on the market for technical analysis. It does not have the startling speed of Trendline II, and it cannot superimpose dissimilar indicator plots. It is also more limited in plotting comparative charts of relative strength. For communications and autoplotting, you will have to come up with ancillary software for MetaStock. Trendline II handles both communications and autoplotting without extra software. But even

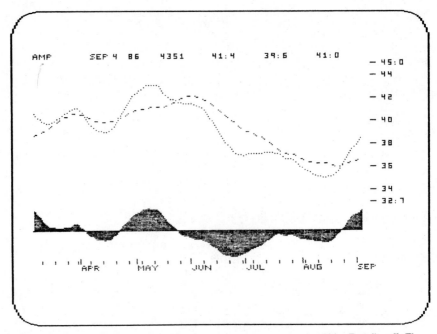

Figure 14.3. An oscillator of the difference-of-averages type as plotted by Trendline II. The filled-in area under the curves is graphically attractive and helps the eye gauge the trend toward or away from a crossover. Moving-average crossovers are commonly read as buy and sell signals. A crossover is indicated every time the oscillator passes through its zero axis.

This type of oscillator can be selected from the Trendline II menu. A series of prompts helps you set up the charting parameters.

after conceding these points to Trendline II, MetaStock comes out ahead. It does more.

Trendline II is designed for beginners and for fundamental investors who may never become fascinated by charts, but recognize the value of checking them. The program is simple and will run right out of the box. However, there is no avenue for growth to advanced skills within the confines of Trendline II. There is no user formula set, so you will always be restricted to using precisely those features supplied with the program. A new and more advanced program is available from Standard & Poor's for investors with a serious interest in technical analysis. It is framed around the RTR TechniFilter concept, so optimization is inherent in it. It does not, however, fall within the moderate price class reviewed in this chapter. As for the price of Trendline II, the $275 seems steep, but it is evidently the gateway to fairly low operating costs. I discussed the price with a Standard & Poor's executive. He pointed out that they have negotiated a special arrangement with Warner Computer, who supplies

HLCV (High, Low, Close, and Volume) data to Trendline II users at favorable rates. The rates are fixed regardless of what time of day the data is brought down. Prime-time users could especially benefit from this arrangement. In addition, he said, the program is supplied with $500 worth of historical data at no charge. In short, the initial $275 price tag for Trendline II can be justified. In considering it, however, you should ask yourself whether you intend to remain a moderately interested observer in the field of technical charting. If you expect to develop your own skills beyond this point, you should look for a more advanced program.

In terms of charting capability, MetaStock is on a par with the big programs (i.e., the $350 to $500 programs), but there is not such a bargain here as it might seem at first. If you stripped down one of the big programs and offered its technical module as a stand-alone product, you'd have something very much like MetaStock, and you'd probably market it at a similar price. If charting is all you want, MetaStock is a brilliant program and a solid value.

15
Comparative Summary of Capabilities

This chapter is designed to help you decide which technical analysis program is best for you. A comparison chart (Table 15.1) indicates the major features of the programs, and the comparative summary in the following paragraphs describes these features in detail.

Use the chart and the descriptive material to evaluate the technical analysis programs strictly on the basis of their relative merits as charting tools. The chapter concludes with subjective recommendations. The emphasis is not on technical analysis viewed in isolation; instead, consideration is given to how well each charting program can be integrated with other programs to create complete computerized investment systems. It is recognized that at this point in the development of the technology of computerized investing, technical analysis owns the center ring of the circus. But it is not the whole show.

Note too that there is no best program overall, though there will certainly be one that's best for you. Select one that reflects your own methods and interests and gives you room to grow.

Smoothing of Data

The Technical Investor

This program provides simple moving averages, weighted moving averages, and exponential moving averages calculated over periods you

Table 15.1. Comparison Chart of Technical Analysis Programs

	Savant	Winning	Active	Dow	MetaStock	Trendline
Smoothing						
Price data	X	X	X	X	X	X
Simple	X	X	X	X	X	X
Exponential	X	X	X	X	X	X
Weighted	X	X	X	X	X	X
Nonprice data						
Directly	X	X	X	X	X	X
Via user formulas only	X	X		X	X	X
Draws channels	X	X	X	X	X	X
Position by std deviation		X				
Position by +/− pct of avg.	X			X	X	X
Via user formula only			X			
Straight Lines			X			
Horizontal	X	X		X	X	X
Vertical	X	X		X	X	X
Specified angle	X	X			X	
Specified slope					X	
Trendlines						
Between specified coordinates	X	X	X			
Moveable			X	X		
Cursor to marker	X			X	X	
H/L/C to H/L/C on command						X
Linear Regression						
Whole screen	X	X	X	X	X	
Adjustable range without rescale		X			X	
Against indicators	X	X	X	X	X	
Parallel Lines	X				X	X
By measuring	X					
Speed Resistance	X	X	X	X		
One third	X	X	X	X		
Two thirds	X	X	X	X		

Table 15.1. Comparison Chart of Technical Analysis Programs (*Continued*)

	Savant	Winning	Active	Dow	MetaStock	Trendline
Oscillators						
Direct command	X	X	X	X	X	X
Rate of change		X			X	X
Difference of averages		X			X	X
The Stochastic			X		X	
Chaikin A/D					X	
By entering a formula	X	X	X	X	X	X
Relative Strength						
Absolute	X	X	X	X	X	X
Relative to a baseline stock	X	X		X	X	X
$100 performance	X	X	X	X		X
Per J. Welles Wilder	X		X	X	X	
Volume Allocation Indicators						
On balance volume	X	X	X	X	X	X
Price volume trend	X	X		X	X	X
Positive volume ind.	X	X	X	X	X	X
Negative volume ind.	X	X	X	X	X	X
Daily volume ind.	X	X		X		X
Accumulation/dist'n			X	X	X	
User Formulas						
Algebraic functions		X	X	X	X	X
Logical functions		X	X	X	X	X
Trig functions		X	X		X	X

Table 15.1. Comparison Chart of Technical Analysis Programs (*Continued*)

	Savant	Winning	Active	Dow	MetaStock	Trendline
Optimization						
Inherent	X	X	X			
Via compatible software	X	X		X		
Sorting per Technical Criteria						
Inherent	X		X	X		
Via compatible software	X		X	X		
Point and Figure	X	X	X	X	X	
Autoplot	X	X	X	X		X
Spreadsheet Interchange						
Inherent	X	X		X	X	
Via optional utilities	X	X		X	X	
Communications Included						
Download data only	X	X	X	X		X
Terminal mode	X	X	X	X		X
Group Analysis						
Directly				X		
Via spreadsheet	X	X		X	X	
Daily Statistical Analysis				X		
Time Frames Adjusted by:						
Rescaling only	X	X		X	X	
"Periscope"			X			X
Zoom in and out			X			X
Functional Color	X		X	X		

stipulate (10-day moving average, 12-day moving average, etc.). Smoothing functions can be freely applied to both price and volume data. All three types of moving averages can be used to draw trading bands. The bands are positioned to contain price swings of plus or minus some stipulated percentage of the moving-average value. The bands are positioned separately, so you might accept a positive deviation of 3 percent and a negative deviation of 2 percent of the moving-average value. Bands and envelopes can be drawn for price or volume data. There are no restrictions on the type of data to which the function is applied.

Winning on Wall Street

This program provides simple moving averages and weighted moving averages calculated over periods you stipulate (10-day moving average, 12-day moving average, etc.), It also calculates and plots exponential moving averages. You can vary the weighting given to the more recent data in the exponential-average calculations. Smoothing functions apply only to price data in the most direct, menu-driven mode of operation, but volume data can be replotted and smoothed with user formulas. Simple moving averages can be used to draw trading bands. The bands are positioned to contain price swings of plus or minus some stipulated fraction of a standard deviation. The fraction can assume values between 0.5 and 3. You cannot use the weighted or exponential moving-average functions to draw trading bands. The program provides a smoothing technique called *adaptive filtering*. The technique is more sophisticated in concept than moving-average smoothing, though the end results appear to be quite similar.

The Active Investor

This program provides simple moving averages, weighted moving averages, and exponential moving averages calculated over periods you stipulate (10-day moving average, 12-day moving average, etc.). Smoothing functions can be applied freely to both price and volume data.

Modified (control key) versions of these commands can be used to smooth the data in the last previous plot, whatever it may be. This feature can be used to smooth, for example, the volume trend indicators. You can also use it to smooth an oscillator function.

All three types of moving averages can be used to draw trading bands, but you will have to employ the user-formula set to create these functions, and so they cannot be flexibly changed in on-screen analyses.

The Dow Jones Market Analyzer Plus

The Plus provides simple moving averages, weighted moving averages, and exponential moving averages calculated over periods you stipulate (10-day moving average, 12-day moving average, etc.). Smoothing functions can be freely applied to price data. Volume bar data must be replotted as a curve before you apply smoothing. All three types of moving averages can be used to draw trading bands. The bands are positioned to contain price swings of plus or minus some stipulated percentage of the moving-average value. The bands are positioned separately, so you might accept a positive deviation of 3 percent and a negative deviation of 2 percent of the moving-average value. Bands and envelopes can be drawn for price or volume data.

MetaStock

This program provides simple moving averages, weighted moving averages, and exponential moving averages calculated over periods you stipulate (10-day moving average, 12-day moving average, etc.). Smoothing functions can be applied freely to price, to volume lines, and to any indicator. The program draws 16 indicators as menu items, more if you invoke user formulas.

All three types of moving averages can be used to draw trading bands.

Trendline II

This program provides simple moving averages, weighted moving averages, and exponential moving averages calculated over periods you stipulate (10-day moving average, 12-day moving average, etc.). Smoothing functions can be applied to price data only.

Trading bands, or envelopes, can be drawn in bracketing moving-average lines. The desired band width is entered as plus or minus a specified percentage of the central moving-average line.

Drawing Straight Lines

The Technical Investor

Horizontal lines and vertical lines are drawn at points selected by a movable on-screen cursor. Lines can also be drawn from any point to any other point if you type in specific coordinates. Families of lines parallel to a given point-to-point line can be generated by successively entering coordinates, but there is no single-command facility for drawing parallel lines.

Dotted horizontal lines to demark preset high and low price flags can be made to appear automatically. Chart grid lines can be turned on and off to facilitate measurement or cut the clutter on screen, respectively. Diagonal $x = y$ lines can be drawn on command to indicate bullish and bearish support and resistance on point and figure charts.

Linear regression lines can be drawn using all the data points on the chart. There is no facility, other that horizontal rescaling, for isolating selected time periods for the application of this function. The linear regression function can be applied to both price and volume plots. Straight-line trading channel boundaries can be created with the linear regression function. You position the boundaries of the channel by stipulating an allowable fraction of a standard deviation from a hypothetical centerline. The linear regression function can be applied to both volume and price data. For prices, it is automatically applied to the close or midpoint values. If it is to be applied to a high or a low, a special file storing those data only must be created. Linear regression is not readily usable for trend line drawing, because it applies to all points on the price curve, and cannot be applied to selected segments without rescaling. This major technique is not very completely developed in the program. Linear regression can be applied only to price and volume, not to calculated indicators. The program will also draw one-third and two-thirds speed resistance lines. It seeks out default values for the major high and low and lets the operator confirm or change either or both of these values. The lines are then drawn automatically. They can be erased one at a time.

Winning on Wall Street

Horizontal lines and vertical lines are drawn at points selected by a movable on-screen wand. There is no facility for drawing point-to-point lines. Diagonal or bullish and bearish support and resistance lines for point and figure charts are not provided.

Linear regression lines can be drawn using all the data points on the chart or for shorter selected time periods marked off within the chart using the wand. The linear regression function can be applied to both price and volume plots. Straight-line trading channel boundaries can be created with the linear regression function. You position the boundaries of the channel by stipulating an allowable fraction of a standard deviation from a hypothetical centerline. The linear regression function can be applied to both volume and price data. For prices, it can be applied to the highs, lows, or closing prices. If you apply user formulas to "pull out" and separately plot indicators such as moving averages, the linear regression function can be applied to these indicator plots as well as to price and volume plots. Linear regression is more fully realized as a technique in this program than in any other I have seen. The program will also draw one-third and two-thirds speed resistance lines.

The Active Investor

There are no special provisions for drawing horizontal or vertical lines. They are put into position using the program's unique ability to move lines on the screen. For a vertical line you might use the wand as a template. Lines cannot be drawn from point to point by specifying co-ordinates. Instead, the line is moved into position to connect the two desired points. This is intuitively more natural but inherently less accurate.

Linear regression lines can be drawn using all the data points on the chart. There is no facility for isolating selected time periods for the application of this function. The linear regression function can be applied to price, volume, and any other plots. It is always applied on a last-plot basis to data which have just been plotted. It cannot be applied to a given set of data points after an intervening plot has been completed.

Straight-line trading channel boundaries can be created with the linear regression function. First, draw a regression line against price. Second, precisely align the "active" drawing line with the linear regression line. Third, use the commands for drawing parallel lines to position the boundaries of the channel.

Linear regression is not readily usable for trend line drawing, because it applies to all points on the price curve, and cannot be applied to selected segments without rescaling.

Freely positioned trend lines are easier to create with this program than with any other program under review, because the whole line can be shifted about with the cursor control keys. There is no cut-and-dried process as there is with other programs; the line is simply coaxed into position. Trading channels based on trend lines are easy to create using the facility for drawing parallel lines. In this mode, a second line can be slipped out from under the first and moved away from it or closer to it while maintaining the perfectly locked parallel alignment of the two lines.

Dow Jones Market Analyzer Plus

Numerically labeled horizontal lines are drawn at points selected by entering a desired x-axis value. Lines can also be drawn from any point to any other point by positioning cursors. There is no special facility for drawing vertical lines, but a movable vertical wand is provided. The wand is meant to demonstrate coincidence only and does not serve to extract numerical data from the chart. (Numerical data can be displayed and scrolled in a window, however.)

Linear regression lines can be drawn using all the data points on the chart. There is no facility for isolating selected time periods for the application of this function. The linear regression function can be applied to both price and volume plots. Straight-line trading channel boundaries can be created with the linear regression function. You position the boundaries of the channel by stipulating an allowable number of standard deviations from the centerline.

Linear regression is not readily usable for trend line drawing, because it applies to all points on the price curve, and cannot be applied to selected segments without rescaling. Linear regression can be applied to price, volume, and calculated volume indicators as charted from menu selections. It can also be applied to any plots created using the system's user-formula set.

The program will draw one-third, two-thirds, and any other speed resistance lines as specified, although this feature has not yet been implemented in the advance copy of the program I examined.

MetaStock

Horizontal and vertical lines can be drawn on command. Vertical lines penetrate both upper and lower charts if both are on the screen. This is very helpful in demonstrating coincidence. Trend lines are drawn from point to point, and the points are set with a cursor. Parallel trend lines are available on command. Lines cannot be drawn from point to point by specifying coordinates. Linear regression lines can be drawn over a specified range, but the range is difficult to specify exactly. The linear regression function can be applied to price, volume, or any indicator.

Straight-line trading channel boundaries can be created with the linear regression function. First, draw a regression line against price. Second, draw parallel lines on command and move them into position with cursor controls.

There are no special provisions for automatically drawing one-third and two-thirds speed resistance lines. Trend lines can be drawn in at specific angles or slopes (Gann angles) entered from the keyboard.

Trendline II

Trend lines are defined by using a movable vertical line, or wand, to define the desired time frame. The wand moves in response to the Left/

Right cursor controls. At each limit of the trend line, you can select H, L, or C to indicate high, low, or close. The program will thus draw trend lines to connect two highs, two lows, two closings, or any combination made up of, say, a high on one end and a close on the other or a low on one end and a high on the other.

Trend lines apply only to price data.

Vertical lines, as noted, appear as a movable wand. Horizontal lines are also movable and respond to the Up/Down cursor controls. The Enter key "freezes" the horizontal line in place on the chart. You can then create another one somewhere else if you wish.

Lines can be drawn on command to parallel a trend line. This is helpful in defining trading channels. If more than one trend line is on the screen, the program will prompt for a choice.

There is no facility for drawing linear regression lines. There are also no facilities for drawing speed resistance lines or any other slanted lines other than the high, low, and close point-to-point trend lines.

Oscillators

The Technical Investor

A single all-encompassing command is provided for drawing oscillators. It can be configured to draw momentum or moving-average oscillators and for miscellaneous types as well. By setting up the oscillator as an automated procedure and then applying the program's Edit Procedure command to progressively change the original oscillator specifications, it is possible to generate families of curves on the screen that represent many related oscillators. This semiautomated process helps you select which oscillator might be most helpful for a particular stock. The Oscillator command is the most difficult command to master in an otherwise straightforward program.

Winning on Wall Street

There are two ways to produce oscillators, via the menu and via user formulas. If you use the menu, you will be prompted with a straightforward general equation for an oscillator. Fill in the blanks, press Enter, and the oscillator will appear—but everything else you may have done to the price plot will disappear as the whole screen is refreshed. If you want to compare the oscillator with another indicator (e.g., a moving-average plot), you will have to apply a user-formula approach. You evidently cannot compare the menu's oscillator with multiple plots, e.g., a plot of price bars plus one or more moving averages. This limitation is troublesome if you use difference oscillators, which follow the periodic convergence, crossover, and divergence of two moving averages.

The Active Investor

There is no oscillator command. Examples of momentum and moving-average oscillators are provided in the user-formula set. Any oscillator would be created via user formulas. Note that oscillators would be subject to smoothing, using the last-plot smoothing functions.

The Dow Jones Market Analyzer Plus

Oscillators are not provided as menu items but can be created easily with the user-formula set.

MetaStock

Volume rate-of-change and difference-of-average oscillators are available from the indicator menu. Price rate-of-change and difference-of-average oscillators are also available from the indicator menu. The system prompts for average periods and rate-of-change periods. More exotic oscillators (e.g., the Stochastic) are on the menu, and more can be created with the user-formula set. Like all indicators, oscillators can be smoothed, regressed, and analyzed by drawing lines.

Trendline II

A menu command initiates a series of prompts that enable you to construct an oscillator of the price difference-of-average type.

Relative Strength

The Technical Investor

Relative strength can be presented in three ways. First, a stock's performance can be compared with that of an index such as the Dow Jones industrial average or with the performance of some other stock chosen as a standard for comparison (such as another stock in the same group). The index, or standard stock, is presented as a straight baseline, and the stock of interest is allowed to vary above and below this baseline. Several stocks can be compared with a standard. Second, relative strength can be measured in terms of dollar holdings. This method assumes that at the outset you purchase $100 worth of each of several stocks. The percentage change in value of each investment is plotted against a zero line. Several stocks can be compared in this way. Third, there is a direct command to display a relative strength measurement as characterized by J. Welles Wilder, which is quite different from the two more conventional measures of relative strength.

Winning on Wall Street

Relative strength can be presented in two ways. First, a stock's performance can be compared with that of an index such as the Dow Jones industrial average or with the performance of some other stock chosen as a standard for comparison (such as another stock in the same group). The index, or standard stock, is presented as a straight baseline, and the stock of interest is allowed to vary above and below this baseline. Five stocks can be compared with a standard. Second, relative strength can be measured in terms of dollar holdings. This method assumes that at the outset you purchase $100 worth of each of several stocks. The percentage change in value of each investment is plotted against a zero line. Five stocks can be compared in this manner. For a measurement of relative strength as characterized by J. Welles Wilder, which is quite different from the two conventional measures of relative strength, you would have to write a user formula.

The Active Investor

Relative strength versus another stock or an index is measured in terms of dollar holdings. This method assumes that at the outset you purchase $100 worth of each of several stocks. The percentage change in value of each investment is plotted against a zero line. Several stocks can be compared in this manner. Color and monochrome graphic devices help you distinguish between the different lines. There is a direct command to display a relative strength measurement as characterized by J. Welles Wilder.

The Dow Jones Market
Analyzer Plus

Relative strength can be presented in three ways. First, a stock's performance can be compared with that of an index such as the Dow Jones industrial average or with the performance of some other stock chosen as a standard for comparison (such as another stock in the same group). The index, or standard stock, is presented as a straight baseline, and the stock of interest is allowed to vary above and below this baseline. Several stocks can be compared with a standard. Second, relative strength can be measured in terms of dollar holdings. This method assumes that at the outset you purchase $100 worth of each of several stocks. The percentage change in value of each investment is plotted against a zero line. Several stocks can be compared in this manner. There is a no-menu selection item to display a measurement of relative strength as characterized by J. Welles Wilder. This is surprising, as the program is strongly influenced by Wilder's thinking. A simple command is provided to plot Welles Wilder relative strength (CS14), and the value appears thematically in tabulated reports compiled by the program.

MetaStock

Relative strength versus another stock or an index is limited to two plots, and so multiple comparisons are not possible. There is a direct command to display a measurement of relative strength as characterized by J. Welles Wilder.

Trendline II

Comparative evaluations are a strong suit in this program, allowing comparisons of up to four stocks or any mixture of stocks and indexes. Comparisons are of three types: (1) absolute, in which the true values of the stocks are displayed superimposed, (2) relative, which flattens one stock to form a baseline for comparison and lets the others range around it, and (3) $100 comparison, which plots the relative performance of several $100 investments in a set of stocks or indexes.

Some historical data are provided as a bonus with the purchase of the program and may be useful in running these comparisons.

No provision is made on the menu for J. Welles Wilder's version of relative strength.

Volume Indicators

The Technical Investor

Five rather standard volume indicators can be calculated and displayed: negative-volume indicator, positive-volume indicator, price-volume trend, daily volume, and on-balance volume. Smoothing functions can be readily applied to volume indicators. Linear regression cannot be used.

Winning on Wall Street

Five standard volume indicators can be calculated and displayed: negative-volume indicator, positive-volume indicator, price-volume trend, daily volume, and on-balance volume. Smoothing and linear regression functions cannot be applied to volume indicators.

The program will draw a unique price-volume relation chart which plots price and volume against a common scale on a common axis over the span of 40 days. This shows whether there is any directly observable relation between price and volume for a particular stock within this time frame.

The Active Investor

Four volume trend indicators can be calculated and displayed: negative-volume indicator, positive-volume indicator, accumulation and distribution, and on-balance volume. Price-volume trend is available as a user formula. Smoothing functions can be readily applied to volume indicators. Linear regression can also be used freely.

The Dow Jones Market Analyzer Plus

Six standard volume indicators can be calculated and displayed: negative-volume indicator, accumulation and distribution indicator, positive-volume indicator, price-volume trend, daily volume, and on-balance volume. The volume indicators are accessible via the menu or via the user-formula set. The user formula for on-balance volume is B3. To smooth it with a 12-day moving average, enter B3A12. Smoothing and linear regression functions can be applied readily to volume indicators.

The basic volume bar chart which first appears when you request a chart cannot be modified and must be replotted for smoothing or other operations. It displays only the tops of the volume bars; this is a sensible way to save space. Also included in the bar display is a dotted line representing the average daily volume over the term of the chart. The average daily volume is also displayed in numerical form under the chart.

MetaStock

Five basic volume trend indicators can be calculated and displayed: negative-volume indicator, positive-volume indicator, accumulation and distribution, on-balance volume, and price and volume trend. A simple volume line chart can be plotted as an indicator so that charting tools can be applied to it. Smoothing functions can be readily applied to volume indicators. Linear regression can also be used freely. Dissimilar indicators cannot be superimposed on each other or on other charts.

Trendline II

This program calculates and plots price-volume trend, on-balance volume, positive-volume indicator, negative-volume indicator, and daily-volume indicator. It will not smooth these indicators. The user-formula set can be used to accomplish this or to create other indicators.

You can draw horizontal or vertical lines over indicators. You can also raise or lower the plots, under cursor control, to achieve a better fit to a price line. It is a useful feature if you are looking for divergence between price and indicator.

Other Indicators

The Technical Investor

You can display the ratios and the differences between any two indicators. This feature is useful in charting the market's daily highs and lows (reported by Warner) and the daily up-volume versus down-volume data. Cumulative differences can also be plotted.

There is no user-formula set. Only those indicators specifically provided in the command set can be plotted.

Winning on Wall Street

This program will draw a unique price-volume relation chart which plots price and volume against a common scale on a common axis over the span of 40 days. This shows you whether there is any directly observable relation between price and volume for a particular stock within this time frame.

The program includes a complete tool kit for writing your own analytical formulas. For this reason it can be said that the program will do just about anything a technical analyst might wish for or conceive. In addition to basic algebraic functions, it includes exponential, logarithmic, and trigonometric functions. This is much more capability than is commonly offered in user-formula sets. It is also possible to employ user formulas to patch up some weaknesses in the program. These mostly involve the application of smoothing techniques to data other than prices.

The Active Investor

Indicators can be created as desired with the user-formula set.

The Dow Jones Market Analyzer Plus

This program has virtually a second language for plotting indicators in its user-formula set, which is compact and easy to learn (A = average, for example). By means of this command set, you can operate the Plus very quickly and directly, bypassing most of the menus and prompts. Command response is immediate; user formulas are displayed without delay.

MetaStock

A number of indicators are provided on the menu which are not widely included in other programs. These include the Stochastic oscillator, the Chaikin A/D oscillator, and volume rate-of-change and difference-of-averages oscillators.

Buy and Sell Strategy Planning Aids

The Technical Investor

This program is compatible with the RTR TechniFilter optimization and chart presorting program. The TechniFilter costs about $300. It evaluates past predictive performance of buy and sell strategies based on dual moving-average crossovers. It tries different moving averages for a given stock and reports results, before commissions, of both long and long-plus-short strategies. Savant's compatibility with this third-party program is a significant feature in my opinion.

Winning on Wall Street

The program includes an optimizer which elevates the past predictive performance of buy and sell strategies based on price and moving-average crossovers. It tries 100 different moving averages for a given stock and reports results, after commissions, of both long and long-plus-short strategies. It is a primitive optimizer, but no one else offers one as a component of a complete technical analysis package. Summa also includes a matrix evaluation feature. This utility examines the past price performance of a stock and makes a prediction, purely on the basis of statistical projection, of the next high and low prices.

The Active Investor

This program includes a technical presorting program similar in function to that of TechniFilter. It enables you to select, from the library of stocks on file, only those meeting certain criteria. You might stipulate, for example, that you want to chart only those stocks currently trading above their 10-day simple moving-average prices.

The Active Investor does not include an optimizer and is not compatible with the RTR optimizer.

The Dow Jones Market
Analyzer Plus

The Plus is compatible with RTR's TechniFilter optimization and chart-presorting program. This program costs about $300. It evaluates the past predictive performance of buy and sell strategies based on dual moving-average crossovers. It tries different moving averages for a given stock and reports results, before commissions, of both long and long-plus-short strategies. RTR wrote both the TechniFilter and the Dow Jones Market Analyzer, and the command language and formula sets are closely compatible.

The Plus is unique among the programs reviewed in terms of its power to create and track indexes reflecting the performance of industry groups of stocks. As a tool for dissecting the stock market, this is an invaluable resource. It also helps you evaluate the performance of your own stocks against that of companies with similar products, markets, competitive pressures, and prospects.

The Plus provides two daily statistical evaluations of stocks and trends. These can be quite helpful in spotting stocks in your portfolio that need attention. It is also useful in helping you establish which stocks are "trading stocks" and which are better suited for long-term investments.

MetaStock

MetaStock enables you to display arrows and notes on charts to indicate significant turning points.

Trendline II

Trendline II provides the basis for a formal and disciplined approach to drawing trend lines.

Other Features

The Technical Investor

Point and figure charting is supported in this program. Up to 38 automated procedures can be stored to single keys. The procedures can be as elaborate as you wish. Each specifies how a particular chart is to be scaled, plotted, smoothed, regressed, and so on. If you have 38 stocks, you can customize an analytical procedure for each one. More likely, you can store frequently used standard procedures (dual moving averages, for example) for application to any of your stocks at a single keystroke. The Savant screen can be used as a full screen or can be split into two, three, or four miniscreens. This is useful for establishing coincident timing and for comparative evaluations using different stocks or different indicators. The four screens can be freely copied, and their positions can be switched. The miniscreens can be addressed separately so that you can perform any operation on any screen. Up to 10 miniscreens can be stored to memory and recalled whole on command.

An automatic printing feature will apply specific charting techniques to each stock, per your request, and print out the finished charts in rapid-fire fashion. If you prefer to review the charts on the screen, you can use a pause command to interrupt the stream of charts in order to examine one. Note that automatic printing applies a single charting procedure (however complex) to all stocks. You can apply different charting procedures to different stocks with a somewhat more intricate procedure.

Savant does not provide for the calculation of user formulas or plot their results. The company sells a separate program to transfer Savant files in and out of the Technical Investor. You are expected to use this utility to make the data available for free-form calculations with Lotus, dBASE, or perhaps customized BASIC programs. The utility costs $145. It is not a substitute, in my opinion, for a built-in user-formula feature. It can, however, be useful in accumulating and importing FM radio or TV cable quotes to the Savant program.

Winning on Wall Street

Point and figure charting is supported. An autoplot feature will apply specific charting techniques to each stock, per your request, and print out the finished charts in rapid-fire fashion. The autoplot cannot be used for reviewing the charts on the screen, however.

The Active Investor

Point and figure charting is supported. The program always helps you distinguish between lines on charts using functional color, monochrome graphics devices, and legends that actually label some lines. These legends could represent the rudiments of a true plot specifier: a target for various different functions. No program has evolved such a thing yet, although they all need one. In its stead, Interactive uses a last-plot specifier to great advantage.

A magnifying glass feature helps you make sense of congested areas on the price chart. Scanning back through time is easy and semiautomatic. Quick zooming from short- to long-term charts and back is one of the program's best features.

An auto-analyze feature will apply a specific set of charting techniques to every stock on the disk, per your request, and print out the finished charts in rapid-fire fashion. The auto-analyze feature can be used to review the charts on the screen as well. The program includes a fairly complete tool kit for writing your own analytical formulas. For this reason it can be said that the program will chart just about anything.

The Dow Jones Market Analyzer Plus

Point and figure charting is supported. You can use the Plus to plot indicators other than price; this is a unique capability. An automatic chart display and printout utility can be programmed in advance so that each stock can be charted in its own way. This is far preferable to plotting all stocks according to a single standard charting procedure.

The screen can be used as a full screen or can be split into two, three, or four miniscreens. Each miniscreen chart is made up of upper and lower screens, so the effective number of miniscreens is actually eight. This is useful for establishing coincident timing and for comparative evaluations using different stocks or different indicators. The miniscreen plotting instructions can be stored for subsequent redisplay. With this technique, miniscreens can be freely copied and their positions can be switched.

The miniscreens cannot be addressed separately, however. You can operate only on the most recently displayed chart. The feature which allows you to store charting procedures in a buffer memory has broad application. Lengthy procedures can be stored for autoplotting or can be assigned to function keys.

MetaStock

Point and figure charting is supported. The program helps you distinguish between lines on charts using graphic devices, i.e., solid or dotted lines. It does not use color functionally, however. The cursor (pointer) "carries" the linear regression function from the lower-screen panel to the upper-screen panel and back.

For autoplotting or keyboard macros, it is suggested that you purchase a third-party program such as SuperKey, SmartKey, or ProKey.

Trendline II

This program can horizontally scroll, or "periscope," across the time axis of charts. It can also zoom in on narrow time frames. This is helpful in gauging the importance of abrupt short- and intermediate-term moves in a stock, because a zoom out to a long view often reveals the more major trends.

An auto-run feature can store up to seven separate sequences of commands. Each sequence can be made up of as many as 50 keystrokes. You might use this feature to store a method of plotting each of seven stocks or storing seven different standard methods with broad application to many stocks.

There is no provision for point and figure charting.

Hardware Requirements, Software Compatibility

The Technical Investor

The Technical Investor requires 256K RAM and DOS 2.0 or higher. It also requires two floppy drives or one floppy drive plus a hard disk. It runs on the IBM PC, XT, and AT; the Compaqs; and the AT&T 6300.

Savant users have reported running the program on Coronas, Columbia, EAGLEs, Panasonics, and Tandy RS-1000 and RS-1200s. It will not run on the Tandy 2000. For IBM computers, the program requires an IBM color/graphics card, an IBM enhanced graphics card, or a dual-mode card such as the Paradise. The program offers functional color only with the enhanced graphics card. (Functional color is used to distinguish among multiple lines plotted on a chart. Decorative color means just that.) If you use the enhanced graphics adapter with a monochrome monitor, the lines will be distinguished by graphic devices (dotted, dashed, etc.). Lines in monochrome are all alike with conventional IBM graphics.

The program has a special utility to make it handier for hard disk users to set up directories. Savant's Technical Investor is compatible with Savant's Fundamental Investor, the RTR TechniFilter (be sure to request the Savant version), and the Savant Databridge program. The Databridge downloads and uploads Savant data in a text file form that is compatible with various application programs, including Lotus, other spreadsheets, dBASE II and dBASE III, and word processors.

Winning on Wall Street

This program requires 192K RAM. It also requires a color or monochrome monitor with a graphics board, two disk drives (one of which may be a hard disk), and a Hayes 1200 or 1200B modem. To print graphics you will need a graphic printer and PC DOX 1.1 or 2.0 or MS DOS (with a graphic dump routine). It will also run on the IBM AT with one or two high-density 1.2-megabyte floppy drives, with a combination of 1.2 megabytes and a conventional floppy drive, and with a combination of the high-density drive and a hard disk.

I have run the program on Compaqs, and it should run on the AT&T 6300, though I have not specifically tested it on that computer. Finally, there is an Apple version of the program.

The Summa Trader's Forecaster is compatible with the Summa Trader's Data Manager and Trader's Accountant programs. The three programs constitute the package, Winning on Wall Street. In addition, Summa offers a series of compatible data transfer programs to exchange files between Winning and various widely available spreadsheets and database managers.

The Active Investor

This program requires an IBM PC, XT, or AT or a computer compatible with 192K RAM and DOS 2.1 or higher. A second floppy disk drive is optional. A graphics card is necessary on IBM machines. The original

IBM version, Anidata's, included a DIF file converter as part of the program so that you could exchange files with Lotus 1-2-3 or other DIF-compatible software. This feature could have been used to chart data retrieved by FM radio modem or via TV cable. It is perhaps not surprising that this feature has vanished from the Interactive version of the program. If you are resourceful, you may be able to locate and review one of the older, open versions of the program. You might ask around at an IBM PC user group meeting.

The Dow Jones Market Analyzer Plus

The Market Analyzer Plus requires 256K RAM, a graphics adapter card (for IBM computers), a compatible monitor, and two double-sided floppy drives. For graphics printouts, the manual suggests an IBM (or an Epson FX or MX) printer with Graftrax Plus. The program will run on the PC, XT, AT, or compatibles, including the Compaqs and the AT&T model 6300. DOS 2.0, 2.1, or 3.0 is required.

MetaStock

This program requires an IBM PC, XT, AT, or true compatible with 256K RAM, DOS 2.0 or higher, and two drives. It fully supports hard disk drives, including multiple directories. It also requires an IBM color graphics adapter or a monochrome graphics adapter. An IBM/Epson dot-matrix printer is needed if you wish to print charts.

Trendline II

Trendline II requires an IBM PC or 100 percent compatible and an IBM graphics card with a composite monitor. It would not run on our IBM PC with a monochrome graphics card owing to boot-up problems. The program is written in Forth. I ran it on our Compaq. It also requires a Hayes 1200-bps modem; an IBM or Epson dot-matrix printer for printing out charts is optional.

Database Compatibility

The Technical Investor

This program can use Warner Computer Systems or Dow Jones. It will access other databases in the terminal mode, but to load data directly into the program, you are restricted to Warner and Dow Jones. One might typically use Warner for historical data and Dow Jones for news and current quotes. To upload FM radio or TV cable data from a spreadsheet, you have to use Savant's Databridge program.

Winning on Wall Street

This program can use Dow Jones and Hale's Dial Data. At this writing there is some discussion of adding Warner Data Systems. To upload FM radio data from a spreadsheet, you have to experiment with Summa's spreadsheet transfer program, the SwitchBoard.

The Active Investor

Interactive Data Systems is used exclusively for the Active Investor version. Warner Data Systems and Compuserve were used in the original (Anidata) version, which is no longer on the market.

The Dow Jones Market
Analyzer Plus

This program uses Dow Jones. A DIF file utility is provided to enable you to upload and download data. This feature could conceivably be used to import data, via a spreadsheet, from sources other than Dow Jones. For FM radio or TV cable data, there could be economies in doing so.

MetaStock

Warner Data Systems connects to the program via Computer Asset Management's communications program, the Downloader. With other communications software, you can use any of six other databases as a source for price-volume data. In addition to Warner, they are Compuserve, Commodity Systems Inc., Hale Systems, IDC (Interactive Data), I.P. Sharp, and Nite Line. The MetaStock program has built-in utilities for importing files from spreadsheets, so you could use a spreadsheet to accumulate FM radio and certain TV cable data for subsequent plotting by MetaStock.

Trendline II

A communications program is part of the package. It accesses Warner Computer Systems.

List Prices

Program	Price
The Technical Investor	$395. Includes communications and technical database. Three disks. Related programs include Fundamental Investor, $395; Databridges (1 fundamental, 1 technical), $145 each; RTR TechniFilter, Savant-compatible version, $299, available from RTR (see chapter on TechniFilter).
Winning on Wall Street	$495
The Active Investor	$495
The Dow Jones Market Analyzer Plus	$349 (introductory offer). Ask about free time on the Dow Jones news retrieval database.
MetaStock	$195 for the MetaStock program only. Downloader program, $49. Both programs purchased together, $224.
Trendline II	$275. Supplied with substantial historical database on disk (e.g., 50 stocks daily data for one year, 25 stocks weekly for five years, 25 stocks monthly for ten years). In addition, about $30 worth of data from Warner can be accessed free.

Remarks

The Technical Investor

This is the most logical, convenient, and controllable of the programs reviewed, though it is not necessarily the best. It was clearly visualized in its design and fully realized in its execution. The portfolio module is not finished at this writing, so you may wish to check on its progress before making a commitment to the program or use a different portfolio manager.

Winning on Wall Street

The Trader's Accountant is an excellent portfolio management program with particular appeal to traders. This should weigh in your decision.

The Active Investor

This program is compact and very fast. It rarely seems to spin the disk. Mnemonic commands require just one letter or one letter plus a command key. On-screen help is excellent—a full-page command dictionary. Documentation is succinct and includes a review chapter on methods of technical analysis. The technical component of the Active Investor is a reasonably good value, a logically organized program, and a bit of a magic show. The limitation is the high cost of the data on which it must run. It is designed to restrict you to a single source for data.

The Dow Jones Market Analyzer Plus

In charting capability the program is rather typical, but the command language cum user-formula set advances it a notch in terms of speed and convenience. The statistical utilities and the power to create and follow group indexes add real value. Group analysis can display the inner workings of the market in action, and I think you will notice the difference it makes in your own performance.

MetaStock

MetaStock is a second-generation technical analysis program, and it shows. The only notable limitation on its capabilities is that it cannot superimpose dissimilar indicators. Each indicator is treated as a separate charting problem. MetaStock is the price/performance leader of the technical analysis programs reviewed in this book. It does not fully duplicate the performance of higher-priced programs at a lower cost, however. Basic components such as keyboard macros, auto-run, and downloading of price-volume data are not included, nor is there a built-in portfolio manager. If you understand the limitations of what the program has set out to do—strictly charting—it is a brilliant success and a bargain.

Trendline II

Trendline II is the fastest program. It does basic, standard charting. There is no user-formula set. It runs right out of the box, without tinkering, and it comes with some attractive bonus offerings of free data. It appears rather costly for its capabilities, but it is economical to operate. Also, programs are often discounted as they find their markets, and this is something to check for.

Manufacturers' Addresses

THE TECHNICAL INVESTOR
Savant Corporation
14814 Perthshire
P.O. Box 440278
Houston, TX 77244

(800) 231-9900
In Texas: (713) 556-8363

WINNING ON WALL STREET
   The Trader's Forecaster
   The Trader's Data Manager
   The Trader's Accountant

Summa Technologies, Inc.
P.O. Box 2046
Beaverton, OR 79075

(503) 644-3212

THE ACTIVE INVESTOR
Interactive Data Corporation
303 Wyman St.
Waltham, MA 02154

(617) 895-4300

DOW JONES MARKET
ANALYZER PLUS
Dow Jones & Company, Inc.
P.O. Box 300
Princeton, NJ 08540

(800) 257-5114

METASTOCK
Computer Asset Management
P.O. Box 26743
Salt Lake City, UT 84126

(801) 964-0391
(800) 882-3040

TRENDLINE II
Micro Services
Standard & Poor's Corporation
25 Broadway
New York, NY 10004

(800) 852-5200, ext. 7

Which Program Should You Buy?

If all you want is a charting package, the answer is simple: MetaStock. If you want more, the range of choice expands considerably.

The best investment package overall is Interactive's Active Investor. It is the only fully integrated investment package. Of the four components that constitute it, one—the portfolio manager—is absolutely first class. The technical analysis package and the fundamental analysis package are very good, but the communications package is the worst feature of the program. It will connect you to just one database—Interactive's—and these data are not competitively priced. For this reason and because Interactive's attitude toward this program and its market seems a bit uncertain, I would very reluctantly put this program into last place.

Next up I would put Winning on Wall Street. The positive features are its trader-oriented portfolio manager, its mathematical sophistication, and its easy assimilation by beginners. In my opinion, it is slow to load and is poorly organized. I suspect that it does not fully exploit the power of IBM hardware.

That leaves Dow Jones and Savant, and I would consider it a toss-up between them for first choice.

The Dow Jones Market Analyzer Plus, like the Active Investor, locks you into a database. However, there are probably ways to circumvent this via the DIF-file utility. It has no fundamental analysis module, but it does have an adequate portfolio manager. The daily statistical breakdown on how your stocks are doing is an attractive and unique feature, as is the power to analyze groups. The program is compatible with an optimizer, the TechniFilter, and shares its formula set. It is a technically oriented program. It may never add fundamental analysis to grow into a complete, integrated package, but you could use it alongside any of the stand-alone fundamental packages.

The Savant program was designed from the beginning as a fully integrated package. The technical component gets a B or a B+, though there are some real limitations. The fundamental component is the best available. Data brought into the price-volume files update price-related items in the fundamental database (betas, P/Es), so it is a truly integrated program. The portfolio manager is not complete at this writing.

The Savant program accesses a number of different databases, so you can shop for data. To make the program work with FM or TV cable data, you need a spreadsheet and a Technical Databridge. To transfer data to and from a spreadsheet from the Fundamental module, you need another utility, called the Fundamental Databridge. By using a spreadsheet, you can compensate for the program's most glaring flaw, the lack of a user-formula set. It seems a shame that this is necessary, but you need access to a spreadsheet anyway, in my view, to use FM or cable data and to keep a portfolio monitor.

Like the Dow Jones Market Analyzer, Savant's program is compatible with the TechniFilter optimization program.

At this point, we have come full circle. Since all these programs must be rather heavily optioned out to create a complete investment computer system, why not start with the most basic building blocks and custom-build your own?

The reason to hesitate before trying this is that it will bring problems with program compatibility and organization. The chief attractive quality of Savant is that it has a strong organizational "spine" that can pull together under one logical menu all the diverse functions of investment analysis. On this score, Savant is the winner. Its designers are meticulous and have seen the problem whole from the very beginning. Interactive's Active Investor was integrated after the fact from four separately conceived components. However, the integration is now a *fait accompli.*

If I were to try to assemble from disparate software components a "best" do-it-yourself integrated investment package and simply accept poor organization and compatibility problems, I would put at its center a spreadsheet such as Lotus 1-2-3. Into this center I would direct quotes from Telemet FM or (somehow) X*Press TV cable. The quotes would be accumulated within the spreadsheet to form a set of files suitable for charting. Incoming quotes would also be used to keep up to date, in nearly real time, a portfolio monitor, again maintained within the spreadsheet.

To chart stocks, I would choose MetaStock.

To run fundamental screens fairly economically, one might use Savant's Fundamental Analyzer as a stand-alone program or try Value/Screen Plus or StockPak II. The advantages of the Value Line program in this application are twofold. It provides a portfolio manager and will transfer data into the spreadsheet so that you can readily update price-based items such as P/Es. (Savant's Fundamental Analyzer will also communicate with a spreadsheet, via the $145 Fundamental Databridge.) The disadvantage of Value/Screen Plus is that it covers too few stocks. StockPak II provides a much broader selection.

You may not have the time or patience to create an integrated private system. The components of the prepackaged products already dovetail. If this appeals to you, favor Savant if you lean toward fundamental analysis and Dow Jones if you are technically inclined. For the highest level of integration now offered, and with equal weight on technical and fundamental analysis and a top portfolio manager, you might consider Interactive's Active Investor—but be aware of the relatively high cost of running it.

16

What-to-Buy and When-to-Sell Programs

Chart Sorting Made Automatic

Suppose you have collected 500 charts of the price and volume performance of as many stocks, each plotted over the span of the past year. The 500 charts comprise a full ream of paper, a stack three inches high. By scanning every single page, you might hope to identify 5 or 10 stocks whose smoothed price curve turned, just yesterday, from downtrend to uptrend or from uptrend to downtrend. If you found 10 such charts in the pile, you might put aside the other 490 and concentrate your analytical attention on just these 10 technically "interesting" stocks, with the expectation, valid or not, of buying low and selling high.

If we edge past the rather chewed over problem of whether technical analysis of charts is worth doing at all (maybe it works, maybe it doesn't), we are left with the practical problem of hunting through 500 charts. If we attacked the job in the traditional way, it would be necessary to actually examine and interpret 500 paper charts. Many of them could be dismissed at a glance, but most would require some slow pencil work to analyze.

You can put the problem on the computer using any of the technical analysis programs reviewed in the preceding chapters. These programs will download from commercial databases the numbers you need to recreate the charts on a PC screen. They file the data and then use the data on command to draw charts. They then enable you to smooth the data in various ways and automate the processes of drawing trend lines, regression lines, speed resistance lines, lines defining trading ranges and envelopes, and other lines of definition and demarcation helpful to technical analysts.

Creating Time to Think

However, as with sorting by hand, much time is sacrificed in the slow, rather artistic detailing that must be drawn on each chart, on paper or on the computer screen: the experimental moving averages, the tentative trend lines, the point-to-point measurements, the trials and the errors and the doodles. This graphic embellishment forms the basis for, and necessarily precedes each judgment call on, the merit of the stock. This painstaking and largely visual interactive analytical process makes the charts more intelligible to human analysts. By contrast, a PC does not need to take time to generate and "look at" a graphic representation to make quick sense of these data. The computer can directly scan the numbers and calculate conclusions. It can make all the obvious save or discard decisions (or at least all the purely objective and quantitative cuts) before it displays a single chart.

This of course speeds the sorting process tremendously. Interactive's Active Investor, for example, will selectively display only those charts which meet the analyst's preset conditions. The conditions may be quite simple (the stock closed above $50, for example) or fairly complex (the 3-day moving average is stipulated to be above the 10-day moving average, say). The specific conditions are not written into the program. Rather, means are provided for the operator to set up the condition desired, including crossovers, turnarounds, ranges, and trends. All this sorting and screening capability is provided by Interactive almost parenthetically as one feature of an integrated technical analysis and portfolio management package.

There is a new, dedicated program that does essentially the same job, perhaps a bit more handily. It is called the TechniFilter. The cost is $299. Given the programming elbow room that comes with trying to do just one or two tasks well, the writers (RTR Software Systems Inc.) have succeeded very well. It would seem to be the program of choice to handle our hypothetical 500-chart problem. It may not be the program most appropriate to your own analytical work, but it establishes a standard you may find helpful in evaluating programs (or features of program packages) of this type.

TechniFilter operates on files created using the Dow Jones Market Analyzer or the Savant Technical Investor. Be sure to specify to RTR which program you will be using, as there are two versions of the TechniFilter, one appropriate to each charting package.

How It Works

TechniFilter works in two steps. First, it calculates and files values of interest for each of the stocks in the system. Five hundred stocks is an upper limit. Typical values might include today's close, the current values of simple moving averages and/or exponential moving averages taken over several short and long intervals (e.g., 6, 10, 12, 24, 30, or 200 days), the slope of the linear regression line, the on-balance volume, Welles Wilder relative strength, and other criteria familiar to market technicians. This is basically a collection of devices to smooth price curves and try to sense their direction.

Once a selection of these values has been calculated, the TechniFilter can use them as the basis for a conditional screening. This second, filtering step is the "filter" part of TechniFilter. For example, the analyst might request a list of all stocks for which today's closing price lies above the 30-day moving-average closing price. If 100 stocks met this condition, the analyst might then stipulate a subset of stocks for which the 30-day moving average exceeds the 200-day moving average, a condition many investors regard as indicative of clear sailing ahead. It would also be possible to link these two conditions with a logical "AND" so that the screen would be accomplished at a single pass.

Result: The Short List of Stocks

At the conclusion of the screening (or filtering) process, the analyst would have in hand a short list of stocks meeting his or her particular criteria for technically appealing stocks. The analyst could then turn to one of the technical analysis graphics programs to visualize and scrutinize in detail the charts of these few stocks of interest.

To help set up the system for a screen, a master list of 48 formulas is provided which is accessible via the program's menu. It is a catalog of questions which can be used to construct the criteria for the screening passes. Most of them are comparative statements that enable you to ask, for example, if today's closing price is higher or lower than yesterday's or if the on-balance volume is rising or falling.

The mathematics underlying the program are nicely hidden from view. To request a calculation of the slope of a least-squares fit to a linear regression for 10 days of volume data for a given stock, you just select or write the formula VW10. To learn how this value compares with the same value as it would have been reported yesterday, you write VW10Y1, where Y1 = yesterday. The notation is easy to pick up if you keep in mind constantly that it is describing something that is graphically obvious: a straight line tending up, a peak, a valley, a saucer, a point position within a bracketing range, or perhaps a point sitting above or below a line.

What the Program Searches For

The combination of standard formulas and conditions enables the program to seek out or weed out stocks on the basis of (roughly) five general types of criteria, as follows.

1. *Reversal tests:* Has the stock price changed direction?
2. *Crossover alerts:* Has the stock's 10-day moving average risen above its 30-day moving average? Has the 30-day moving average plunged through the 200-day moving average?
3. *Tests of position within a range:* Has the stock broken out of its characteristic trading range? Is it approaching, to within some stipulated percentage of the range, its historic high or low?
4. *Volatility:* How fast does the stock move? How frequently does it ricochet back and forth within its trading range?
5. *Measures of position and trend:* Where is the stock relative to its five-day simple moving-average line? Where is the 12-day exponential average relative to the 12-day simple moving average? What is the slope of the least-squares-fit line over the span of the past 30 days? What is the trend of the on-balance–volume line?

One cannot use all 48 model formulas in a screening operation. Instead, the user makes a selection of six or eight formulas (or writes his or her own) and then sets the conditions to be met by the results calculated using these formulas. If formula 1 is a calculation of a 10-day moving average and formula 2 is a calculation of a 30-day moving average, a typical condition might require that the result of formula 1 must exceed that of formula 2 for the chart to be considered acceptable. Again, this describes a relation of two curves (one lies above the other) that you would note at a glance on a chart but would grow weary of noting on 500 charts in a row. Seven preset formula sets with conditions already established are provided with the program as "examples."

Stock Pickers for Free

It is a nice aspect of the way the program is presented that the examples it provides, which are in fact capsule programs that will select stocks, are not urged upon the user as methods of choice, money-makers, or anybody's favorite formulas. You can run them right out of the box, however, and get a quick feel for what the program can do before settling down to customize formula sets in accordance with your own technical criteria.

The Optimizer

The program does one more thing that is somewhat different in kind. Once you have picked a stock chart that holds your attention, you can test different buy and sell strategies to learn what would or would not have worked for this stock in the past. Thus, instead of applying some blanket strategy to all stocks, you can devise a strategy uniquely appropriate to each of the stocks you trade.

A prototypical strategy might stipulate, for example, that you always buy whenever the 10-day moving average rises above the 30-day moving average and that you always sell short when the 10-day moving average falls back through the 30-day moving average. The program will examine the price history of the stock, keep track of the mock transactions executed in accordance with your strategy, and report your net percentage gain or loss as of the most current close. It will also report the results obtained by simply buying at the price recorded for the first day on file and selling at the last close. These reports can be an embarrassment to the whole concept of stock trading, but they sometimes pinpoint highly profitable strategies. The testing process is automated to a degree. You can have the program automatically vary and test several different terms of the moving averages to discover the best strategy.

This strategy "optimizer" is not as highly automated as it might be and its work should not be understood literally as an optimization process. It might be interesting to see it teamed with a built-in number generator, perhaps a random number generator. You'd have to start it in the morning and walk away, of course, but by the evening of the following day you might have in hand a rather comprehensively tested strategy.

It would also be nice if one could experimentally vary the term over which the strategy is tested. It is my view that when these strategies do work, it is purely fortuitous; they just happen to work, for whatever reason or for no reason whatever. There are no underlying principles to name, grasp, and use. The thing to be grasped and used is the moment (or the week, weeks, or even months) during which the strategy succeeds. TechniFilter may or may not help you seize these profitable moments, but there is no question that it can improve the quality of the time you spend doing technical analysis.

There are several other optimizers on the market. One is inherent in the Summa's Winning on Wall Street. This utility tests only a single moving average against the curve of unaveraged prices. TechniFilter tests the crossovers of more than one moving average. A still more complex program, the MicroVest Profit Optimizer, is designed to test 22 separate technical indicators and four types of stops. Pardo's Swing Trader runs multivariable models and is the top-priced optimizer (for micros) at $1440. I am aware of a mainframe model-building program for com. ..dity trading that consumes $45,000 to $80,000 worth of computer time every time it is run, so that one might say that the problem has magnitude. Maybe it is too ambitious to expect a microcomputer to compete in this arena, but if there was ever a little engine that could, the micro is it.

Optimization programs should be understood as the cutting edge of the technology of computerized investing. They are primitive and slow, but they can indeed produce the most "rational" buy and sell strategies for short- and intermediate-term traders. Whether a rational strategy will work better for you than an irrational one, such as a coin flip, is something you can perhaps determine with a coin flip.

Sources and Prices

TECHNIFILTER
RTR Software Systems Inc.
444 Executive Center Boulevard, Suite 225
El Paso, TX 79902
(915) 544-4397

List price: $299

Requires: PC with 128K RAM and two drives or XT. DOS 2.0. Operates on files generated with the Dow Jones Market Analyzer program on the Savant Technical Investor

THE ACTIVE INVESTOR
Interactive Data Corporation
303 Wyman Street
Waltham, MA 02254-9113
(617) 895-4300

List price: $495

Requires: 192K RAM, a PC, PC Jr, XT, AT, or compatible. Monitor, graphics card. Will not work on a Hercules color graphics card. DOS 2.1 or higher. 1200-bps modem. Graphics printer. One or two drives or single drive plus hard disk.

PROFIT OPTIMIZER
MicroVest
P.O. Box 272
Macomb, IL 61455
(309) 837-4512

List price: $495

Requires: 256K RAM, two drives. DOS 2.1. Operates on files of High Tech charting program ($495), which is another MicroVest program. Tests 22 separate technical indicators and four types of stops.

WINNING ON WALL STREET
Summa Technologies, Inc.
P.O. Box 2046
Beaverton, OR 97075
(503) 644-3212

List price: $695

Optimization is an integral feature of the Trader's Forecaster program. It is called the Strategy Command. Tests one moving average against price.

SWING TRADER
Pardo Corporation
1615 Orrington, C202
Evanston, IL 60201
(312) 866-9342

List price: $1440

Requires: 256K RAM, two drives, DOS 2.1 or later, modem. Runs multivariate analyses.

PART 4

Fundamental Analytical Software

17
Fundamental Screening Programs

How to Discover Top-Performing Companies

Fundamental stock analysis is a tool to help investors judge the inherent value of a stock relative to its current market price. The idea is to pinpoint undervalued stocks to buy and overpriced stocks to sell. Fundamental analysis is an enormous subject—a profession, in fact—but investors from many different backgrounds use its basic techniques to good advantage. The questions it poses are indeed fundamental: Is this company making money? How much, how soon? How is it likely to be parsed out among the suppliers, lenders, stockholders, management, and idea people? How well is the company doing relative to every other publicly held company in the universe of companies you may wish to invest in?

This last question is really one for your PC to answer. Perhaps a half dozen major programs are now available for fundamental stock screening. They enable you to extract, from a universe of up to 10,000 stocks, a short list of stocks which meet the fundamental criteria you consider most important.

Automating the Process
of Elimination

You may favor only those companies which faithfully distribute generous
dividends. Another investor may prefer exponential sales growth fueled
by retained earnings. Once you have specified what you want, the programs list the stocks that meet your requirements. As these programs
mature technologically, they appeal to a wider range of investors. If you
already use fundamental analysis, you may have come to feel that you
are working and reworking a stale universe of 50 or 100 or 300 stocks.
A PC can suddenly expand the scope of your attention to include many
thousands of stocks that are new to you. If you are a market professional
with established sources of fundamental data, you may be surprised and
pleased by the power of the newest software to pare your research expenses. If you have never tried fundamental analysis, you will find that
learning to use a screening program is a good way to feel your way into
this mode of thinking about and evaluating stocks.

How Screening Works

All the programs are supplied with or provide access to a deep database
of fundamental stock information. In a typical screening protocol, you
might begin by extracting from the database a list of all the companies
that happen to be in the pharmaceutical manufacturing business. From
this list a second, smaller list could be drawn, made up of all pharmaceutical companies with revenues in excess of $100 million, and a third,
still smaller list composed of pharmaceutical companies with revenues
in excess of $100 million and profit margins in the range of 10 to 14
percent. With each screening pass for an added logical condition, the
list shrinks. You ultimately print a short, manageable list of stocks that
look quite attractive to you. Criteria for screening typically include stip-
ulations about the current ratio, rates of growth, return on equity, volatility of the stock, level of institutional holdings, amount of stock
outstanding relative to gross revenues or sales, and many other considerations.

The Big Pitfall:
A $6000 Download

Screening is useful, certainly, but if you are not alert to the major pitfall
in the process, it can turn into one of the truly expensive things you can
do with a PC. This pitfall is downloading. Its cost will come as a shock

particularly if you routinely use a computer for technical analysis. The price-volume data which support technical analyses come down via modem for about $100 per 360 kilobytes, which is not at all unreasonable. But if you download fundamental data (i.e., anything other than price-volume data, including earnings per share, institutional holdings, dividends, net income, shares—altogether about 200 different items of information you might wish to scrutinize in fundamental analysis), the price of a fill-up for a 360-kilobyte floppy can shoot up to $6000. How do the various programs deal with this price barrier? What compromises must one accept in order to get around it?

The do-it-yourself solution costs least. You can set up your own fundamental database under a database management program such as dBASE III and enter data manually from off-line sources (print or microfilm), some of which cost nothing at all. Easy to use sorting, ranking, and screening procedures are written into database management programs. A system of this type is discussed in Chapter 18. The major compromise involves your time. To manually maintain a database on more than about 500 stocks will require more time (yours or that of your support personnel) than makes good sense. If you have a specialized investment interest, e.g., high-technology stocks, a 500-stock database can be sufficient. But to screen stocks in a generalized way, you will probably find it helpful to work from an initial universe of 1500 to 2000 companies.

Buying Fundamental Data on Diskettes

One answer is to buy the data on floppy disks. Value Line, Inc., and Standard & Poor's Corporation both offer fundamental data on diskettes on a subscription basis, along with the programs you need to access and analyze the data. These are useful and popular packages. The prices are not directly comparable since Standard & Poor's distributes the price of its program across the price of the data diskettes while Value Line does not; no two disks cover the same set of companies. However, the prices seem to fall in the range of $20 to $30 per disk of 1500 to 1650 companies. Standard & Poor's markets its disks in 12-month subscriptions, as does Value Line, but Value Line also sells a quarterly subscription. Including the Value/Screen Plus program and program maintenance charges, this quarterly service costs $211 the first year and $162 in subsequent years. Fundamental data are reported quarterly by companies, and there is a major reporting cycle ending December 31; thus a four-disk subscription will suffice for many investors. Both Standard & Poor's and Value Line disks offer tremendous improvements over the cost of downloaded data. The compromise here involves timeliness. The information canned on your monthly or quarterly disk has already aged a bit by the time you receive it. Until recently there was no way to update it either manually or by modem.

The Importance of Current Data

Updating is notably a problem with price-related items such as price/earnings and price/sales ratios, dividend yields, and volatility. Fundamentally oriented investors are seldom slam-bang traders, and they tend to take a long-term view of the market. But their overarching interest is the measurement of value against price—today's price—so the value of data sealed up on a floppy decays rapidly with time.

The Interactive Solution:
Don't Interact

Interactive Data has developed a means of transmitting monthly updates for both price and fundamental data items on its disks via modem. The service is made accessible only to users of Interactive's excellent integrated software package, the Active Investor (see Chapter 21). The Active Investor software incorporates the predecessor program of Value/Screen Plus, and it taps the Value Line database. This software was called simply Value/Screen by Value line and is called Fundamental Analysis on the Active Investor's menu. Updates are provided weekly over the phone on 125 stocks. At this rate you can completely refresh your Value Line database of 1650 stocks once per quarter. In the meantime, you can also enter updates manually. The on-line updates are provided on a subscription basis to users of the Active Investor; the price is $40 per month. The on-line service is reasonably priced because it is a prepackaged, high-speed dump. You do not go on-line for long, and you do not waste time interacting with the database to request data item by item. Instead, you pull the lever and stand back while the mainframe empties its hopper into your micro.

At the opposite extreme in terms of on-line efficiency (i.e., cost efficiency) is the Dow Jones Market Microscope. This program operates exclusively on selectively downloaded data and is thus very costly to operate.

The Value/Screen Plus program, which supersedes Value Line's earlier Value/Screen offering (the company recalled and replaced all the older programs), differs from the original in several ways, but the basic screening concept is unchanged. See Figure 17.2.

The newer program is better organized. Instead of scrolling willy-nilly through a list of 37 different screening criteria, the new program organizes the screening criteria into four distinct groups. Each group is presented in a window, on request, as you set up a screening run. They include (1) ratings and estimates, (2) market data, (3) historical measures, and (4) growth projections. The screening criteria are essentially the same as those of the original program, but their presentation in groups improves the operating convenience of the program and tends to police your logic as you set up screens.

New features include a portfolio manager and the ability to transfer to spreadsheets both the manager and any other reports on which you wish to operate. The portfolio manager is unique in that you can keep in view, along with the usual valuation data, some facts about your stocks that you might not otherwise consider every day. Projected return, earnings, and earnings growth rates are examples. You can take your choice from among the 37 fields of data in the database or display all of them.

These ancillary data are helpful, especially in a spreadsheet presentation. The extra information informs your daily decisions about the continuing wisdom of holding the stocks you happen to own. It is chiefly useful, of course, if you happen to own stocks included in the Value Line database. If you trade heavily in over-the-counter stocks, you won't get much use out of this program or its features. Otherwise, it's excellent.

One of These 10,000 Stocks Is the Best One

Savant's Fundamental Investor combines three approaches to data gathering. Savant offers monthly subscriptions to data on floppy disks, but you are free to write updated information onto the disks. The updates can be accomplished automatically via modem or manually from the keyboard. Both fundamental and price-related items can be kept current. The fundamental data selection can be expanded slightly with downloaded data items for all companies or hugely enriched for a few stocks of particular interest. See Figure 17.1.

Two sets of three floppy disks are made available to subscribers every month. The first set includes data on 5500 companies altogether, sorted in order of asset value. These are the commonly traded stocks of both major exchanges and the over-the-counter market. The other three diskettes cover 4500 more stocks, most of which are rather obscure and

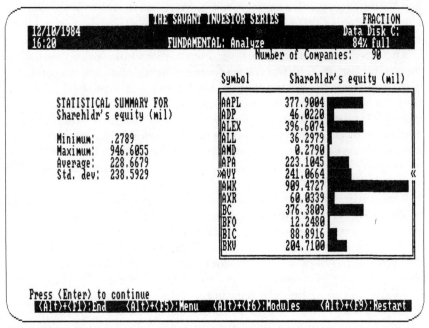

Figure 17.1. One facet of Savant's Fundamental Investor. You can scroll the information in the window up and down to review the range of results from a screening or ranking operation. A horizontal bar graph helps your eye gauge the data as you scroll. In general, horizontal rather than vertical bar graphs make the most efficient use of screen space and thus convey more useful information.

infrequently traded. The first trio of disks is obviously the bread and butter item, but the second is available to those adventurers and archivists who are interested. The total is 10,000 stocks. You can subscribe to one or more diskettes per month as you wish. A 12-disk annual subscription costs $275, or about $23 per disk, the typical price. The Fundamental Investor program costs $395, a one-time expense.

The Economies of Selective Downloading

For each company in the database, 35 data items are provided to subscribers on the disk. These are the items most investors would probably wish to use in an initial screening. At the conclusion of an early screening, one can begin downloading data. But because the rough cuts have already been made (you have dismissed all companies which are not pharmaceutical companies, for example), the economies of downloading fundamental data are suddenly much more attractive. You can update the 35 items already on file for the remaining companies of interest and expand these files to include as many as 200 items per company. You can transfer data into a spreadsheet for modeling purposes via a separate Savant program called the Fundamental Databridge. It costs $145. Value/Screen Plus will move data into a spreadsheet without any accessory software, which is a point in its favor, but there is no facility for moving dial-up quotes into the same spreadsheet. You would have to purchase a separate spreadsheet link program to accomplish this. A minimal spreadsheet link program, Market Link, costs $85. FM or TV cable quote can be transferred to the spreadsheet without additional software, however.

When you download prices into Savant's Fundamental Investor, all price-related items such as price/earnings ratios (P/Es) and price/sales ratios (PSRs) are recalculated automatically by the Fundamental Investor. Price quotes come in over the phone for one-sixtieth the cost of

OVERALL FINAN POS		Assets	Liabils	LTDebt	Sales	NetWorth	EPSyrend found 69—
TDY	TELEDYNE INC	2790.70M	1631.40M	1070.70M	3494.30M	1159.30M	37.69
F	FORD MTR CO D	27.49B	17.65B	2110.90M	52.37B	9837.70M	15.79
GM	GENERAL MTRS	52.00B	27.93B	2772.90M	83.89B	24.07B	14.22
C	CHRYSLER CORP	9062.70M	5756.79M	760.10M	19.57B	3305.90M	11.75
IBM	INTERNATIONAL	42.81B	16.32B	3269.00M	45.94B	26.49B	10.77
MD	MCDONNELL DOU	6191.30M	3847.50M	40.50M	9662.60M	2343.80M	8.10
SC	SHELL TRANS&T	69.19B	39.63B	8344.00M	73.71B	29.56B	6.82
CBS	CBS INC	3261.76M	1708.82M	364.29M	4831.45M	1552.94M	6.59
JCP	PENNEY J C IN	7438.00M	3879.00M	1709.00M	12.08B	3559.00M	6.25
DG	ASSOCIATED DR	2084.43M	1098.96M	333.14M	4106.65M	985.47M	6.07
COT	COLT INDS INC	1023.54M	679.82M	124.59M	1868.27M	343.72M	5.99
DEC	DIGITAL EQUIP	5593.25M	1614.03M	441.31M	5584.43M	3979.22M	5.73
GTE	GTE CORP	26.47B	18.20B	8523.24M	14.55B	8267.94M	5.45
PG	PROCTER & GAM	8898.00M	3818.00M	630.00M	12.95B	5080.00M	5.35
GE	GENERAL ELEC	24.73B	12.16B	753.00M	27.95B	12.57B	5.03
SW	STONE & WEBST	489.37M	222.31M	17.25M	343.03M	267.06M	5.02
LSI	LEAR SIEGLER	1469.21M	899.90M	346.99M	1941.67M	569.31M	4.96
MA	MAY DEPT STOR	3046.70M	1680.70M	532.90M	4744.00M	1366.00M	4.96
UK	UNION CARBIDE	10.52B	5594.00M	2362.00M	9508.00M	4924.00M	4.84
KO	COCA COLA CO	5958.07M	3180.00M	740.00M	7364.00M	2778.07M	4.76

[↑][↓][←][→][PgDn][PgUp] [G]rph [E]xpd [O][^O]Sort [C]hng [^F]Save [P]rt [esc]_

Figure 17.2. The basic principle of fundamental stock screening is to start with a long list and extract from it a short list. Value Line's Value/Screen Plus program gives you 1650 stocks to start with. Note that this shorter list is ranked in order of earnings per share at the year's end. You might select the top 25 from this list and proceed to another screening step, perhaps by specifying sales in excess of $1 billion.

fundamental data, so this is quite economical. Fundamental downloading is handled selectively. Savant's arrangements call for the data to be downloaded from Disclosure Inc. via Warner Data Systems. Rather than download every item of data available for a given company (and probably more than you want to know), you can preselect the items you want. Similarly, you might select one item of interest (institutional holdings, say) and download it for every company on the disk. If you prefer, you can enter such data from the keyboard.

The program has many other intelligent features (statistical summaries, a horizontal bar graph presentation that can be scrolled up and down to scan the results of each screen and ranking, a set of useful standard equations and tools to write your own), but it is selective downloading that matters most. It makes fundamental data more economical—and therefore accessible—without sacrificing much of anything.

Interactive came close to providing this much capability within the Active Investor, but this program will not recalculate price-related values. The rather high cost of retrieving price data from Interactive makes it impractical to update the price values across the database of 1650 Value Line stocks. The weekly download of data on selected Value Line issues can update prices on about 125 stocks but not on all 1650.

By comparison, you could download prices from Warner Computer, one of Savant's sources, for a reasonable price if you happened to have 1650 stocks in the Fundamental Investor.

Given a spreadsheet, enough files, and enough patience, one could download FM or TV cable quotes on 1650 stocks for no more than the cost of downloading a single quote on one stock. There are no usage charges. This would certainly be the best and most economical means of maintaining up-to-date prices and price-volume–related data within a large fundamental database.

In terms of operating cost, performance, and detailing, Savant has the best-developed fundamental screening program you can buy. It costs more going in, but the operating costs are realistic.

The Value/Screen Plus and the Standard & Poor's StockPak II floppy services share second place. Value Line gives you a built-in portfolio manager and the power to transfer fundamental data (but not on-line price data) into a spreadsheet. Standard & Poor's provides a far wider choice of stocks to screen.

The Interactive integrated program is low in initial price and includes a technical analysis program and a portfolio manager in addition to the fundamental screening capability discussed here. The low initial cost is a gateway to rather high operating costs on the technical side of the package, but the massive download of current Value Line data is attractively priced. For an average investor interested in the basic set of 1650 stocks it is a good choice, but professionals and serious private investors interested in a wider range of stocks would probably prefer the Savant or S&P packages.

Sources and Prices

THE FUNDAMENTAL INVESTOR
Savant Corporation
P.O. Box 440278
Houston, TX 77244-0278
(713) 556-8363

List price: $395 for the Fundamental Investor, $275 per 12-disk subscription to monthly data. Downloaded data additional. Fundamental Databridge to spreadsheet, $145.

Requires: 256K RAM and two disk drives. Hayes Smartmodem is recommended.

Database: Disclosure, Inc. 10,000 stocks.

VALUE/SCREEN PLUS
Value Line, Inc.
305 E. 46th Street
New York, NY 10017
(212) 687-3965

List price: Value/Screen program, Fundamental data disks on 1650 stocks, about $29 per disk, subscriptions monthly or quarterly. Monthly subscription, $348 a year. Quarterly subscription, $211 first year, $162 in subsequent years.

Requires: 64K RAM, one drive.

Database: Value Line, Inc., 1650 stocks.

STOCKPAK II
Standard & Poor's Corporation
25 Broadway
New York, NY 10004
(212) 208-8581

List price: $30 initial setup charge. $245 per 12-disk subscription to monthly data. Subscriptions available to 1500-company composite from NYSE, ASE, and OTC; to 1500 NYSE companies; to 800 ASE companies; or to all OTC (2200 companies, two diskettes, $490 for both).

Requires: 128K RAM, two drives preferred, graphics card optional.

Database: Standard & Poor's. 4600 stocks.

MARKET MICROSCOPE
Dow Jones & Company, Inc.
P.O. Box 300
Princeton, NJ 08540
(800) 257-5114

List price: $349

Requires: 128K RAM, asynchronous communications, DOS 1.1 (only). Hayes Smartmodem or 1200B recommended.

Database: Media General, 3150 stocks.

THE ACTIVE INVESTOR
Interactive Data Corporation
303 Wyman Street
Waltham, MA 02254-9113
(617) 895-4300

List price: $495

Requires: 192K RAM, a PC, PC Jr, XT, AT, or compatible. Monitor, graphics card. Will not work on a Hercules color graphics card. DOS 2.1 or higher. 1200-bsp modem. Graphics printer. One or two drives or single drive plus hard disk.

Database: Value Line, 1650 stocks, and Interactive for prices.

18

How to Set Up
a Private
Stock Market
Database

Intensive fundamental stock analysis calls for a great deal of data on each of just a few companies, say 10 or 20. You can do it with a calculator. Extensive fundamental analysis calls for somewhat less data on each of hundreds or even thousands of companies. I bought an IBM PC primarily for this purpose.

A Quick, Calculated Reaction
to the Latest News

Extensive analysis is supported by a few specialized database management programs, as outlined in Chapter 17, but in terms of time expended, timeliness of results, and cost, I think a generalized database manager such as Ashton-Tate's dBASE III or dBASE III Plus offers a valuable alternative to dedicated software.

This is the case because existing dedicated software makes only limited provision (if any) for manual data entry. The data you buy for the dedicated program will be canned on a floppy and therefore aged or will be brought down via modem. Downloaded data are not as expensive as in the past, but they have not yet become inexpensive. Nor are downloaded data necessarily up to the minute. You receive the data over the phone in moments, but there may be a significant lag between the day the data are reported by the company and the day the report actually becomes available to users of on-line databases.

Keyboard entry to dBASE III keeps you current at relatively low cost. Within a day after a quarterly report is issued on a stock you follow, you can reevaluate your position in the stock, taking the new data into account. The option is realistic for resourceful investors who are willing to roll up their sleeves, program their computers, and take time to enter data.

Favorable Costs of Interest to Professionals

If you are in the investment business with a smaller firm, the appeal of a private database is surprising. The cost of keying in data from printed sources is usually lower than the cost of downloaded or even recorded data purchased from the same sources. One skillful keyboard operator can save you as much as 90 percent of your outlay for equivalent on-line fundamental data. Once the database is loaded, you own it. You will not find yourself repeatedly purchasing changeless historical data. You will require only the most current data. This further reduces costs.

It is important to recognize the limitations of this approach. Operating problems arise and must be coped with in the areas of quality control, comparability of data, and database magnitude. About 500 companies is a working limit, assuming that you store about 250 data items per company.

The Creation and Contents of a Private Database

Custom programming for this task is not costly if you supply the programmer with a tool such as dBASE III and specific instructions. You may wish to learn to program it yourself. (I programmed our system in dBASE II and look back on the experience as an absolutely heroic effort. dBASE III and dBASE III Plus are so much further along technologically, you may find the same task pretty easy.) I used eight coordinated databases. Here is an enumeration of what's in them.

Five databases contain the data items that go to make up quarterly and cumulative income statements (two hold numerical data, and three hold annotations). A sixth database holds current balance sheets and institutional and insider stock holdings. A seventh holds company addresses, phone numbers, ticker symbols, SIC (industry group) codes, and other information of the type that rarely changes. The eighth database, a rather crucial one used daily for recalculation, sorting, and ranking, contains values calculated or extracted from all the other databases plus the most current closing prices.

Following is a discussion of sources, costs, and techniques for maintaining one of the eight databases, a rather simple system which files and operates on quarterly income data. It can be used as a prototype for all the various fundamental databases you may wish to create in order to do extensive fundamental analyses.

Surprising Value of the Data

You can obtain quarterly income statements in print or on microfilm from Disclosure, Inc., or from the companies themselves, but the best source, at least initially, is the daily business press. It's readily accessible, it's virtually free, and it's daily.

One month after the close of a major reporting quarter (December 31, March 31, June 30, and September 30), the "Digest of Earnings Reports" section of *The Wall Street Journal* begins to expand from its typical fraction of a page, composed of 50 or fewer reports, to a full page and sometimes two. The "Digest of Earnings Reports" includes about 150 reports per page per day at the flood tide of quarterly reports. *The New York Times* has a similar feature, as do other major newspapers.

These useful capsule reports are based on quarterly income statements. Suppose you were to download into your computer 150 quarterly income statements over the phone, via modem, from a commercial database. It could cost about $2 per report, or $300 per day, to match the pace of the newspapers, report for report, for several days running during the peak reporting weeks. The data you'd get over the wire would be cleaner and would indeed constitute a complete income statement rather than a digest. But even acknowledging these limitations on the data in the newspapers, it is difficult to simply drop the *Journal* or the *Times* into the wastebasket day after day without mentally ticking off those hundreds of dollars ($300 . . . $600 . . . $900 . . .). The topical value of these data is obvious, as is the bargain price. How can we realize this apparent value in terms of better stock market decisions?

Power of the Database

Earnings digests are just point observations, and they don't mean much in isolation. The real value of gathering these data follows from the power of dBASE III to piece them together with other data. One must have a record of the preceding and intervening quarters, as well as the current quarter and the year-ago quarter, to get a clear picture of the company. But in a private database, we will have accumulated within one year eight quarterly reports per company. We're picking them up from the newspaper at the rate of two quarters per entry. We can quickly collect and load historical data from many supplementary print sources as well.

When you associate these quarterly income data with balance sheet data (perhaps entered from the Standard & Poor's *Stock Guide,* from the company's own 10Q or 10K reports, or from Value Line and Disclosure, Inc.) and with current closing prices, you'll have enough data to run extensive fundamental analyses using your private database. You will be able to judge the significance (good news, bad news, no news) of earnings reports the day they are published and decide for yourself whether they have been properly or completely discounted into the market.

The Actual Work

To rapidly capture "Digest of Earnings Reports" data, numbers are entered into a screen configured to look just like a blank version of the report which is published, in this case in the newspaper (Figure 18.1). When a blank screen is called up by the operator to begin the entry process, the stub headings ("Revenues," "Sales," "Income," "Extra Credit," "Net Income," "Shares," and "Earnings per Share") should be displayed automatically. The description of the period (the quarter ending January 31 in the example) and the year headings (1987 versus 1986) can also be made to appear automatically. This gives the operator the basic skeleton of a report. Once the company's name has been entered, a record is established in the quarter's database for that company.

If you are going to program this system, note that the numeric key pad must never be expropriated, in spreadsheet fashion, for cursor control. The operator needs the numeric key pad for numbers, and manual cursor control will waste time in this application. Commas and decimals should be displayed automatically. This saves about 10 keystrokes per report.

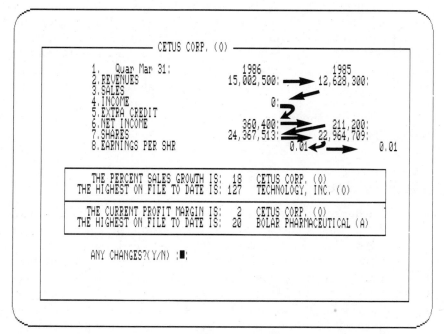

Figure 18.1. This is the quickest way to load earnings digests directly from the newspaper. The entry screen looks exactly like the newspaper report, but the numbers are left blank. You enter them from the keyboard.

A basic Z pattern of cursor positioning is programmed in so that you need only the number pad and the entry key. Cursor positioning logic skips past blank fields to save time and keystrokes. One earnings digest takes 10 seconds to enter. It is worth, in on-line dollars unspent, about $2.

The value of the program to my firm is about $600 per operating hour. This is no trivial saving for an individual or a smaller investment business. Moreover, you get the data into your system immediately. You need not wait for the data to be cleaned up and made available on-line. Keying in the data is quick and dirty. I find that quick data are worth more to us than delayed data, however pure.

Essential Shortcuts

The system can be made to deduce where to put the cursor after each numerical entry. The basic image for the cursor's flight is a repetitive Z pattern. It would be practical to let this Z play from the top of the tabulation to the bottom, simply entering zero by means of a carriage return where no data are supplied by the newspaper. But it speeds up entry to create shortcuts for the cursor.

For example, if no entries are made on the income line, we know in advance there will be no extra-credit entries to modify them. From a zero current income entry, the cursor is thus free to skip all the way down to the current net income line. Having noticed this, we can incorporate it into the program's logic: If current income = 0, i.e., a carriage return, then jump down to current net income. Full fields opposite earnings per share can trigger a cursor jump without a carriage return keystroke. Logical jumps speed up entry considerably. For the report shown in the figure, the operator keyed in six numbers and hit the carriage return six times. Ten seconds and *fini*. A more complex earnings digest report takes more time.

$600 per Hour

There is an impressive dollar value attached to keystroke efficiency. With the help of automatic cursor-positioning logic, an experienced operator can load a fairly complete earnings digest in 10 to 12 seconds. At this rate, the operator is entering five reports per minute, or the equivalent of about $600 worth of on-line data per hour. We are not in fact capturing $600 worth of data, since these are digests and not complete reports. But if you use the information for preliminary sorts and cuts and supplement it with information keyed in from other print sources, you will indeed be able to save the retrieval cost for the vast majority of the complete reports.

Finishing Up—and Using the Results

After each skeleton report has been filled in, the program can roll up another blank screen, ready for the next entry. The completed report is stored. The beauty of the database manager is that it can logically link the company's newly entered quarterly report with its cumulative income statement, balance sheets, price history, calculated results, and other records scattered about in the other seven databases.

The other databases are loaded from print sources using rapid-fire entry techniques very similar to those which have been detailed here for capturing quarterly reports. The techniques are common to any sort of tabular data, with one notable difference. Newspaper earnings digests require just two data columns, and other major sources (the S&P *Stock Guide* and Value Line, for example) have many columns. For these larger tables, you will find it helpful to incorporate the automatic panning and scrolling of capture screens. Finally, bear in mind that these data are for your own internal use.

Whether you approach extensive fundamental analysis using dBASE III or via the (certainly easier) dedicated database programs, it will prove worthwhile. Extensive fundamental analysis—ranking, sorting, sifting, and scanning through truly large volumes of diverse data—is at this point exclusively a pursuit of computerized investors. It is perhaps our main advantage, the capability which distinguishes our machines, in actual combat, from advanced electronic calculators.

Source and Price

dBASE III PLUS
Ashton-Tate
10150 West Jefferson Blvd.
Culver City, CA 90230
(213) 204-5570

List price: $695 (typical discount price is $370).

Requires: 256K RAM, two drives. Runs on PC, XT, AT, 3270 PC, and compatibles.

Database: Off-line sources. Lotus 1-2-3 will transfer files to dBASE III, and this feature can be useful in transferring, into a dBASE III database, price and volume data accumulated in the spreadsheet from FM radio or TV cable broadcasts.

19

Compustock:
A Stock Tester
for Income-Oriented
Investors

How to Weigh a Stock's Price
Against Its Intrinsic Value

Here is a good program for steady, income-oriented investors who like to remain aloof from the market's daily turmoil and examine the long-term value of a few carefully selected stocks. Compustock is a basket of useful fundamental analysis programs. It doesn't do much that you couldn't do with a programmable electronic calculator, if you knew exactly what you hoped to accomplish before sitting down to calculate. The value of the computer in this application is its ability to structure the problem and to teach. If you are not a seasoned fundamental analyst, this program will virtually take you by the hand and show you how to test the current price of a stock against its inherent value. If you already use fundamental analysis, Compustock will automate many routine aspects of your work.

It costs $59, including the most comprehensive documentation I have seen with any low-cost program. There is an electronic tutorial as well. The program uses a larger number of data, and its creators, A.S. Gibson & Sons, provide monthly diskettes at $30 each, preloaded with 100 to

150 stocks. It is this follow-on service that justifies the low front-end cost of the Compustock program, since a full year's subscription will bring the total cost of the service and program to about $350. However, the program will operate on manually entered data and provides tablets of blank data collection forms to help you gather data from print sources. By referring to Value Line and/or the S&P *Stock Guide*, you should be able to find the data you need.

Gibson & Sons offers by monthly subscription a diskette of data on 100 to 150 stocks at about the same price you would pay Savant, Value Line, or S&P for a diskette to screen over 1000 stocks. There is nothing inequitable about this. Recall the distinction between intensive and extensive fundamental analysis. In extensive fundamental analysis, the computer operates on a few items of data on each of a great many companies. In intensive fundamental analysis, the computer scrutinizes a large number of data on just a few companies. Compustock puts companies under a microscope. For each of a few companies, it operates on income and balance sheet data accumulated over a period of six years.

This approach works best for the stocks of·big industrials and utilities that are virtually woven into the American economy. The numbers emerging from such companies (there are precious few of them in my opinion) seem to have a certain rolling inertia, so that the trends established in the past usually do indeed run true through the present and into the future. Such companies are regarded as "mature industrials" in that their periods of dramatic growth have passed. The program is specialized for stocks of this type. I would not use it to evaluate growth stocks, but it can be helpful in identifying turnaround situations.

What the Program Does

Compustock provides the tools you need to ask and answer five basic types of questions about a given stock.

1. Is it priced correctly for its rate of earnings growth?
2. Is the rate of return sufficient to justify the risk?
3. Are there any tragic flaws evident from balance sheets and income statements?
4. Sometimes important recent data are submerged in analyses of long-term averages. Do recent earnings and the short-term financial picture indicate any special new vulnerability or strength?
5. How attractive is the PSR? What about the price/research ratio?

As you work through the program, you will find answers to all these questions in turn. If the stock were one of your own and you were checking to make sure you should continue to hold it, it would be helpful to work through all five steps. If you were stock hunting, you could use just the first two steps as a screen to determine whether a given stock was properly priced and offered an adequate return. For the few good stocks that passed the test, you could then proceed to run the entire program.

This is not a program for massive screening, however. The monthly diskette service from Gibson & Sons identifies 10 stocks which are all prescreened and worthy of a closer look. Alternatively, for rapid-fire screening, you could use Value/Screen, the Savant Fundamental Investor, or the Standard & Poor's Stocktrak to narrow the field to 10 or 15 stocks and then use Compustock to arrive at a final selection.

Earnings Growth and Pricing

The faster a company grows, the greater the price of its stock. We can look at the past earnings of a company to determine how rapidly it has been growing. From statistical history, we know approximately how much a given growth rate is likely to be valued by the market. By putting these facts together, it is possible to estimate the "fair" price of a stock from its earnings growth rate. Compustock will do this for you automatically. It calculates the growth rate of a stock, consults a table of price/earnings multipliers historically associated with ranges of growth rates, and computes a range of fair values for the stock.

Figure 19.1a shows the results of these calculations at the bottom of the screen. The term *investment value* refers to the maximum acceptable price level, and the *discounted investment value* is the minimum typical price level. The range of prices in between is the area where stocks with this earnings growth rate have typically been valued by the market in the past. A stock like this one, with a current price below the discounted investment value, is a potential buy. A stock priced near its investment value is one you should consider selling. A stock priced above its computed investment value should, according to this program, be sold straightaway.

If You Don't Like It, Change It

One is immediately skeptical of this approach, since no simple absolute relation exists between growth rates and price/earnings multipliers. My own feeling is that one approximation is about as good as another and that the particular assumptions written into the program seem appropriate to the types of stock under consideration. Moreover, a $59 computer program of this size and scope is beyond criticism.

What the program promises is a good guess at what the maximum price of the stock should be. The maximum acceptable price is the so-called investment value. If the actual price is much lower than this good guess, look deeper into the stock. If the actual price is higher than the good guess, the stock is either overpriced or a growth stock and therefore is not really susceptible to further analysis by the Compustock program. In short, this system provides an adequate first screen. The program provides two other measures of price appropriateness, so we are not being asked to accept its built-in assumptions about the growth-price relation as the last word on this subject.

The table from Gibson & Sons is based on a broad, long-term statistical history of the stock market. If you don't like the generalization which results, you can go into the program and make changes. The calculations use a weighted version of the six-year average earnings growth rate shown in Figure 19.1a. The BASIC program is not compiled. You can locate the growth rate versus earnings multiplier table around line 3500. I suggest you examine the assumptions and, if you can make better approximations of the slope and intercept of the multiplier "curve," write them in. I would be inclined to insert values peculiar to the historical valuation of growth by the market for each individual stock group. The author of the program, a utilities industry analyst, has already included such separate treatment for utilities in the program.

The Railway into the Future

Figure 19.1b tells quite a bit about the method used by Compustock to project future earnings and dividends. To estimate the return for this stock, we must first determine where the stock price will be three and five years from now. We must also estimate future earnings and dividends. Finally, we need some measure of the quality of our own guesswork so that we will know if the estimates are solid enough to bet on.

The one basic line projected into the future is the earnings line. All future prices and dividends are calculated from this projection of earnings performance. The earnings performances for the past six years represent the raw input data. Regression analysis is used to project each new year's earnings from that of the preceding years. The projection process begins with the earliest available data points. The early predictions (that for 1980, for example, which is a projection from 1978 and 1979 data) can be compared with the actual earnings produced by the company in the subject year. For 1980, regression analysis projected

```
DIVIDEND HISTORY FOR BRISTOL-MYERS,  $/SHARE: 10-18-83

          ACTUAL        PREDICTED        PAYOUT         CORRELATION   GROWTH
  YEAR    DIVIDENDS      DIVIDENDS        RATIO,%        COEFFICIENT   RATE,%
  77      0.53          0.53            39.0
  78      0.60          0.60            39.0
  79      0.70          0.69            40.0
  80      0.78          0.78            38.2
  81      0.89          0.89            38.9
  82      1.02          1.02            39.4
                                                        .9993643      13.9
  83                    1.16            39.3
  84                    1.32            39.3
  85                    1.51            39.3
  86                    1.72            39.3
  87                    1.95            39.3

                        INVESTMENT       DISCOUNTED     CURRENT
                        VALUE            INV. VALUE     PRICE
                        57.0             37.6           41.5

                                             Press any key to continue.
```

(a)

```
          ACTUAL    REGRESSION  PREDICTED  GROWTH RATE   CORRELATION   DISCOUNT
  YEAR    EARNGS.   EARNINGS    EARNINGS   % PER YEAR    COEFFICIENT   PERCENT/YR
  77      1.36      1.36        1.36
  78      1.54      1.55        1.54
  79      1.75      1.76        1.75
  80      2.04      2.01        2.04
  81      2.29      2.29        2.29
  82      2.59      2.61        2.59
                                           13.93         .9993881      0
  83                2.97        2.95
  84                3.38        3.36
  85                3.85        3.83
  86                4.39        4.36
  87                5.00        4.97

                    CALCULATED PRICE/EARNINGS RATIO

                    78        79        80        81        82      5 YR.AVG.

  AVG.PRICE.FOR YR.  17.0     16.5      19.0      25.0      28.0
  P/E RATIOS         11.0      9.4       9.3      10.9      10.8      10.3

  DATA FOR BRISTOL-MYERS:10-18-83          Press any key to continue
```

(b)

earnings of $2.02. The actual earnings in 1980 came in at $2.04. The program notices the error and takes it into account as a correction factor for subsequent calculation.

By examining six years of past data, the projection process can be gradually refined by means of correction and recorrection. The column of predicted earnings shows the effects of correction. Thus refined, regression analysis is used to project earnings five years into the future. The correlation coefficient shows how faithfully the predictive process has mirrored reality in the past. Correlation coefficient values close to 1 suggest that earnings have stayed pretty much as predicted from year to year.

The screen in 19.1a shows what happens when the same techniques are used to project dividends. Our best hope calls for a consistent payout ratio. (The payout ratio shows how much of the year's earnings are actually paid out as dividends to shareholders.) Again, the correlation coefficient suggests a good performance in predicting past dividends, and a glance at the columns comparing actual and predicted dividends shows that the prediction usually comes within a penny of the actual dividend. Note that there is no particular magic in the method. What we have here is a very consistent stock.

The Prediction Box

To this point, we know that the stock is acceptably priced for its earnings growth rate, and we have projected an earnings line into the future. From this line we can deduce future prices, dividends, and total returns, but we must plug in some assumptions to derive these results. The program provides a set of prompts to collect these assumptions.

It asks, for example, if you have an optimistic, pessimistic, or neutral view of the future of the economy. (I did not get into the program to determine the numerical consequences of these qualitative terms, but

---

Figure 19.1. Screen a projects dividends; screen b projects earning's. Look first at the bottom line in screen a. The investment value is the price at which this stock, Bristol-Myers, should be sold. The discounted investment value is a price level at which the stock is an attractive buy. The current price suggests that at this early point in the scrutiny of the stock, it looks good enough to warrant a closer look. Two more evaluations of the price of the stock lie ahead. The price will be evaluated in light of the risk the buyer must accept in making the purchase (or in continuing to hold). It will also be evaluated in terms of the current price/sales ratio.

The tabulation on the upper half of screen b shows the work of the earnings projector. It operates first on historical data, and you can see how well it succeeds by noticing the differences between regression earnings and actual earnings. The projector corrects itself as it moves toward the present, and the predicted earnings column shows the corrected results.

you should if you will use the program, and you might wish to change them.)

It asks for the current rate of inflation so that this can be taken into account in measuring the ultimate return on the investment.

The program redisplays the historical five-year average P/E ratio as computed in Figure 19.1*b* and asks whether you think it will remain constant or change. You can be pretty sure it will change. The documentation includes historical charts of P/E ratios versus time for many of the stocks preloaded onto the program disk. You can consult these charts as one approach to a realistic guess about the future course of the P/E. The value you enter will be used to calculate, from the already completed earnings projections, the price of the stock three and five years from now. The results of this projection are shown in Figure 19.2

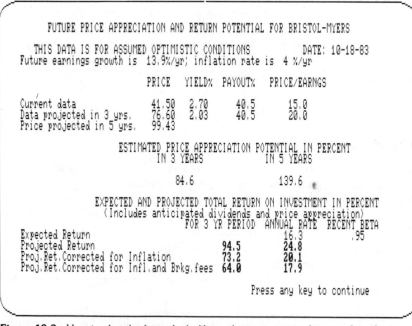

```
      FUTURE PRICE APPRECIATION AND RETURN POTENTIAL FOR BRISTOL-MYERS

    THIS DATA IS FOR ASSUMED OPTIMISTIC CONDITIONS          DATE: 10-18-83
   Future earnings growth is  13.9%/yr; inflation rate is  4 %/yr

                          PRICE   YIELD%  PAYOUT%   PRICE/EARNGS

   Current data           41.50   2.70    40.5      15.0
   Data projected in 3 yrs.  76.60  2.03    40.5      20.0
   Price projected in 5 yrs.  99.43

                     ESTIMATED PRICE APPRECIATION POTENTIAL IN PERCENT
                          IN 3 YEARS              IN 5 YEARS

                            84.6                    139.6

                  EXPECTED AND PROJECTED TOTAL RETURN ON INVESTMENT IN PERCENT
                     (Includes anticipated dividends and price appreciation)
                               FOR 3 YR PERIOD  ANNUAL RATE  RECENT BETA
   Expected Return                                  16.3         .95
   Projected Return                      94.5       24.8
   Proj.Ret.Corrected for Inflation      73.2       20.1
   Proj.Ret.Corrected for Infl.and Brkg.fees  64.0  17.9

                                        Press any key to continue
```

Figure 19.2. Here is what the future looks like to the program—and to you. In order to develop these numbers, you must key a set of assumptions into the program to let it know your expectations for inflation and other critical factors. You would display this screen again and again as you tried out different sets of assumptions ranging from the most optimistic circumstance through the worst case. Future prices are based on earnings projections and on your estimates of future price/earnings ratios.

The expected return is that return which would be demanded by a hypothetical prudent investor, given the risk the investor must accept with the purchase of the stock. In this tabulation, the prudent investor would look for a return on investment of 16.3 percent. Under the given assumptions, Bristol-Myers is supposed to return 17.9 percent at the bottom line. This makes it look like a buy for the prudent investor, since the return exceeds the investor's minimum expectation.

on the upper half of the screen. Note that the basic assumptions are detailed at the top of the report.

Beneath the price projection is a panel which reports on expected versus projected return on the investment. This is, if you will, the program's bottom line. To make sense of it, however, it is necessary to examine the concept of an expected return. This is discussed below. At this point, simply note that every one of the *projected* values reported here can be dialed up and down with the assumptions you load into the program. You can raise and lower your expectations for the future P/E ratio, payout ratio, and rate of inflation.

This part of the program is like a black box, with dials you can set to correspond with your expectations of the future. Different investors would elicit different results, and each investor could produce several different scenarios for the stock. By trying various assumptions, you can set future goals and cutoff values for the stock, and these can be helpful as you monitor its future performance. We haven't bought the stock yet, however.

The Buying Decision and Expected Return

Whether you select a stock to buy or to discard depends heavily on a comparison of the projected return on the investment versus the expected return.

Just what is this expected return? Who expects it and why?

The *expected return* is what a prudent investor should be willing to accept. We know that there is such a thing as a risk-free rate of return, which is the return on Treasury notes. The stock under consideration is more risky than a Treasury note, since its value fluctuates in the stock market. To accept this risk, the prudent investor will expect to be paid a higher return than that offered by the risk-free Treasury note. How much higher the stock's return must be to get the prudent investor to buy it will depend on the degree of risk involved.

It turns out that it is possible to construct a risk/return line like that shown in Figure 19.3. The horizontal axis is scaled in fractions of a number called *the beta*, which is a measure of risk. A beta of 1.0 corresponds to the risk associated with a portfolio consisting of every single stock in the S&P 400. A beta of zero corresponds to the risk associated with Treasury notes, which is no risk at all. The return on Treasury notes (say, 10 percent) marks the low end of the risk/return line. The return on "the market," as indicated by the return on the S&P 400 portfolio, can be plotted as 15 percent at the point where beta = 1. This gives us a second known point to use in positioning the risk/return line.

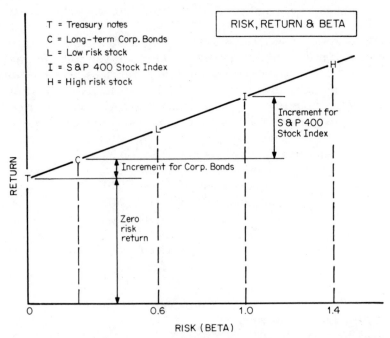

Figure 19.3. This chart shows how to determine how much you should demand to be compensated for your risk. Treasury notes define the rate of return available at zero risk. Let's say this is 10 percent. The return on the S&P 400, set at about 15 percent in this chart, shows the return associated with a beta of 1.0. Connecting the two return levels with a line produces a risk/return line. For real numbers to plug in, check the current business press.

From the line we can read out the return which would be appropriate, in the eyes of a prudent investor, to any beta level. Thus, if you know the beta of a stock, the return on the market, and the return on T-bills, the program can calculate what the stock's ROI should be. This will tell you whether the stock is expensive or cheap. Either way, find out why.

The return on the S&P 400 is published at intervals by the business press and by brokerage research services.

Given the risk-free rate of return, the market rate of return, and the beta associated with the particular stock under consideration, the computer can read out a value of expected return. This is the minimum acceptable rate of return a prudent investor should be paid to take on the risk associated with the given stock.

Figure 19.2 shows the Compustock report on potential return. The expected return on Bristol-Myers is 16.3 percent given the current risk (beta value) associated with the stock. If your projected rate of return for the stock, corrected for inflation and brokerage fees, is less than 16.3 percent, it will not be a good buy. It turns out that for the given assumptions, a projected return on Bristol-Myers is 17.9 percent. This is better than the prudent investor would demand, and so the stock is a potential buy.

In order to derive the expected return value, you have to enter two numbers, the current beta for the stock and the rate of return for 20-year corporate bonds. The beta is published in brokerage research reports and by various investment advisories, including Value Line. It is also recalculated daily and reported by a number of computer programs, including Savant's Fundamental Investor. The rate of return on 20-year corporate bonds is published in *The Wall Street Journal.*

As a practical matter, you can determine the fair return on any stock from Compustock by digging out these two numbers and entering them into the program when you are prompted for them. The program documentation tells you exactly where to look in the *Journal* and how to extract the bond return number you need. Betas are easy to find and clearly designated.

As a theoretical matter, you may note that 20-year corporates are not risk-free. They do, however, give us a reward value associated with a certain level of risk, and this serves to pin down one point on the risk/reward line. The other point we need to draw the line, the return on the S&P 400 at beta = 1, is not included among the data points requested by the program. In fact, the risk/return equation has been rewritten with this market return value treated as a constant. It isn't a constant; it is sort of constant. You'll need to venture into the program to change it. I am not a purist in these matters, but I would want to update the S&P 400's return from time to time. However, at $59 you don't pick nits in a program with so much basic value. Either live with the nits or pick up a wrench and fix them.

As a final comment on how much return to demand on your investment, note in Figure 19.2 the striking effects of inflation and brokerage fees. This stock is actually less risky than the market, and the projected return is almost 25 percent annually. Yet the "take home" after inflation and commissions is just 1.6 percentage points above the prudent investor's expectation.

Ratio Tests

Have we bought the stock yet? No.

We have determined that the price is commensurate with the growth rate and that the return on the investment is in line with that acceptable to a prudent investor. We have not tested the inherent strengths of the company's balance sheet and income statements. To do so, we proceed into Part II of the program (Figure 19.4).

```
RATIOS AND OTHER FINANCIAL DATA FOR BRISTOL-MYERS: 10-14-83

        COMMON     BOOK     ASSET    NET PROFIT  RETURN    FINAN.   RETURN ON
YR.     SHARES     VALUE   TURNOVER   MARGIN    ON ASSETS LEVERAGE COM.EQUITY
       Millions  Per Share  Ratio     Percent    Percent    Ratio    Percent
77     130,200     7.09     1.47       7.96      11.68      1.65     19.26
78     130,400     8.05     1.44       8.28      11.97      1.61     19.34
79     130,800     9.11     1.43       8.41      12.04      1.61     19.42
80     131,400    10.43     1.43       8.57      12.25      1.61     19.74
81     132,400    11.81     1.41       8.75      12.29      1.59     19.56
82     134,000    12.79     1.31       9.69      12.65      1.61     20.34

       EFFEC.TAX  INVENTORY  CURRENT    CAPITAL    R.& D./  OP. EXPEN./    DEPR/
YR      RATE,%    TURNOVER    RATIO    EXPENDIT.  REVENUES   OP. REV.    OP. REV.
                   Times               Millions   Percent    Percent     Percent
77       46.0      0.00       2.33      72.900     3.693      85.3         1.4
78       46.0      0.00       2.37      82.100     3.697      84.7         1.5
79       45.3      0.00       2.45      95.500     3.742      84.6         1.5
80       45.0      5.79       2.38     131.400     4.072      84.4         1.5
81       44.6      6.19       2.38     159.300     4.118      84.2         1.5
82       42.5      6.44       2.33     170.000     4.472      83.2         1.7

                                                   Press any key to continue.
```

(a)

```
FINANCIAL DATA IN MILLIONS OF DOLLARS FOR BRISTOL-MYERS: 10-14-83

       OPERAT'G.  OPERAT'G.  OPERAT'G.    OTHER     OTHER      GROSS     INCOME
YR.    REVENUES    EXPENSE    PROFIT     INCOME    EXPENSE    INCOME     TAXES
77    2,233.700  1,904.700    329.000    0.000     0.000     329.000    151.300
78    2,450.400  2,074.700    375.700    0.000     0.000     375.700    172.700
79    2,752.800  2,329.500    423.300    0.000     0.000     423.300    191.800
80    3,158.300  2,666.700    491.600    0.000     0.000     491.600    221.000
81    3,496.700  2,944.800    551.900    0.000     0.000     551.900    246.100
82    3,599.900  2,993.800    606.100    0.000     0.000     606.100    257.400

          NET     DEPREC.&    CURRENT    CURRENT    TOTAL    LONG-TERM SHR.HLDRS.
YR      INCOME    AMORTIZ.    ASSETS     LIABIL.    ASSETS      DEBT     EQUITY
77     177.700    32.300  1,102.000    472.500  1,521.800    93.700    923.700
78     203.000    36.300  1,226.900    517.100  1,696.300    90.200  1,050.700
79     231.500    40.200  1,380.900    563.700  1,922.000   120.100  1,193.100
80     270.600    47.300  1,587.700    667.200  2,209.400   111.900  1,371.900
81     305.800    51.700  1,769.800    744.000  2,488.500   102.200  1,564.500
82     348.700    60.100  1,941.700    833.000  2,756.200   113.500  1,714.400

                                                   Press any key to continue.
```

(b)

Figure 19.4. The program is thorough. Here is a six-year accumulation of balance sheet (a) and income statement (b) data and a battery of ratio tests to help evaluate financial condition. On color monitors, values outside an acceptable range for each ratio test are flagged in red and exceptionally good numbers are displayed in green. On a monochrome monitor, dubious values blink and laudable numbers are intensified.

These tabulations appear on two successive screens. You can buy the data on diskettes from Gibson & Sons or enter the data yourself. The first screen is a six-year summary of financial statements and balance sheet items. The second screen is a compilation of accounting ratios calculated from those statements. The second screen is essentially a judge's scoring card. For each of the values tabulated here, there is an acceptable range. If the calculated value falls outside that acceptable range, it is flagged in red on color monitors. Similarly, if a calculated value exceeds the commonplace, it may be flagged in green. In monochrome versions of the program, dubious values blink and laudable numbers appear intensified on the screen.

At a glance you can identify problems and spot exceptionally promising trends.

Ratio test screens are basic to fundamental analysis programs, and many short programs offer little else. All such programs fairly bristle with judgmental yardsticks, and Compustock is no exception. Gibson & Sons, Inc., does supply with the program documentation a complete table of threshold values and ranges for the flags. If you program, you can reset them to suit your own tastes or attune them to particular stock groups.

I think the values assigned by the writer of the program are widely accepted. If they err, it is on the conservative side. This is the responsible way to write a program of this sort. If you don't agree with the way the flags are set, simply disregard them in favor of your own set of limiting values. If you do like the preset limits on the accounting ratios, you'll enjoy the one-quick-look evaluation of a huge collection of data. This is the sort of work analysts used to pore over at length with their notoriously sharp pencils, and it is an essential step in fundamental stock evaluation. You will find that you can breeze through it with Compustock, since the program directs your attention instantly to problem areas and special strengths.

The basic picture can be graphed on the screen using pie charts for financial statement data on three selected years and line projections for trends in the underlying data as well as trends in the accounting ratios.

Short-Term Trends in High Relief

It is a standing criticism of long-term fundamental analysis that it tends to obscure the most recent trends by lumping them into averages, with equal weight, with data on the events of six years ago. The Compustock program is careful about this problem. Weighted averages are used in calculations of earnings growth, for example, to favor the most recently received data. A final module in the program deals exclusively with recent earnings and short-term financial data. The report on this module is reproduced in Figure 19.5.

The earnings for the past three years can be charted in stacked fashion, much as they are tabulated here. This way you can visually compare results from each quarter with results from corresponding quarters in the past. Often this reveals cyclic strengths and weaknesses. For example, if third-quarter results are typically down, one can note this recurring pattern. One might consider it a positive sign if the most recent third quarter took less than the usual dip. The same recent data, viewed in a linear graph, would show only that the third quarter was a bad one, relative to the second and the fourth.

Short-term financial data are evaluated against preset limits. Danger-ous numbers appear in red on a color monitor; on a monochrome mon-itor they blink. Green or highlighting is used to indicate exceptional

```
        QUARTERLY EARNINGS ($ PER SHARE) FOR BRISTOL-MYERS: 10-14-83

        YEAR        Q U A R T E R S (For Fiscal Yr End'g, DEC. 31)

                     1      2      3      4

        81         0.51   0.53   0.65   0.60
        82         0.59   0.61   0.75   0.64
        83         0.68   0.70   0.00   0.00

                  SHORT-TERM FINANCIAL DATA

        NET QUICK    SHORT-TERM  TOT. EQUIV.  EQ.DEBT  INTEREST  AFDC/
         ASSETS         DEBT        DEBT        RATIO   COVERAGE  NET INC.
YEAR     Millions     Millions    Millions    Percent    Times   Percent

 81      460.600      156.600     505.200      24.4     10.35      NA
 82      549.600      167.800     527.700      23.5      9.87      NA

Recent Value for Price/Book Ratio = 3.50
Common Equity as % of Capitalization, for Year  82 = 93.77
Recent Value for Price/Sales Ratio=   1.67
Recent Value for Price/Research Ratio=  37.2

                          Press any key to continue.
```

Figure 19.5. Sometimes excellent recent results are obscured in long-term evaluations. The recent numbers may be averaged in with (and thus swallowed by) the results of business transacted six years ago. The Compustock program provides an analytical module that gives due consideration to recent earnings and short-term data. As a final test of current price, the module computes price/sales ratios and price/research ratios.

strength. The key short-term ratio tests are net quick assets and equity to debt.

Having passed all these tests, can we buy the stock? Sure.

The program's writer has, perhaps as an afterthought, thrown in two additional criteria you may wish to consider. These are the price/sales ratio (PSR) and the price/research ratio. The PSR is particularly valuable in examining growth stocks, where the P/E is not particularly meaningful. It is not clear that for mature industrial stocks, for which this program is specifically intended, the PSR can help much. The price/research ratio is, in my opinion, meaningful chiefly for pharmaceutical stocks. In other technology-based stocks, the research value reflected in the ratio has a tendency to wander out the back door. It subsequently reappears as an asset of some other company, a start-up. The ratio may thus help account for the remarkable efficiency of brand-new technology companies, but it does not reliably point to the future promise of a company spending these dollars on research.

Conclusions

The Compustock program accomplishes most of what a conservative investor might expect of a computer system. It evaluates and selects stocks for optimum return on investment, makes sensible judgments about buy and sell prices, and provides a tool to determine whether stocks currently in the portfolio deserve to be held.

It also spots trouble brewing in the balance sheet and income statements. If you are a conservative, income-oriented investor, you can put Compustock together with a basic portfolio management program and have everything you need. If you already subscribe to Value Line or another print service, you can key in data from those sources. The database from Gibson & Sons would be more convenient and probably more economical, but it is not complete at this writing. The capital asset pricing model, which is the formal designation for the risk/return methodology discussed above, is widely recognized and used. The program will work best for companies with a nice, orderly stream of earnings, and it will alert you (via the correlation coefficients) to companies for which the predictive power of the program is not good. Eliminating unpredictable stocks is part of the culling process. Use the program for mature industrial, utility, and transportation stocks.

For somewhat more growth-oriented investors, the program can be useful in identifying turnaround situations in basically very solid companies.

If you buy growth stocks, you may find that the program rubs against the grain, but the ratio test section is a good discipline and could keep you out of some companies with really glaring problems.

The program should not be used in evaluating the stocks of insurance companies, banks, and other financial stocks. The earnings projector will function, but the ratio alarms are not designed for such stocks.

For the price, Compustock is a superb value, even if you regard it purely as a cost of education. If you already know your way around fundamental analysis, it can save you a great deal of time. Some written-in assumptions may need a bit of tweaking to suit you, but the method is stepwise, thorough, and complete.

Source and Price

COMPUSTOCK
A.S. Gibson & Sons, Inc.
1412 Vineyard Drive
Bountiful, Utah 84010
(801) 298-4578

List price: $59 for the program and $30 per month for the database service (100 to 150 stocks per month).

Remarks: The database is accumulating as the service proceeds. Ultimately it will include data on 1500 to 2200 stocks. For each stock it includes earnings and dividends histories for the past six years and projections for each of the next five years. It includes income statement and balance sheet data for the past five years and a history of P/E ratios.

PART 5

Portfolio Management and Fully Integrated Software

20
Portfolio Management Programs

Look for the right one, not the best one. There is no best portfolio manager, just as there is no best style of investing. The best portfolio manager for you is one that keeps track of the transactions and holdings peculiar to your own style of investing.

If you are a speculative trader, you need to keep track of options, futures, margin accounts, and minute-to-minute changes in the markets.

If you are an income-oriented investor, you want a detailed accounting of streams of dividends and some means of projecting income expectations. Among other things, you may wish to see the averaged results of repeated (dollar cost averaged) investments in one stock. You may also require some means of measuring the performance of all your stocks relative to that of your debt securities so that you can, as necessary, adjust the apportioning of capital between stocks and bonds. Finally, you may wish to evaluate the allocation of your portfolio among a fixed set of stocks in the interest of minimizing the risk you must take to achieve a given rate of return.

If you are a broker or adviser, you may want search and sort capabilities so that if a particular stock turns sour, you can instantly determine which of your customers hold it in which portfolios. You will certainly require the ability to store and retrieve multiple portfolios—far more of them than the typical individual investor could conceivably need.

One of the top software writers in the investment field has been working for the past two years on a comprehensive portfolio management program. It should handle everything from zero-coupon bonds to pork belly futures.

He does not like to be asked how he's doing with this project. The resulting program will be, I am sure, all things to all people. It will be helpful to market professionals, who may handle all types of securities. Why an individual investor would want to purchase all this excess capability is beyond me. The fact is, if you are fascinated by pork belly futures, you are probably indifferent to zero-coupon bonds, and vice versa. If you buy a universal portfolio manager, you will be paying for much more software than you will ever actually use.

The Excellent Spreadsheet Alternative

If you are handy with a spreadsheet, you can tap in a portfolio management file to suit your own particular needs. It will take a Saturday or two, and there are guidebooks to tell you how to do it. You are also welcome to use or adapt one I wrote under Lotus 1-2-3, which is shown in Figure 20.1. The cell contents are indicated in Figure 20.2.

If you have never used a spreadsheet, a portfolio management system is a very good workbook-type problem on which to learn. I would not buy a spreadsheet just to manage an individual stock portfolio, but if you already own a spreadsheet or need one for other purposes as well, use it. A spreadsheet will do a better job for you than most dedicated commercial portfolio management programs.

The spreadsheet has three advantages over dedicated programs.

1. It is huge. You can "fly" the viewing port around over a vast reporting sheet. Dedicated programs are restricted by single-screen viewing area to one-page reports, each of fixed format. This breaks up the data made available for viewing into several discrete and rather redundant little reports. If you are looking at a summary report of gross profit and loss and you suddenly become curious about the price you paid per share versus the current price of a particular stock, you may have to slog back through a series of menus and request a different report. With a spreadsheet, every fact pertaining to your portfolio is on view all the time. You can shoot over to the exact site of the information you want to see with just two or three keystrokes.

One dedicated program (from Dow Jones) uses the Page Up and Page

Down controls to deliver two or more reports, detailed and summary, without a return to the main menu. Most reports offered by most programs can be scrolled to a bottom line of portfolio totals, but none of the programs' reports can be panned from side to side like a spreadsheet. In researching this chapter, I found that shifting from a spreadsheet-based portfolio manager to a fixed report type of portfolio manager creates a sense of confinement. It is as if one had suddenly tried on a set of side blinders.

2. As your own customized portfolio manager, you can make the spreadsheet program do exactly what you want it to do, no less and no more. Spreadsheet programs can be expanded and changed as your needs change. You are not locked into a fixed style of reports. You can use the spreadsheet's built-in utilities to sort, group, and graph any parameters you choose. Bar graphs are particularly helpful in portfolio evaluation.

3. A spreadsheet can load and store FM radio and TV cable broadcast data. This means you can update your portfolio automatically at a reasonable cost, every few seconds if you wish. It also means you can accumulate on the spreadsheet your own 250- to 500-day database of high, low, close, and volume data for each of your stocks, for their groups, and for any other stocks and groups of interest to you.

Every source of microcomputer data promises to "put you on the exchange floor." In practice, because of the relatively high cost of data via telephone modem, most private investors tend to take their data in sporadic sips and samples. But with FM or TV cable, you can actually get a torrent of data in real time, all the time, and you can afford it. You can even afford to let most of the data go by and store your data points just once a day after the close of the market.

I follow two portfolios of eight stocks each. I monitor these 16 stocks (rather, the computer does) in real time. I also monitor the statistical environment surrounding these stocks—their groups, various indicators—and this entails collecting data on 350 other securities and indexes a day. This costs, via FM, $25 per month. If you brought down via telephone modem the daily closing data on 350 stocks only once per day from one of the better databases, you'd exhaust $25 in three days. You would not have monitored your own stocks closely enough to catch an intraday stop-loss or high limit, and you would have only just barely begun to accumulate data on the statistical environment in which your stocks move.

Days in positions: 10

Portfolio I

Option Ticker	Stock Ticker	Strike Price	Current Close	Entry Close	No. of Shares	Entry Price	Current Price	Percent Change	Dollars Invested	Current Value	Absolute Change
AAQ(VU)	AAPL	$12.50	$0.000	$15.000	2000	$0.250	$0.0625	-75.00%	$500.00	$125.00	($375.00)
GEQ(VI)	GENE	$45.00	$49.500	$47.250	400	$1.625	$0.5000	-69.23%	$650.00	$200.00	($450.00)
								-71.74%	$1,150	$325	($825)

Portfolio II

Option Ticker	Stock Ticker	Strike Price	Current Close	Entry Close	No. of Shares	Entry Price	Current Price	Percent Change	Dollars Invested	Current Value	Absolute Change
IGQ(VF)	INTG	$30.00	$27.500	$30.500	300	$1.750	$3.0000	71.43%	$525	$900	$375
LOQ(VE)	LOTS	$25.00	$18.500	$26.375	300	$1.563	$6.7500	332.00%	$469	$2,025	$1,556
								194.34%	$994	$2,925	$1,931

{GOTO}C38~/FCCEFMOP~

TO PULL IN A PANEL OF FRESH FM DATA FROM THE FILE, "FMOP"
PRESS ALT I

FM data panel as imported via a DIF file:

Both portfolios:
51.60% $2,144 $3,250 $1,106

SYMBOL	AAPL	AAQVU	GENE	GEQVI	IBM	IGGVF	INGR	LGQVE	LOTS	ZRA
TYPE	S	S	S	S	S	S	S	S	S	I
LAST	0	0	49.5	0.5	129.375	3	27.5	6.75	18.5	1339.27
HIGH	0	0	49.75	0.625	130.5	3.125	28	6.75	19.75	1342.85
LOW	0	0	48.75	0.5	129.25	2.75	26.75	6.5	17.75	
VOL	0	0	469	0	11037	2	4000	0	7122	0
CLOSE	0	0	49.5	0.75	129.125	3.75	26.75	5.75	19.75	1335.69
DATE	9/9/1985	9/9/1985	9/9/1985	9/9/1985	9/9/1985	9/9/1985	9/9/1985	9/9/1985	9/9/1985	9/9/1985
TIME	15:43	15:43	15:43	15:43	15:43	15:43	15:43	15:43	15:43	15:43

/MC52..M3
/CC40..M4
/CD45^C52

TO ENTER
CLOSE INT
DATABASE.
ALT A

250-Day Database:

DATE:	AAPL	AAQVU	GENE	GEQVI	IBM	IGGVF	INGR	LGQVE	LOTS	Z
9/9/1985	0	0	49.5	0.5	129.375	3	27.5	6.75	18.5	1339.27
9/6/1985	15	0	49.5	0.75	129.125	3.75	26.75	5.75	19.75	1336.52
8/05/1985	14.88	0.125	48.5	0.75	126.625	4.5	26	4.625	20.5	1334.6
8/30/1985	14.875	0.1875	49.5	0.375	126.625	4	26.5	5.25	20.5	1334.6
8/28/1985	14.88	0.1875	49.75	0.75	126.75	3.75	26.5	4.75	20.75	0
8/23/1985	14.75	0.25		0.75	126.75	3.375	27.5	2.25	23.875	0

Figure 20.1. This Lotus 1-2-3 portfolio monitor imports FM radio data from the Telemet Service. The FM data file is outlined. It is first downloaded as a .DIF file from the Telemet program, Personal Gains. Using Lotus menu commands, the .DIF file is translated into a .WKS file called FMOP.

The Lotus portfolio file is then opened and displayed. When the command ALT I is keyed in, the outlined block is automatically filled with the most current quotes from the radio. All portfolio values—percentage changes, net performance—are instantly recalculated. Once a day, to permanently store the entire stack of historical data (dotted outline) down by one row and salts in the FM data as of today's close on top of the stack.

Days in positions:@TODAY-@

Portfolio I

		A	B	C	D	E	F	G	H	I	J	K	L	M

Option Ticker	Stock Ticker	Strike Price	Current Close	Entry Close	No. of Shares	Entry Price	Current Price	Percent Change	Dollars Invested	Current Value	Absolute Change
AAQ(VU)	AAPL	12.5	+E43	15	2000	0.25	0.0625	(+K18-J1	+J18*I18	+I18*K18	+N18-M18
GEQ(VI)	GENE	45	+G43	47.25	400	1.625	0.5	(+K20-J2	+J20*I20	+I20*K20	+N20-M20
								+O22/M22	@SUM(M18	@SUM(N18	@SUM(O18

Portfolio II

Option Ticker	Stock Ticker	Strike Price	Current Close	Entry Close	No. of Shares	Entry Price	Current Price	Percent Change	Dollars Invested	Current Value	Absolute Change
IGQ(VF)	INTG	30	+K43	30.5	300	1.75	3	(+K30-J3	+J30*I30	+I30*K30	+N30-M30
LOQ(VE)	LOTS	25	+M43	26.375	300	1.5625	6.75	(+K32-J3	+J32*I32	+I32*K32	+N32-M32
											@SUM(O30

`(GOTO)C38~/FCCEFMOP~`

TO PULL IN A PANEL OF FRESH FM DATA FROM THE FILE, "FMOP"
PRESS ALT I

FM data panel as imported via a DIF file:

```
                                                              +O34/M34 @SUM(M30 @SUM(N30
                                                              Both portfolios:
                                                              (O22+O34 +M22*M34 +N22+N34 +O22+O34
```

	SYMBOL	AAPL	AAQVU	GENE	GEQVI	IBM	IGGVF	INGR	LOQVE	LOTS	ZRA
	TYPE	S	O	S	S	S	S	S	O	O	I
/MC52..M3	LAST	0	0	49.5	0.5	129.375	3	27.5	6.75	18.5	1339.27
/CC40..M4	HIGH	0	0	49.75	0.625	130.5	3.125	28	6.75	19.75	1342.85
/CD45~C52	LOW	0	0	48.75	0.5	129.25	2.75	26.75	6.5	17.75	
	VOL	0	0	469		11037	2	4000	0	7122	0
TO ENTER	CLOSE	0	0	49.5	0.75	129.125	3.75	26.75	5.75	19.75	1335.69
CLOSE INT	DATE	9/9/1985	9/9/1985	9/9/1985	9/9/1985	9/9/1985	9/9/1985	9/9/1985	9/9/1985	9/9/1985	9/9/1985
DATABASE.	TIME	15:43	15:43	15:43	15:43	15:43	15:43	15:43	15:43	15:43	15:43
ALT A											

250-Day Database:

DATE:	AAPL	AAQVU	GENE	GEQVI	IBM	IGGVF	INGR	LOQVE	LOTS	Z
9/9/1985	0	0	49.5	0.5	129.375	3	27.5	6.75	18.5	1339.27
9/6/1985	15	0	49.5	0.75	129.125	3.75	26.75	5.75	19.75	1336.52
9/05/1985	14.88	0.125	48.5	0.75	126.625	4.5	26	4.625	20.5	1334.52
8/30/1985	14.875	0.1875	49.5	0.375	126.625	4	26.5	5.25	20.5	1334.6
8/28/1985	14.88	0.1875	49.75	0.75	126.75	3.75	26.5	4.75	20.75	0
8/23/1985	14.75	0.25	49.5	0.75	126.75	3.375	27.5	2.25	23.875	0

Figure 20.2. This is the template for the portfolio monitor. You will have to replace the ticker symbols shown with those appropriate to your own portfolio. The FM data panel is a sample. The data are imported automatically to this spreadsheet block by the macro command Alt I. Be sure to transcribe the two macros in the left-hand margin. The first imports the line of FM data. The second (Alt A) shifts down the block of accumulated price-volume data and layers on top of these data each new day's trading results. Data for the 251st day "fall out the bottom," but if you have sufficient memory, you can adjust the size of the block to accumulate more days. A 640K RAM system should accommodate over 2000 days of data.

We use this system, with multiple files, to accumulate data on 350 stocks every day. This costs $300 a year from Telemet America, i.e., $25 a month. An equivalent accumulation of data from one on-line service would cost close to $2400 a year.

Spreadsheet Links for FM and TV Cable Data

Three of the four FM and TV cable services provide software that is designed to download data into DIF (Data Interchange Format) files. A DIF file is a file written in a standard format which most spreadsheets will readily accept. This is why, at this early point in the technology of using broadcast data, a spreadsheet is attractive. Telemet America's Radio Exchange, Lotus Broadcasting's Signal, and Data Broadcasting Corporation's MarketWatch will all download files of data you can upload into a spreadsheet. X*Press will not download data, but I understand that the user underground is alert to this problem. You might raise the question at a user group meeting and see what sort of ideas or programs surface.

The portfolio management spreadsheet shown in Figure 20.1 is one I designed for monitoring, displaying, and accumulating FM data from Telemet America's service. Although it runs on FM data, the spreadsheet is presented here as a general prototype for either FM or TV cable data. In the spreadsheet, the two portfolios are stacked one atop the other. Below both is a third tier of data. This is what price and volume data look like when brought in from the FM radio modem. The importation of this block of data requires three steps, as follows.

1. Using the FM (Telemet America) Personal Gains software, the data are first stored in a DIF file. The creation of the DIF file is an option on the Personal Gains menu, so you can do it with a keystroke. The file is stored on a disk accessible to Lotus 1-2-3.

2. A Lotus 1-2-3 utility is used to translate the DIF file from the DIF format into Lotus's own .WKS format.

3. With Lotus 1-2-3, the main portfolio management file is opened and displayed. At this point, what you will see on the screen is what you see in Figure 20.1.

The cursor is positioned at the upper left-hand corner of the panel of "old," previously imported FM data. A Lotus command to combine files is used to bring the new panel of FM data into the spreadsheet, where it is precisely superimposed over the old data. The new data replace the prior data price for price, volume for volume.

Once the file containing the latest sampling of FM data has been imported, the rest is automatic. Cell addresses refer the last reported prices from the FM data panel up into the appropriate positions in the current price columns of the portfolio management panels. Recalculation is virtually instantaneous. As soon as the latest file of FM data is imported, one can read the actual and annualized performance of the portfolios, the proximities to stop-loss prices, the absolute and percentage gains and losses for particular stocks, and various totals of interest.

For the purposes of explanation, this process has been presented as it would be worked through manually using single commands. Lotus 1-2-3, Symphony, and Framework can be programmed to accomplish these file-shuffling and cursor-positioning tasks using macros, i.e., stored sequences of commands. If you use macros, you can automate the spreadsheet part of the process to such a degree that you need only ask yourself, "How'm I doing?", push a button, and read the latest answers. Lotus's Signal software is supplied with sample templates for portfolio managers (see Chapter 6). By means of macro looping, the transfer of incoming data into a spreadsheet can be made repetitive and fully automatic. Signal spreadsheet portfolios are thus updated constantly so that you can monitor your spreadsheet portfolio "live." With the Telemet and DBC systems, spreadsheet transfers cannot be as fully automated, but live portfolio monitor screens are inherent in the basic software. A once-daily transfer to a spreadsheet is thus sufficient.

How to Build a Price Database from FM Quotes

When new FM data are brought into a spreadsheet via the Combine File command, the data are superimposed over the previous day's FM data. The old data are lost. You can save the data for eventual charting by moving them down to get them out of the way before the fresh data are brought in from the modem.

Define a huge block on your spreadsheet, 250 rows deep and as many columns wide as you need to accommodate the close and volume data for your stocks. For, say, 16 stocks, you might allow a width of 32 rows. This massive block will become the data accumulator.

Now write a macro command to move the whole block down one row. When it moves, it will carry with it the top row, which contains yesterday's price-volume data. This downshift gets yesterday's data out of the way, leaving a blank top row ready to receive today's closing data. After the close of trading tomorrow, you can apply the block downshift macro again. This will carry today's data down one row and clear the top row to receive tomorrow's closing prices and volume figures.

The system requires two macro commands. The first downshifts the block, using the Lotus Move command. The second pulls in the day's fresh data with the Lotus Combine File command. You can combine the two commands into a single sequence.

This sample system has the capacity to store 250 days of data. You can actually store as many days as you have memory to accommodate just by specifying a bigger block. The sample system stacks the daily data by piling the new data on top and letting the oldest data sink toward the bottom of the block. This is easier to visualize and is thus used for the purpose of explanation. You can load the block from the bottom up just as easily or reverse whichever stacking order you have chosen by invoking the Lotus data and sort facilities.

The transfer of prices and daily volume into the database is typically made once a day, after the close. Our system has 640K and provides plenty of room for 250 days of data on each of the portfolio stocks. There is room for a lot more, but it seems good practice to use many files rather than just one. You can organize database files by stock groups.

You can chart spreadsheet data in a primitive way using the graphics software associated with the spreadsheets. Or you can transfer the spreadsheet data into a DIF file and upload the data into a technical analysis program such as MetaStock, Savant's Technical Investor, and Summa's Winning on Wall Street. Savant and Summa sell special bridge programs to get spreadsheet data into their programs. MetaStock imports files directly. It is possible that the Dow Jones Market Analyzer Plus can be made to do this as well, although I have not tried it. Assume that you will have to do some fiddling to accomplish these data transfers. It is worth experimenting.

When you need historical data to get started on a file for a particular stock, you can bring the data in over the phone from Warner Computer Systems, a specialist in historical data, at relatively low cost. A spreadsheet link program will get it into your spreadsheet, or you could bring it in via your charting package.

In summary, FM or TV cable can save you much of the high cost of telephone updating. You can bring in broadcast data on as many stocks as you care to and accumulate the data daily in your spreadsheet.

The spreadsheet is a superior tool for portfolio management even if you forgo FM or TV links and simply enter the data manually or via the telephone with a spreadsheet link program. As a parking place for FM and TV data being accumulated for subsequent charting by a technical analysis program, the spreadsheet is obviously a makeshift, but it is the only approach now readily available to individual investors for doing this valuable job. Window on Wall Street, an advanced portfolio manager well suited for market professionals, will directly accumulate data from the Signal radio modem. It seems best suited for managing multiple portfolios. TSA Proforma offers a program which will operate directly on X*Press TV cable data. See Chapters 6 and 7 for details on these programs.

But If You Hate to Tinker . . .

Several dedicated portfolio management programs are commented on here, including the Xor Blu Chip, Dow Jones, Summa, and Interactive Data offerings. None of them run directly on FM radio data. They are designed for manual entry or for updating via telephone modem, with the exception of the Xor program, which accepts manual data only.

Figures 20.3, 20.4, and 20.5 suggest the basic elements of any complete portfolio manager. These are (1) a database containing all the essential information available about each position in the portfolio, both current and closed, (2) an accounting of realized revenue from dividends and from actual security sales, and (3) an accounting of unrealized profits in positions which are now open. These three figures were printed out from the Xor Blu Chip portfolio manager, a program written by John Blu. The program costs about $80, and it is probably one of the least expensive programs that truly measure up to the problem of portfolio management. (Note that in the stock-monitoring program I wrote with

Stock	Coops International		Ticker Symbol		COOP
Brokerage Firm	A. Discount Firm		Date		8/18/82
Broker Name	Some Broker		# Shares		400.000
Tax Deferred	N		Price per Share		8.06250
Total Price		3,225.00			
Commission		32.41	Remaining Shares		300.0
Misc. Charge		0.00	Est. Net Price		10.93750
Interest		0.00	Est. Value		3,281.25
SEC/Postage		2.00	Est. Gain/Loss		836.69
Total Amount		3,259.41			
Notes					

	SALE DATE	# SHARES	$ per SHARE	SELLING COSTS	NET AMOUNT	GAIN/LOSS
→	8/19/83	100.0	9.25	34.00	891.00	76.15

Display current Help

■ Help ■   Find   Estimate   Analysis   Portfolio   Dividend   Split

Figure 20.3. This is the screen which first appears when you run the Blu Chip portfolio manager. It is a page which presents all the information on file about a given stock in the portfolio. To turn the page, in effect, you use the Pg Down key. Another page, for the next stock on file, will be displayed. The Find command speeds you to a page on a specific stock. Both realized and unrealized gains are noted in the file.

```
                    SALES ANALYSIS AND DIVIDEND REPORT

 STOCK                      PURCH. DATE  SALE DATE   GAIN/LOSS    GAIN CATEGORY

 Ajax Computers              2/14/83      7/15/83        387.36   SHORT TERM
 Ajax Computers              2/14/83      7/19/83        643.61   SHORT TERM
 Ajax Computers              2/14/83      7/30/83        237.36   SHORT TERM
 Coops International         8/18/82      8/19/83         76.15   LONG TERM
 Harrison Company            4/16/83      7/16/83        704.42   SHORT TERM
 International Trading Co.   2/15/78                     132.40   Y-T-D DIVIDENDS
 International Trading Co.   2/15/78      8/20/83      2,770.37   LONG TERM
 Magma Exploration          8/10/82      8/15/83      2,017.50   DEFERRED
 Norton Enterprises         2/14/82      8/15/83      1,030.06   LONG TERM
 Price Systems              4/18/83      8/15/83          5.00   SHORT TERM
 Quick Starts               5/05/83      7/15/83        -98.94   SHORT TERM
 Rapid Starts               1/15/83      4/15/83      1,745.00   SHORT TERM
 Slick Oil and Gas          4/15/83      7/15/83      1,818.80   SHORT TERM
 Tough Beef                 4/04/83      8/20/83        257.75   SHORT TERM
 Ultra Products            12/31/82      1/01/83       -288.50   DEFERRED
 Ultra Products            12/31/82      8/18/83        121.25   DEFERRED



 <Esc> = Abort     <any other key> = Continue
```

```
        --- SALES ANALYSIS and DIVIDEND REPORT SUMMARY ---

             TOTAL SHORT TERM            5,700.38
             TOTAL LONG TERM             3,876.58
                                       --------------
             NET CURRENT GAIN/LOSS       9,576.95

             TOTAL DEFERRED              1,850.25
                                       --------------
             TOTAL GAIN/LOSS            11,427.20

             TOTAL Y-T-D DIVIDENDS         132.40










 Press any key to return
```

Figure 20.4. This is the report of realized gains for both individual stocks and the entire portfolio. Note that dividends are included here, along with a tabulation of the tax status (long-term and short-term) of each gain and loss.

```
              ESTIMATED PORTFOLIO VALUE and GAIN/LOSS ANALYSIS

                    Purchase  Remaining  Estimated    Estimated    Estimated
   Stock Name         Date      Shares   Net Price      Value       Gain/Loss

 Better Inventions   1/01/80    1,000       0.06         62.50      -1,284.00
 Coops International  8/18/82      300      10.94      3,281.25         836.69
 Equity Enterprises  1/01/83      200      37.88      7,575.00       1,655.12
 Harrison Company    4/16/83      500       1.13        562.50         300.92
 International Tradi  2/15/78       50     120.00      6,000.00       2,799.00
 International Tradi  8/20/82      100     120.00     12,000.00       6,516.00
 Joberts             1/15/83      100      21.13      2,112.50         883.25
 Lawtons             8/18/82      100      12.63      1,262.50         -34.00
 Orchard Development  8/18/83      400       5.06      2,025.00       1,156.75
 Slick Oil and Gas   4/15/83    3,000       0.34      1,031.25         829.95
 Ultra Products      12/31/82     200       2.63        525.00        -484.00
 Ventures, Inc.      8/18/82    1,000       0.44        437.50        -846.50
 Walker, Inc.        1/01/82      100      19.13      1,912.50         632.00
 Xor                 8/31/83      200      20.00      4,000.00       1,969.23
 Yellow Bird         5/15/83      400       1.25        500.00         398.00
 Zenon Computers     7/15/83      300       6.50      1,950.00         -34.00
                                                   ------------    ------------
                                                     45,237.50      15,294.42

 Press any key to return
```

Figure 20.5. A report of unrealized gains and losses: your active portfolio. The use of the term *estimated* in the tabulations is ambivalent. It means you can plug in hypothetical prices to see how you might do—sit and dream, in other words. In most circumstances the columns headed "Estimated" will contain values based on actual reported prices you have entered from the keyboard.

Lotus 1-2-3, there is no sharp partitioning of realized versus unrealized gains. This is a basic and essential feature you should look for in a commercial program.) The Xor Blu Chip has been popular for a long time. You won't have to worry about bugs.

What you see in the three figures is pretty much what you get. Figure 20.3 shows the screen which comes up when you boot the program. The boxed section is the format of the portfolio database and is the first page of many. As you successively press the Page Down key, you "turn" these pages of neatly boxed data, or leaf through the database. These records include all positions, both open and closed. All the information in the system about each stock can be read from its respective record in the database.

Across the bottom of the screen runs a loop menu. Menu items are selected by cursor. Some menu items are self-explanatory, and some aren't. The item labeled "Help" is a guide to function key commands, which you use to help enter, edit, and delete data and to record buy and sell transactions. When you buy a stock, you fill in a blank record which is then stored in the database.

The Find command will display on the screen the database record for any company you request, so you don't have to page through alphabetically to reach the one you want.

"Estimate" does not mean *estimate* at all. You use this command when you want to enter a current price, which the program regards and calls out as an "estimated price." You can play what-if by entering any estimated price for the stock and reading out its result in terms of profit and loss. This may be helpful on the downside (How much downside are we going to tolerate in this turkey?), but on the upside the Estimate command looks like a device to automate wishful thinking.

The Analysis command elicits the report on realized gains and losses shown in Figure 20.4. The Portfolio command produces the report on unrealized gains and losses shown in Figure 20.5.

The Dividend and Split commands are for entering dividends as they are paid and splits as they occur, respectively.

The program recognizes that you may sell some but not all of your position in a stock. Below the record for Coops International in Figure 20.3, the program notes that 100 shares of the original 400-share purchase have been sold, for a realized gain of $76.15. The remaining 300 shares show an unrealized gain of $836.69. The term *remaining shares* is used throughout in lieu of the simpler but less strictly logical term *shares*. This is why you find the term *remaining shares* in the report on unrealized gains and losses (Figure 20.5). The term reserves the possibility that you might have owned more shares at one time.

What You Get and What's Missing

The program does all the absolutely necessary expansion arithmetic (e.g., 100 shares × $2.375 per share = $237.50) but no more. It does not show percentage gains and losses for individual stocks, nor does it calculate annualized gains and losses. There are no provisions for entering acceptable price limits and using them to trigger alarms. These are all mere embellishments you don't really need, but I would miss having them. Percentage calculations and limits help focus your attention on problem stocks and stocks that are getting ahead of themselves.

The program describes in detail the tax consequences of realized gains and losses, as shown in Figure 20.4. You can view multiple portfolios with it by storing one portfolio per disk. It is an excellent program to put your house in order, and for long-term, income-oriented investors the Xor Blu Chip portfolio manager should prove satisfactory. It should be understood as a bookkeeper, however. Slightly more elaborate portfolio managers are more than that. They can provide you with an early-warning system that will help you judge when to sell what.

The Value/Screen Plus Portfolio Manager

Figure 20.6 shows the basic portfolio display supplied with the Value/Screen Plus fundamental analysis program. It is of interest because it can be loaded into a spreadsheet for updating and because of the diversity of data it will array on each of your stocks. The data are selected from the Value/Screen Plus data disk, which is provided monthly or quarterly by subscription. For each of your stocks you can display, alongside the usual valuation, information about future growth estimates, the most current earnings, P/E, or any or all of 37 different data items stored for each stock on the disk.

If you keep the portfolio manager on a spreadsheet, you can update both the prices and the price-related items (P/Es, PSRs, etc.) from day to day with FM, TV cable, or dial-up data. The portfolio manager and Value Line data can be transferred directly into the spreadsheet. You will need other software to get the prices into it. The necessary software comes with both FM services and with TV data from Data Broadcasting. For X*Press, no link is available. For the major daily dial-ups, linking software costs $85 from Market Link. (See Chapter 22 for details.)

The range of information you can display to help you make judgments about your portfolio is wider with this system than with any other. Note, however, that it will help only if your portfolio stocks are to be found among the set of 1650 Value Line issues. If you own or follow very many over-the-counter stocks, for example, you will probably be disappointed in this program.

Two Programs in the Middle Range: Dow Jones and Summa

In the middle range of complexity and usefulness are the Dow Jones and Summa portfolio managers. Both can be updated automatically via modem. Dow Jones provides an exceptionally wide range of reports.

```
GAINS & LOSSES
Data:  Apr 1986
Shares                     Purchase  Current  Value of    Gain or   % Gain
  Held   Company Name       Price     Price   Holdings      Loss    or Loss
------  ----------------   --------  -------  ----------  --------- --------
   200  GENERAL MOTORS      70.375   76.375   15275.00     1200.00     8.5
   500  INTL BUS MCH       155.500  148.125   74062.50    -3687.50    -4.7
   350  MERCK & CO         137.000  186.375   65231.25    17281.25    36.1
   200  VIACOM              54.500   60.125   12025.00     1125.00    10.3
------                                        ----------  --------- --------
  1250  Totals/Averages                       166593.75   15918.75    10.6


ANALYTICAL REPORT
Data:   Apr 1986
                  Time-   Recent Current Current % Return  Est % Chg
  Company Name    liness  Price   P-E    Yield  Net Worth  EPS FY
----------------  ------ ------- ------- ------- --------- ---------
MERCK & CO          2    161.125  19.3    2.2     19.4      14.8
                  ------ ------- ------- ------- --------- ---------
Grp Totals/Avgs    2.0   161.125  19.3    2.2     19.4      14.8

GENERAL MOTORS      3     86.125   7.3    5.8     18.8     -17.3
INTL BUS MCH        3    148.000  12.4    3.0     20.5      18.6
VIACOM              3     55.000  32.4    0.9      6.1      -8.3
                  ------ ------- ------- ------- --------- ---------
Grp Totals/Avgs    3.0   127.643  14.0    3.2     18.5      10.0

                  ------ ------- ------- ------- --------- ---------
Totals/Averages    2.6   140.753  16.1    2.8     18.9      11.9

INCOME REPORT
Data:   Apr 1986
Shares                    Current  Value of  Current Estimated Current
  Held   Company Name      Price   Holdings    Div    Income    Yield
------  ----------------  -------  ---------- ------- --------- -------
   200  GENERAL MOTORS     76.375   15275.00   5.00    1000.00    5.8
   500  INTL BUS MCH      148.125   74062.50   4.40    2200.00    3.0
   350  MERCK & CO        186.375   65231.25   3.60    1260.00    2.2
   200  VIACOM             60.125   12025.00   0.50     100.00    0.9
------                             ---------- ------- --------- -------
  1250  Totals/Averages            166593.75   3.86    4560.00    2.8
```

Figure 20.6. The Value/Screen Plus portfolio management facility produces several standard reports and can be customized to produce others. Three of the standard reports are shown here. It is the special power of this program to tap the Value Line database disk for helpful information you would not ordinarily expect to find in a portfolio manager. Note in the analytical report, for example, the array of data on the percentage return on net worth and the estimated change in EPS. Any of 37 different database fields can be included in a portfolio report. The sorting and ranking capabilities associated with the program's main task, which is fundamental stock screening, can be applied to the portfolio as well as to the database. The fundamental data in the portfolio can be updated with the monthly disk from Value Line. The prices can be updated from the disk, by hand, or by means of a spreadsheet coupled with a spreadsheet link program. There is no inherent facility for direct telephone updates of fundamental or price data. The program is an excellent choice for investors who concentrate on exchange-listed securities.

Summa's program is particularly careful in informing you about cash and margin accounts; this is a real plus for active stock traders.

Dow Jones has the more powerful program. It is cumbersome, perhaps even cranky, but once you catch on to its operating procedures, you will come to appreciate it. You can configure the finished reports in many different ways to extract the specific information in which you are in-

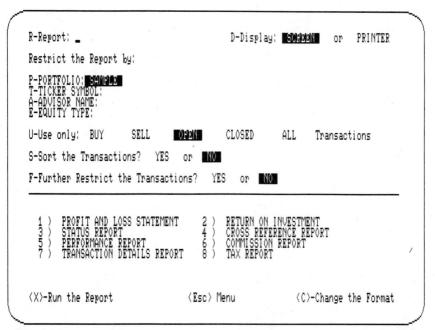

Figure 20.7. The unusual menu of the Dow Jones portfolio manager. You can use it to custom-tailor any report you wish to see. The basic types of reports are enumerated at the bottom of the menu. Having selected a profit and loss statement, for example, you might restrict it, by using menu item E, to bonds only or stocks only. If you run several portfolios, you would specify which one you wanted the report on by using menu item P and then typing in the appropriate portfolio name. From this single menu myriad reports can be generated.

terested. The basic reporting menu is shown in Figure 20.7. It is less a menu than a panel of toggles. You use cursor arrow controls to position highlighted blocks behind the options you choose. Letter selections position the cursor in the part of the panel on which you wish to operate. If you want to print out your reports, for example, you select option D for "display" and then position the highlighted block behind the word PRINTER. The item designated as U, "for use only," can be used to define whether you want to view reports on all stocks, on unrealized gains and losses only (the OPEN positions), or on realized gains and losses only (the CLOSED positions). In addition to these basic three groups, you can also restrict reports to long and short positions. You highlight SELL to elicit reports on short positions and BUY to elicit reports on long positions. Note that there are five basic reporting groups as opposed to the three (realized, unrealized, and both) types offered with simpler programs. Moreover, there are eight different types of reports as opposed to a single standard statement of position. Particularly

```
      Profit and Loss Statement    PORTFOLIOS: SAMPLE

                   Basis      Basis      Current                Short
 Symbol  Shares    Date       Cost       Value      Profit      or Long

 DSY     100.00    05/30/84   2,663.00   3,012.50    349.50     LONG
 ABF     100.00    05/30/84   1,913.00   2,175.00    262.00     LONG
 AMT     200.00    05/30/84   3,850.00   2,950.00   (900.00)    LONG
 DJ      100.00    06/12/84   4,089.90   4,325.00    235.10     LONG




                  <PgDn>-page down                 <Esc>-menu
```

```
           Realized: Short Term Profits:        0.00
                     Long Term Profits:         0.00

                 Total Realized Profits:        0.00


         Unrealized: Short Term Profits:        0.00
                     Long Term Profits:       (53.40)

               Total Unrealized Profits:     (53.40)


                       Total Profits:        (53.40)


                   Total Percent Gain:        (0.43)
              Annualized Percent Gain:        (0.18)


                    Liquidation Value:     12,462.50



         <PgUp>-page up                       <Esc>-menu
```

Figure 20.8. A profit and loss report. Note the split in the totals between unrealized and realized gains and losses. We could also have used the menu to restrict the report to only realized or only unrealized gains and losses.

helpful among them are the reports reproduced in Figures 20.8, 20.9 and 20.10.

Figure 20.8 shows a profit and loss statement constructed for the group of all the stocks in a mock portfolio called SAMPLE. If you viewed this report on the screen of your computer, you would find that it is actually a dual report. The upper panel of tabular information is accessible with the Page Up key. The lower panel summary and totals are displayed by pressing the Page Down key. Note the split in the totals between realized and unrealized gains and losses. We could also have restricted the tabulation to a display of only realized or only unrealized gains and losses.

Percentage gains are calculated and presented along with annualized percentage gains. The annualized gain provides a yardstick for comparing the annual performance of the stock with that of some other investment, e.g., a T-bill. Note, however, that these gain and loss percentages represent capital gains and losses. They do not include dividend distributions.

The program uses expanded figures almost exclusively. For example, the entry price for the investment in CBS is reported as a total, $6950, under the heading "Basic Cost." This is fine, but you must do a bit of mental arithmetic to determine that you paid $69.50 per share to get into CBS. Similarly, its current value per share, which is $112, must be deduced from the "Current Value" total of $11,200.

This little calculation is not too taxing if you are working with nice round lots, ideally of no more than 100 shares. If you bought an odd lot or if the stock has split 5 for 4 and then 3 for 2 so that you have wound up with 187.5 shares of the stuff, you may have to resort to a calculator to backtrack on the adjusted entry price and figure out the current price. This is not convenient, but then, why would you wish to know the per-share prices anyway? The expanded numbers show the bottom line on your gain and loss.

The answer is this: Suppose one of your stocks suddenly falls $2. You learned this from a televised business report, and you want to put it into perspective. A $2 shift on an $8 stock is a disaster; a $2 shift on an $80 stock can be written off to a day's profit taking. To react, or decide not to react, you need the per-share price levels in plain view on the monitor. The use of basis cost and current value totals tends to obscure the significance of day-to-day changes. A long-term, income-oriented, round-lot investor would probably not be troubled much by this problem. A trader, an OTC market enthusiast, or a short seller using this program would have a constant sense that something important was hidden and, like an iceberg, dangerous.

In only one of the report formats do the entry price per share and the value per share appear juxtaposed, and that is in the transaction report on realized gains. This is too late to be of any use. The status report, which ought to deliver this information, shows only the basis price per share and then remarks verbally about the stock's current position relative to the stipulated stop-loss ("Above," the program might say). This is not enough.

The return on investment report is shown in Figure 20.9. If you compare the percentage return on investment (%ROI) with the percentage gains in the value of the stocks in the profit and loss report, you can judge the effect of dividend distributions on the overall performance of each security. As with all reports, this ROI report can be restricted to unrealized or realized returns. You can also sort the information within the tabulation so that the top-performing stocks appear at the top of the table, for example. You can also impose conditions on the reports, so that only stocks meeting those conditions (they are losing money, for example, and are candidates for pruning) will be included in the report. Sorting and conditional restrictions can be applied to any of the eight different report types.

A performance report is available to tabulate the performances of

```
              Return on Investment    PORTFOLIOS: SAMPLE

   Symbol     Cost      Price Gain      %ROI     Ann. ROI    Current Yield

   CBS      6,950.00    4,250.00       64.39      52.69
   DSY      2,663.00      349.50       16.50       7.40          3.98
   ABF      1,913.00      262.00       16.05       7.20          2.76
   AMT      3,850.00     (900.00)     (22.60)    (10.13)         2.71
   DJ       4,089.90      235.10        7.22       3.29          1.39


                       Total ROI:      4,646.60

                       Total %ROI:       23.87

                       Annualized %ROI:  19.22

                       Average Yield:     1.35




              <PgDn>-page down                    <Esc>-menu
```

Figure 20.9. A return on investment report. By comparing it with the profit and loss report, you can see the effects of dividend distributions on the overall performance of each security. You could sort this tabulation per performance so that the top-performing stock appeared at the top of the list.

your positions in stocks, bonds, options, mutual funds, and T-bills. If you are forming decisions about how to apportion your invested capital among these particular types of investments, the report will show where your money has performed best.

A cross-reference report can be assembled in any of three different ways: by equity type, adviser, or symbol. If, for example, you manage several portfolios and are anxious to know which ones contain IBM, you can enter the symbol and get back a report naming those portfolios and detailing their respective positions in the stock. If you sort by equity type, you can enter the type (bonds, for example) and receive a report on all bonds drawn from all portfolios.

Finally, if you actually can't remember who tipped you to buy 300 shares of the XYZ Corporation the day before trading was suspended forever, you can tabulate your stocks under the name of the adviser who recommended them and thus identify the culprit. You can use the same reporting technique to see who has had a "hot hand" lately.

The tax report is shown in Figure 20.10. It is organized so that you can transfer the information directly to an Internal Revenue Service

```
         Capital Gains and Losses-Information for Schedule D (Form 1040)
                           PORTFOLIOS: SAMPLE
   Part I. Short Term Capital Gains and Losses

     a. Property      Acquired     Sold      Sales Price    +Fees      f. Gain
                      b. Date   c. Date      d. Gross     e. Cost

                                     Net Short Term Gain or (Loss)      0.00
   Part II. Long Term Capital Gains and Losses

     a. Property      Acquired     Sold      Sales Price    +Fees      f. Gain
                      b. Date   c. Date      d. Gross     e. Cost

     CBS INC.         05/30/84  08/19/85    11,338.00    7,088.00    4,250.00

                                      Net Long Term Gain or (Loss)   4,250.00

   Part III. Summary of Parts I and II

                      Net Gain or (Loss)                       4,250.00

                      Net Long Term Capital Gains               4,250.00

                      40% of Net Long Term Capital Gains         1,700.00
```

Figure 20.10. The Dow Jones tax report is formatted just like Schedule D, and short- and long-term capital gains are nicely itemized, ready to transcribe. Other programs tag and total long- and short-term gains, but this is the only one reviewed here that virtually prepares the reporting form.

(IRS) Form 1040 Schedule D, reporting on long- and short-term capital gains and losses. In the figure, only the results for CBS Inc. are shown, since this was the only realized gain in the sample portfolio. In a real tax report, you might have several realized capital gains and losses and the pencilwork could be considerable. This report makes the preparation of year-end tax data a push-button project. All the portfolio managers reviewed here provide a reporting of short- and long-term gains for tax purposes, but only Dow Jones has so faithfully followed the actual format of the IRS's Schedule D. After the tax transition year of 1987, this will no longer be an important feature.

Summa's Trader's Accountant

If you trade stocks much, the Trader's Accountant program is a better choice in my opinion than the Dow Jones portfolio management program reviewed above. The Trader's Accountant does not have as diverse a selection of report formats as that offered by Dow Jones. It does not provide utilities for sorting or conditionally extracting data about securities. In lieu of these capabilities, Summa provides some important accounting features that well help you determine from one day to the next exactly where you stand with your investments. This can help you put surplus cash to work and anticipate, with a few simple calculations, any margin calls that might be looming. Here's how it works.

The Trader's Accountant maintains, in addition to your securities records, a cash-margin database. If you buy a stock, the program will automatically diminish your cash position by an amount equal to the stock purchase. When you sell a stock, your cash balance will be raised by the amount of the sale. In this way you can keep records in parallel with those maintained by your broker, much as you keep your own checkbook record in parallel with the accounting services provided by the bank. If you sell short, the proceeds of the sale will be made evident in the cash balance. When you purchase stock to cover the short sale, the cash balance will drop by the amount of your purchase. One hopes, naturally, that the cost of this purchase will be substantially less than the proceeds from the sale. But if you do take a loss, that too will be reflected in your cash balance.

The account keeps records of both cash and margin positions. If you used a 40 percent margin to purchase $1000 worth of stock, your cash balance would drop by $600 and the margin of $400 owed your brokerage would be noted in the database. You will have to calculate the proximity to a margin call. The program cannot do it for you, though it provides the numbers you need.

Dividends paid, interest paid by you on margin accounts, interest paid to you against cash in the account—all these items are noted in the database and duly added to or subtracted from your cash position. When you are wondering where you are exactly, you can print out a report called the Margin Account Transaction Report and you'll know. Note that even if you never trade on margin or venture into short positions, the accounting of your cash position is still an invaluable aid in managing your investments.

There's Cash, and Then There Is Liquidity

The cash-margin account reflects the condition of your account with your broker. It does not include your checking accounts, money market funds, savings accounts, or other cash positions. Accordingly, Summa has provided a separate database for this other cash. It gives you a place to keep track of bank deposits, withdrawals, and interest earned. The program's formal designation for this little database is the Investor's Liquid Fund. Within it you can keep a separate record for each bank or money market fund with which you do business.

Realized and Unrealized Gain and Loss Reports

The program provides the two basic requisite types of reports: statements of realized and of unrealized gains and losses. The Summa reports include a column reflecting the margin and margin percentage associated with each security position.

The averaged report is a summary of the detailed report, in which values associated with more than one position in one stock are compressed into a single entry for that stock. The number of shares is added, and the price is presented as a weighted-average price. This is a useful feature for investors who use the technique of dollar cost averaging.

Tax Reporting

The tax report totals interest and dividend income. Although it marks long-term capital gains with the code letter L, no attempt is made to assemble a short- and long-term capital gains total or to format these data for the tax form. The information is provided, but you have to do some arithmetic to pull it together. Bear in mind that the whole orientation of the Winning on Wall Street package is toward meeting the special needs of traders rather than investors. If a trader shows a long-term capital gain, it can often be explained as the residue of an ill-starred short-term trading strategy that never quite worked out. A typical trader's game is supposed to produce short-term capital gains so exalted that the tax consequences can be, if necessary, gracefully accepted. In any event, the capital gains effects won't matter much after 1987.

The Masterpiece

I have remarked that there is no best portfolio management program. The best one for you is the one that does just what you need—no more, no less. If you need a trader's portfolio manager, I unhesitatingly recommend the Summa program. If you just need to clean out your desk drawer so you know what's happening with your stocks, get the Xor. If you hold or manage a few income-oriented portfolios, try Dow Jones.

But having said all that, I must also express my admiration for the author of a program that does everything well. You probably won't need to use half of what it can do (it even keeps track of valuable *stamps*), but it is a jewel. It comes as one component of the fully integrated software package from Chase Manhattan's data-purveying subsidiary in Boston, Interactive Data. The package is called the Active Investor, and its other two components, for fundamental and technical analysis, are reviewed elsewhere in this book. The portfolio manager combines in a well-organized package the transaction recording, accounting, and reporting capabilities of the portfolio managers discussed above, and it does more in each area. The range of transaction types is wider than that of any other program considered here and provides for all sorts of trades in options, stocks, warrants, bonds, tangibles—you name it.

The program draws charts and diagrams based on various reports. These are extremely helpful in evaluating your positions at a glance. It also displays a calendar schedule of projected income from interest and dividend payments over the span of a year. Not only prices but also dividends and splits can be updated automatically via modem.

The reporting capability is extensive, and a midget programming language is provided (on a menu) so that you can design your own custom reports. Sorting and conditional extraction of securities can be accomplished both within single portfolios and globally, using all portfolios under the management of the program.

Many programs provide a portfolio management feature as an adjunct to some major capability, e.g., technical or fundamental analysis. Portfolio managers tend to be thrown in as an extra buying incentive. Interactive's is in contrast a fully realized program, a tour de force.

Types of Transactions

Here are the types of securities and other assets the system will specifically handle:

Stocks

Bonds

Municipal bonds

Discount instruments (T-bills, commercial paper, liquid asset funds)

Warrants

Calls

Puts

Index options

Commodities

Funds

Cash

Tangibles

An asset is pretty much an asset by whatever name, but the types of transactions associated with each type can be quite specialized. Accordingly, the program makes specific provisions for selling and covering short positions, for margin transactions, and for all sorts of trading in options. You can buy and sell, exercise, or write options, including covered calls and puts, without befuddling the program.

The program has no slant toward traders or investors. It is a superior tool in both arenas.

Report Smorgasbord

The main menu is reproduced in Figure 20.11. The detailed report and the history reports provide information about realized and unrealized gains. The Interactive program provides averaged summary reports in which values associated with more than one position in one stock are compressed into a single entry for that stock. The number of shares is added, and the price is presented as a weighted-average price. This is a good feature for investors who use the technique of dollar cost averaging.

The expanded detail report shown in Figure 20.12 combines the current unrealized gain report for a particular stock with a panel of information gleaned from the complete database record on the stock. The

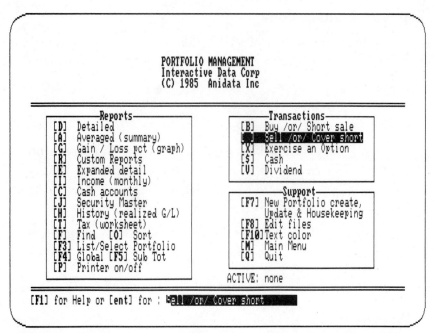

Figure 20.11. The main menu of the Active Investor's portfolio manager. This is the best one. Detailed and history reports (unrealized and realized capital gains) are terms that survive from the program's antecedent, the Anidata manager. Everything else is new and different. Color is used functionally. Bar graphs make trends apparent.

panel presents the ticker, the stock group, and dividend data including the pay cycle, the pay date, and the dividend itself. It also presents the upper and lower price limits you many have set in order to trigger alarms on excessive price moves. It includes earnings per share, yield, and if the security is an option, the current price of the stock or index underlying the option. Not all the stocks in the system are accessible through this reporting option, only those in the portfolio which is currently "up." To examine the entire database, including open and closed positions in all portfolios, you can display the portfolio master report.

An income report is shown in Figure 20.13. Note that it projects income from dividends and interest, in a convenient calendar format, over the span of the next year. Since it is a projection, it must be understood that the numbers will change and that dividends and interest are actually paid out. Nevertheless, it helps to have such a clear representation of one's expected income.

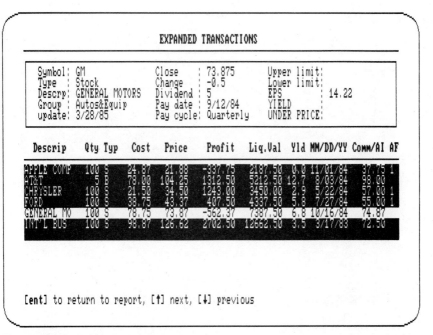

EXPANDED TRANSACTIONS

Symbol: GM	Close : 73.875	Upper limit:
Type : Stock	Change : -0.5	Lower limit:
Descrp: GENERAL MOTORS	Dividend : 5	EPS : 14.22
Group : Autos&Equip	Pay date : 9/12/84	YIELD :
update: 3/28/85	Pay cycle: Quarterly	UNDER PRICE:

Descrip	Qty	Typ	Cost	Price	Profit	Liq.Val	Yld	MM/DD/YY	Comm/AI	AF
APPLE COMP	100	S	24.87	21.88	-337.75	2187.50	0.0	11/01/84	37.75	1
AT&T	5	B	78.00	104.25	1312.50	5212.50	12.7	8/03/84	98.00	
CHRYSLER	100	S	21.50	34.50	1243.00	3450.00	2.9	5/22/84	57.00	1
FORD	100	S	38.75	43.37	407.50	4337.50	5.8	7/27/84	55.00	1
GENERAL MO	100	S	78.75	73.87	-562.37	7387.50	6.8	10/16/84	74.87	
INT'L BUS	100	S	98.87	126.62	2702.50	12662.50	3.5	3/17/83	72.50	

[ent] to return to report, [↑] next, [↓] previous

Figure 20.12. The expanded detail report. This is essentially a peek into the database. By running the full-width bar cursor up and down the alphabetical list of stocks, the operator selects the panel of data which appears across the top of the screen. Note that you can set alarm limits. The pay cycle and pay date let you know when to look for dividends. The list of stocks below the panel contains information on unrealized gains and losses.

Performance Graphs

Under the two options labeled gain/loss and custom reports you will find the jewel at the center of the program, a spindly bar graph that is displayed adjacent to each tabulation of portfolio performance. It is instantly apparent from these bar graphs which of your stocks are winners, which are promising, and which are neither winning nor promising. See Figure 20.14 for a display of gain and loss. The graphs are just simple ornaments, but they make the program; they are the essential luxury.

Note that the stocks in this portfolio can be sorted in order of profitability. The graph is redrawn automatically to reflect the new order, as shown in Figure 20.15. The sorted stocks can be arranged in order of ascending or descending profitability.

You can use any criterion for sorting you like: Price, profitability, return on investment (ROI), and weighting of the portfolio are typical

	Aug	Sep	Oct	Nov	Dec	Jan	Feb	Mar	Apr	May	Jun	Jul
AT&T	-	-	-	-	331	-	-	-	-	-	331	-
CHRYSLER	-	-	25	-	-	25	-	-	25	-	-	25
FORD	-	63	-	-	63	-	-	63	-	-	63	-
GENERAL	-	125	-	-	125	-	-	125	-	-	125	-
INT'L BU	-	-	110	-	-	110	-	-	110	-	-	110
INT'L BU	-	-	110	-	-	110	-	-	110	-	-	110
INT'L BU	-	-	110	-	-	110	-	-	110	-	-	110
MARY KAY	-	-	3	-	-	3	-	-	3	-	-	3
PENNZOIL	-	28	-	-	28	-	-	28	-	-	28	-
sub-tot	0	215	358	0	546	358	0	215	358	0	546	358
Interst	203	203	203	203	203	203	203	203	203	203	203	203
	5391	203	418	561	203	749	561	203	418	561	203	749	561

[↑][↓]line [PgDn][PgUp][^PgDn][^PgUp]page [P]Prt [D][A][G][R][E][F][O][I][C][J]_

Figure 20.13. This income projection is laid out in the form of a calendar. It shows forthcoming dividends for the next year and totals the monthly income to be anticipated in each
month. It is a very helpful feature I have not seen included in other programs.

choices. You can also make conditional sorts (list all stocks priced lower
than $12, for example). Finally, the sorts and conditional extractions can
be applied to single portfolios or globally to all portfolios. If you are an
adviser, for example, you might use a global search to locate all stocks
with the ticker symbol IBM in all the portfolios of all your clients and
thus produce a list of those clients. You might wish to display a list of
all your options that happen to be in or out of the money at the moment.

The system provides logical and arithmetical operators and a "work-
bench" menu to help you plug together your conditions for sorting and
extraction. The conditions can be stored so that if you use a custom
report frequently, you need not recreate the conditions for it again and
again. This is typical of the thoughtful and well-organized quality of the
whole program.

Other Reports

The other reports are self-evident from the menu. They program a tax
report, an accounting of your cash positions, and a list of portfolios. The

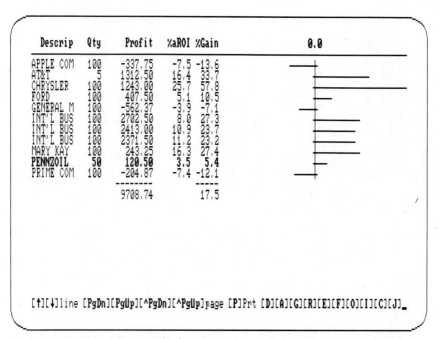

```
 Descrip   Qty    Profit  %aROI %Gain                     0.0

APPLE COM  100    -337.75  -7.5 -13.6        ——————+
AT&T         5    1312.50  16.4  33.7              +————————————
CHRYSLER   100    1243.00  25.7  57.8              +——————————————————
FORD       100     407.50   5.1  10.5              +———
GENERAL M  100    -562.37  -3.9  -7.1          ————+
INT'L BUS  100    2702.50   8.0  27.3              +—————————————
INT'L BUS  100    2413.00  10.9  23.7              +————————————
INT'L BUS  100    2371.50  11.2  23.2              +————————————
MARY KAY   100     243.25  16.3  27.4              +————
PENNZOIL    50     120.50   3.5   5.4              +——
PRIME COM  100    -204.87  -7.4 -12.1          ————+
                 --------
                  9708.74        17.5


[↑][↓]line [PgDn][PgUp][^PgDn][^PgUp]page [P]Prt [D][A][G][R][E][F][O][I][C][J]_
```

Figure 20.14. The bar chart included with this gain and loss report makes it instantly apparent which of your stocks are doing well and which are not. The winners' lines extend to the right of the zero line, and the losers' lines extend to the left. The program has built-in communications to retrieve quotes from the Interactive database. You can review this graph daily after the close of the market or as often as you like.

directory of portfolios is surprisingly missing from most other portfolio managers reviewed here. It will be most useful to advisers, brokers, and other professionals.

Accessory and Specialized Portfolio Software

Frederick Barthelme, the novelist, wrote for his own use a combination portfolio manager and portfolio database. It is available in the public domain; a $100 contribution should be sent to the author if you keep the program. It maintains a broad array of data on each of several sets of stocks, somewhat in the manner of the Value/Screen Plus portfolio manager. It does more, however, in that Barthelme has coded in judgmental algorithms to tell you when to buy and sell. These are generally based on the precepts of "value investing" (see Benjamin Graham, et al.) and on Barthelme's own experience. It also takes into account some

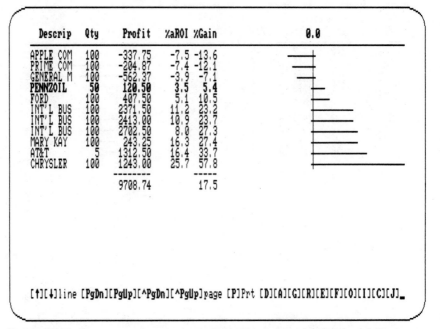

Figure 20.15. The program has sorting capability. Here a gain and loss report is shown which has been sorted in order of ascending profitability from top to bottom. Note that the bar chart reflects this ordering of the stocks and indexes. Bar charts are actually most helpful in columns of unsorted data. They draw your eye to the extreme values. Horizontal bar charts are *de rigueur*. It is astonishing how much more efficiently than vertical bars they use the space on the screen.

technical factors, such as the current price of the stock relative to its moving average. The program is distributed in compiled BASIC. It runs fast. You need not use any on-line service to keep it up to date. All entries are hand keyed from widely available print sources such as the Standard & Poor's *Stock Guide,* the Value Line service, and the financial press. It is a stand-alone program for investment management, but because it is compiled, you cannot examine or change the buy and sell criteria. Otherwise, the program is very helpful. It should prove useful in evaluating and controlling your own portfolio and in assembling and evaluating multiple mock portfolios. You need not agree with its hard-coded judgments to make good use of the program.

If you would like to reduce your portfolio's exposure to risk, you might consider a special program designed for this purpose. It is called the Stock Portfolio Allocator. Examine its output, which is reproduced in Figure 20.16. These are two portfolios which differ only in terms of the allocation of stocks. The risk associated with the lower portfolio is

```
Your allocation:

Stock name    % of funds   No. of shares   Price per share   Amount invested

IBM             24.33           100            123.0             12,300
DEC             38.38           200             97.0             19,400
WANG B           4.55            50             46.0              2,300
BURROUGH         7.52           100             38.0              3,800
PRIME           16.32           150             55.0              8,250
GENERAL          4.95           100             25.0              2,500
DATAPOIN         3.96            50             40.0              2,000

                Total invested            $50,550
                Expected return            11.57%
                Standard deviation         19.78%

                Portfolio value after one year

                Expected value            $56,397
                Best case                  76,396
                Worst case                 36,398
                Spread (best-worst)        39,998
```

```
Minimum risk allocation with same return as your allocation

Stock name    % of funds   No. of shares   Price per share   Amount invested

IBM             33.09           136            123.0             16,728
DEC             34.35           179             97.0             17,363
WANG B           9.55           105             46.0              4,830
BURROUGH        14.58           194             38.0              7,372
PRIME            8.05            74             55.0              4,070
DATAPOIN         0.32             4             40.0                160
GENERAL          0.00
CASH             0.05                                                27

                Total invested            $50,550
                Expected return            11.56%
                Standard deviation         14.98%

                Portfolio value after one year

                Expected value            $56,395
                Best case                  71,537
                Worst case                 41,252
                Spread (best-worst)        30,286

Minimum risk allocation has reduced spread by 24.3 percent.
```

Figure 20.16. Look first at the number-of-shares columns. The upper portfolio was built with the purchase of round lots primarily, without regard to risk optimization. The lower portfolio has been reallocated among the same set of stocks. It offers the same projected return at almost 25 percent less risk. Note that in the process of reallocation, one stock was assigned zero shares and was thus pruned from the portfolio. The program computes the safer allocation in accordance with the tenets of modern portfolio theory. It is called the Stock Portfolio Allocator, and it costs $60. The assumption here, as in many such calculations, is that the standard deviation is a mirror of risk. The higher the standard deviation, the higher the risk.

almost 25 percent lower than the risk associated with the upper portfolio. The rates of return are identical. In a nutshell, this is why you might wish to invest $60 in the Stock Portfolio Allocator.

The upper portfolio looks like mine. The number-of-shares column reflects the typical purchases of nice round lots of 100 or 200 shares of a stock. This is, as it turns out, the wrong thing to do. Note the number-of-shares column in the lower portfolio. The allocation to one stock has been reduced to zero, and the others have been considerably modified. The changes reflect the insights of modern portfolio theory into the risk/reward problem. The mathematics are too complex to present here, but the resulting reduction of risk is impressive. If you are in the process of dollar cost averaging, the Stock Portfolio Allocator can show you how much of which stocks to buy in order to bring your portfolio closer to the ideal allocation for minimum risk.

The program looks at 60 days of price data and at estimates of future return. The prices are entered by hand. The estimates are potentially the weak point in the concept. They would have to come from sources such as Value Line or brokerage research reports. You might prefer to enter historical returns.

The program will print out the optimum allocation for minimum risk at a given level of return. It can also allocate for the maximum return at each stipulated level of risk.

Summary and Conclusions

The portfolios can be ranked in terms of capability in the order in which they were presented in this chapter. Interactive has the most comprehensive system, and Xor the most basic. In between lie Value Line, Dow Jones, and Summa. Value Line's power to display current fundamental data on portfolio stocks can be helpful to any investor in exchange-listed securities. It is more of an information projector than a portfolio manager, however. The Dow Jones Portfolio Manager is a good choice for investors, and Summa is a better choice for traders.

Finally, you can make your own portfolio manager with a spreadsheet or transfer one in from Value/Screen Plus or other sources. I think the spreadsheet approach is the best one, particularly now that workable spreadsheets can be found for as little as $100. The spreadsheet can be updated from FM radio modems or TV cable decoders, and this is economically a big advantage. One other portfolio manager provides access to low-cost FM and is suitable for professionals. This is the Window on Wall Street program (not to be confused with Winning on Wall Street or Wall Street Window).

A number of other portfolio managers are available. In evaluating them, I suggest you look for four basic minimum features: (1) a report of unrealized gains, (2) a report on realized gains, (3) access to the underlying database so that you can scan for all the information in the system, and (4) at least a minimal accounting of your cash position. The last feature will help you make comparative checks on the statements you receive from your broker or brokers.

Some brokers provide on-line or off-line portfolio managers as part of their services to computerized investors. Charles Schwab's Equalizer software includes a particularly nice portfolio manager. It will go on-line to retrieve current data, but it keeps your files at home. Most portfolio managers from brokers will keep your files on the broker's mainframe, which means it will cost you something to look at them. This is not good. Brokers' portfolio management facilities are discussed in some detail in Chapter 23, but I think you will find that independent software is a better choice. One should select a brokerage by comparing commissions, not software.

Sources and Prices

MARKET MANAGER PLUS
Dow Jones & Company
P.O. Box 300
Princeton, NJ 08540
(800) 257-5114
Price: $249

THE ACTIVE INVESTOR
Interactive Data Corporation
303 Wyman St.
Waltham, MA 02154
(617) 895-4300
Price: Included with integrated package

THE TRADER'S ACCOUNTANT
Summa Technologies, Inc.
P.O. Box 2046
Beaverton, OR 97075
(503) 644-3212
Price: $249, or included as part of the Winning on Wall Street package

BLU CHIP PORTFOLIO MANAGER
Xor Corporation
5421 Opportunity Court
Minnetonka, MN 55343
(612) 938-0005

Price: $79.95

STOCKTRACK
Frederick Barthelme
201 Sherwood Drive
Hattiesburg MS 39401

List price: $100

Requires: IBM PC or compatible. DOS 2.0 or higher. One drive.

STOCK PORTFOLIO ALLOCATOR
Portfolio Software
14 Lincoln Avenue
Quincy, MA 02170
(617) 328-8248

List price: $60

Requires: IBM PC or compatible. 192K RAM. DOS 2.0. One drive. Also runs
on Wang PC.

21
Integrated Investment Software

Levels of Integration

There are four basic types of programs specifically designed for investors: (1) technical analysis, or charting, programs, (2) fundamental analysis programs, (3) portfolio management programs, and (4) communications programs. Any package containing all four components qualifies for definition as integrated investment software—provided that there are some pathways for data to pass between the various components.

If you retrieve prices for technical analysis, for example, you should be able to use the same price data to update your personal portfolio without going back on-line to a financial database or making a manual transfer of data, i.e., printing the data out and then keying them back in.

An integrated program should also transfer calculated values. If your technical analysis program calculates betas, for example, it would be nice if you could insert them into your files of fundamental data each day to reflect the most current prices. In fact, any values in the fundamental database which are calculated from price—price/earnings ratios, price/sales ratios, price/book ratios, volatility—should be updated automatically in an integrated package.

Integration is typically achieved by setting up a common database, or pool, of price-volume data. One can maintain this database with a daily or weekly phone call via the communications program to a commercial financial database (Warner, Dow Jones, Compuserve, etc.). Once you have retrieved and stored the most current data, the data are accessible to any of the three major components of the integrated package: the charting program, the fundamental screening program, or the portfolio manager.

Most of the major investment software companies offer at least limited integration at this point, and some are working their way toward fully integrated packages.

Savant, for example, offers a well-integrated fundamental and technical package, though it does not yet offer a portfolio manager. Dow Jones offers an integrated technical and portfolio management package, as does Summa. All these programs are provided with a communications program to retrieve data and one or more common databases in which to store data for subsequent access by the technical, fundamental, and portfolio management packages. Savant will undoubtedly progress to a fully integrated package, as the company is known to be at work on a portfolio manager, the final component. Dow Jones offers a fundamental analysis package, the Market Microscope, but it is not supported by an off-line database, so there is no place to park the data you bring down. It is thus a stand-alone program and cannot be regarded as a part of an integrated or complete package. All the pieces for it are there; they just don't fit together.

Interactive Comes in First

The first producer to offer a four-component package of investment software was Interactive Data, a Chase Manhattan subsidiary in Boston. Interactive's primary business is maintaining for mainframe access vast financial databases such as the Standard & Poor's CompuStat and Value Line.

Interactive's package for individual investors is called the Active Investor. The technical analysis component is a direct lift, through a buyout arrangement, of the Anidata Market Analyst. The fundamental package is, in essence, Value Line's old Value/Screen program. It operates on data retrieved over the telephone instead of on floppy disks. The portfolio management component, which is a real beauty, was evidently worked out by Interactive. The three components are tied together with a communications and filing utility which links the system to the Interactive database (and to no other).

The individual components of the Active Investor are reviewed individually in this book. See Chapters 12, 17, and 23. The Active Investor is priced at $495. This is about the value I would place on just two of its three components, the charting and portfolio packages, so it is an attractive software value.

Look Closely at Operating Cost

The cost of operating the Interactive package after you purchase it will be higher than the cost of running the component packages that make it up.

Here is a specific example. On a Saturday morning I brought down into the Savant Technical Investor, from the Warner Computer Systems database, 250 days of high, low, close, and volume data on Genentech. By my stopwatch, it took about a minute. The non-prime-time rate for 1200-bps data retrieval from Warner is 60 cents a minute at this writing, so I spent 60 cents for Genentech's chart. Interactive lists a fixed charge of 3 cents for one day's high, low, close, and volume for a given stock, so the same chart, loaded into the same technical analysis program, would have cost $7.50 from Interactive. If I had used Warner during prime time, I would have spent more for the chart ($1.70), but this is still less than a quarter of Interactive's price.

Whether the higher cost of data will be acceptable to you will depend on your mode of investing. If you trade actively and frequently require complete stock charts, you would do better to accept the higher front-end cost of some other program in order to save forever after on data. But if you are a more typical investor and are chiefly interested in monitoring charts on your own portfolio and perhaps a few related or similar stocks, the steep one-time cost for a single chart from Interactive will not add up to much. After the initial recovery of a chart, you need update it only once each trading day or, if you prefer, once a week. Daily updates on 10 stocks mount up to only $78 per year. Viewed in this light, the Active Investor may be a superior choice. The portfolio manager, which is superb, is updated with the same numbers you bring down to update your charts.

The fundamental data, which is Value Line's, cost $25 or $40 per month, depending on whether you select reported data only or the fuller data provided by the complete Value Line service. The complete service includes Value Line's timeliness and other ratings and will probably be helpful if you'd rather read earnings projections than run them.

The complete service puts you in touch with a body of opinion which is scrutinized by professional and private investors alike. The service's opinion may be accepted wholesale, piecemeal, or not at all, but it is part of the daily lore of the marketplace and is therefore important to you. Whether it is worth $480 a year will depend once again on your approach to investing. A Value Line executive told me that the company's most successful floppy subscription service is the Quarterly, which then cost about $100. The floppy service, as purchased direct from Value Line, has two flaws. Both are associated with the decay of the value of the data. Price data recorded on the disk could go stale in the mail on the way to you. Earnings and other fundamentals change more gradually with the passage of time, but they certainly do change.

The Interactive Investor does not completely solve the problems inherent in the original (and ongoing) floppy-based Value/Screen subscription program, but it certainly represents an improvement. First, you can manually update fundamental data on any individual company. Second, fundamental (and price and price-based) data on about 125 companies per week are updated over the wire as part of the service. Value Line covers about 1650 stocks, so Interactive's electronic updating will completely refresh your database once a quarter.

No provision has been made for the automatic modification of prices and price-based information in the fundamental database (including betas, price/earnings ratios, etc.). You can manually change these values, but there is no automatic update and recalculation feature, as there is in the excellent Savant Fundamental Investor program. You do get complete price updates, along with all other data, on the 125 stocks per week. You could not separately bring down 1650 prices over the wire and expect the program to plug them automatically into the fundamental database. This would be a rather costly ($48 at Interactive's rates) but occasional exercise—and necessary.

It seems pointless (to me, anyway) to launch a fundamental screen without the most current P/Es, PSRs, price/book ratios, and betas. The program is not as "integrated" in this area as it can be. The other limitation is the number and type of stocks Value Line tracks. The 1650 stocks are drawn chiefly from the ranks of exchange-listed and high-marketability stocks; the selection itself is part of the service. But if you want to follow over-the-counter growth stocks, you would do better with a broader database. Savant's, which is based on the Disclosure database, includes up to 10,000 stocks. This is excessive, but you can select and retrieve your subset of data from this broad universe. These are "as reported" data, however, and are therefore likely to be less reliable in comparative analyses than Value Line's data.

Note that the fundamental data service provided by Interactive is not necessarily billed to you if you buy the program. You can sign up for the service or leave it alone. When you consider the low initial price of the Active Investor, you must conclude that one of the three major components (fundamental, technical, or portfolio) has been in effect thrown in for free.

If you do technical analysis primarily (as most computerized investors probably do at this stage), the Active Investor is not the best choice. It provides excellent charting and portfolio management capabilities, but the cost of quotes from Interactive is so high as to discourage extensive charting. Similarly, if you do fundamental analysis primarily, you might save by going to Value Line directly, using its floppy service (with all its limitations), and using the Value/Screen Plus or a stand-alone portfolio manager. If you do fundamental analysis in deadly earnest, Savant's Fundamental Analyst coupled with a third-party portfolio manager is the best approach. When Savant finishes its own portfolio manager, you might look at that component as well.

If you have no particular bias toward fundamental or technical analysis and want a beautifully packaged product that does it all, I recommend the Active Investor. The analytical packages are still state of the art. The portfolio manager is easily the best choice for individual investors, and the documentation is excellent. You can save on operating costs by piecing together a similar package from available stand-alone components, but there is a compelling discount if you buy the three offered by Interactive—and they are, to a degree, integrated. It isn't just a software sandwich. The components can access a common pool of data retrieved by a common communications utility.

One reservation: The Active Investor is hermetically sealed against any source of data other than that offered by Interactive. You can't get into Dow Jones or other sources for news, searches, and gossip, so you'll need some other communications capability (program) for that crucial function. The market is not just a stream of numbers. You need qualitative information as well, and in this regard the program falls short of complete integration. Many modems are supplied with a communications program tucked into the box, so you could use one of these programs for access to news. I frequently resort to Smart Com II, the communications program which came with my Hayes 1200B, for this purpose.

Telescan: An Integrated Program You Can Buy for $49.95: Do It

I am going to invent a story about the moment of conception for this unique program. Let's say somebody associated with Telescan, perhaps its author, was seated in front of a monitor watching as 24 days of closing prices were being retrieved in the conventional manner from one of the conventional databases. It was his intention to capture these numbers, store them, and then use them to plot a stock chart.

But he happened to notice, sitting there, that in order to paint just 48 little numbers on the monitor screen (24 closing prices and 24 volume totals), the monitor had to go through the same motions it might in painting a detailed picture, e.g., a TV picture or, more to the point, a stock chart.

Well, why not just send the stock chart over the phone instead of the numbers? And so, in this apocryphal story anyway, Telescan's business was born. It consists of a program that costs $49.95 and a deep database of charts on 6500 stocks, extending back as many as 12 years.

It turns out that the cost to the customer of receiving a complete stock chart is far lower than the cost of bringing down the numbers it would take to plot that chart. The cost of using the database is $15 an hour in off-prime time. It is thus permissible to go on-line to Telescan's database and simply *stay* on-line, luxuriating in the data for an hour at a stretch, sifting and analyzing charts. Telescan is the ultimate low-cost on-line chart service. It has 6500 stocks and groups of stocks in the database, covering the NYSE, the AMEX, and the OTC markets, with data ranging back 12 years.

A Fundamentalist's Chart Service?

Telescan's designers have been compelled by the medium they invented for broadcasting charts over the telephone to convey all sorts of information, both technical and fundamental, by means of charts.

The technical charting capabilities are similar in kind but slightly less comprehensive than those offered by the conventional charting programs from Dow Jones, Savant, MetaStock, and Summa. The fundamental charting capability is available in no other widely marketed program. Telescan's concerted effort to illustrate fundamental data may turn out to be the more profound and lasting innovation associated with the program. It represents investment software "integration" in a new sense of the word: Telescan applies the program utilities associated with charting to the display and analysis of fundamental data.

In most cases, fundamental charts link balance sheet and income data to stock prices by illustrating various ratios and their historical extreme values. Figure 21.1 shows how this works for the price/earnings ratio. It is a prototype for charting many fundamental ratios.

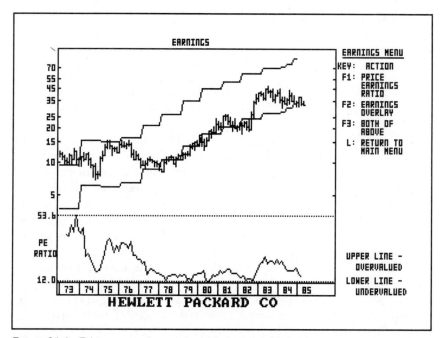

Figure 21.1. Telescan typically provides both fundamental and technical data on a single screen. This chart relates price to earnings via the familiar price/earnings ratio and is a prototype for Telescan's charting method. The bars represent the usual plot of high, low, and closing values for Hewlett-Packard stock. Bracketing the price bars are two staircaselike plots. These brackets represent upper and lower limits on the price. They are calculated from the current earnings and the historical high and low P/E ratios. The lower panel is a 12-year plot of the P/E ratio. Telescan's data go back to January 1, 1973. Most conventional charting programs focus on the just-current trading year. Telescan data cost less to transmit, and the program thus offers great value.

The lower panel is a 12-year plot of the P/E of Hewlett-Packard from 1973 to 1985. The extreme high and low values are noted at the vertical axis. The historical low value is at the baseline of the chart.

The upper panel of the screen is a standard high/low/close price bar chart. Superimposed on it, however, and bracketing the price values, are two lines resembling parallel staircases. They are meant to be understood as limiting values on the price of the stock. The most recent points along the upper boundary are calculated by multiplying the highest historical price/earnings ratio by the most current earnings. The computer then retreats into the past one year and repeats the calculation using that year's earnings. It repeats the calculation using earnings as reported for each of the years on the chart. The result is a staircase plot of maximum reasonable prices.

Here is the annual calculation:

The year's earnings × price/earnings (highest ever) =
price at the upper limit of plausibility

Similarly, the calculation of the lower boundary line requires the computer to multiply each year's current earnings by the historical *low* for the price/earnings ratio.

Between the two boundary lines is a price range, based on current earnings, which I would designate as historically plausible or reasonable. Telescan has somewhat higher ambitions for the overlaid price boundaries. The documentation and the screen both urge that prices above the upper boundary indicate overvaluation and that prices below the lower boundary indicate undervaluation. In my view a price below the lowest boundary and trending down may indicate a stock that is simply sinking out of sight. This does not diminish the effectiveness of the two boundary lines as a tool. For a quick sense of the meaning of today's stock price, it is a superb presentation. It helps you ignore as trivial most of the daily whimsies of the marketplace. If you are a long-term investor, you can use the program to view a selected stock's P/E within a 12-year frame of reference.

The Price/Book Ratio

Figure 21.2 shows a price/book value ratio. Note that the ratio, which expresses the current price as a percentage of book value, is plotted in the lower panel. As with the P/E ratio, maximum and minimum values are noted along the vertical axis. These maxima and minima are used to calculate the boundary lines bracketing the price in the upper chart. The purpose is to establish a historically plausible range of prices in terms of this ratio. Note that in the lower panel, when the price is below 100 percent of book value, the chart is filled in with a solid background. When a stock is selling below its book value, it should (theoretically) actually rise to the level of the book value in the event of bankruptcy. Book value is the liquidation value of the company on paper. Be skeptical and careful about these values.

Some speculators hunt for special situations among companies selling below book. They specifically look for a company for which bankruptcy would be unthinkable. An unthinkable bankruptcy would be, for example, that of an aerospace contractor manufacturing some component crucial to the national defense. Things have a way of working out all

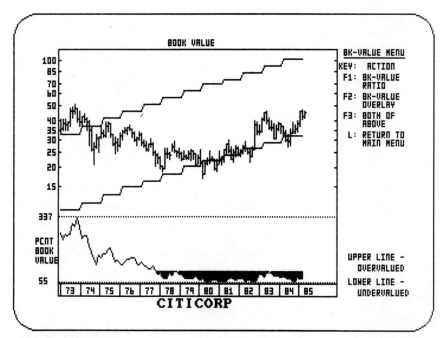

Figure 21.2. The price/book value ratio plotted for Citicorp. The calculation of the upper and lower limits bracketing price is similar in principle to that used for price/earnings ratios in Figure 21.1. Note that in the lower panel, when the price drops below 100 percent of book value, the chart is filled in with a solid background. It is an elegant graphic technique and a vivid way to show that the stock price has submerged beneath its book value.

right after all for such companies, and stocks selling below book are very cheap indeed.

The program uses solid inlays of the type shown in Figure 21.2 beautifully both in this type of application and in technical oscillator charts, e.g., plots of momentum and moving-average differences.

The Price to ____ Ratio Carried to Its Logical Conclusion

Altogether, Telescan will construct six different ratios relating fundamental data to price: price/earnings, price/book value, price/cash flow, price/dividends, price/capital spending, and price/sales. In addition, it will plot a price/composite indicator assembled from any or all of the six fundamental value denominators. If you are a hunter of growth stocks, for example, you might favor a composite of price/capital spending and price/sales. The basic notion can and probably will be extended to include even more fundamental indicators. In every case, a chart like those shown in Figures 21.1 and 21.2 is produced, showing the historical plot of the ratio and an overlay of plausible price limits derived from its historical extreme values.

Nonprice Indicators

Telescan uses the lower panel to plot two types of indicators which will not naturally conform to the price ratio structure. These are the short-interest ratio, which relates the current short interest to the current volume in the stock (or index), and the insider trading indicator. Figure 21.3 shows short interest in the lower panel of the screen. The largest

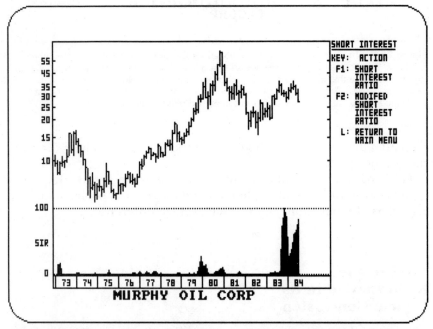

Figure 21.3. Short sellers must eventually buy a stock to cover their positions, and so a large number of short sales create a latent demand for a stock. The demand can become overt quite suddenly in the form of panic buying. Some traders therefore use the short-interest ratio as a bullish indicator. It is plotted here for Murphy Oil over the span from 1973 to 1984. If you chart short interest for various stocks, you can check on its validity as a leading indicator for those stocks. No other program offers this capability.

value for the ratio is adjusted to 100, and the indicator thus varies between 0 and 100. Very high levels of short interest in a stock are believed to presage a rally because short sellers must buy the stock to cover their purchases. Sometimes panic buying on the part of short sellers can be induced by a sudden rally in the stock, and this fuels a further rally. If you notice from the chart a surge in short interest, you can often consider it a bullish signal. It is not a sufficiently strong signal, however, to warrant a buy in the absence of other positive signs.

Figure 21.4 shows the treatment of insider transactions. This information is not commonly presented as an indicator in graphic form. More often one sees direct transcriptions of tabular reports to the SEC of stock transactions on the part of officers, directors, and large shareholders. Telescan sorts the buy and sell transactions and arranges them against a time base. The price bar chart in the upper panel makes it possible to judge how to use the indicator. It comes as a surprise to some investors that insiders often have rotten luck with the timing of their buying and

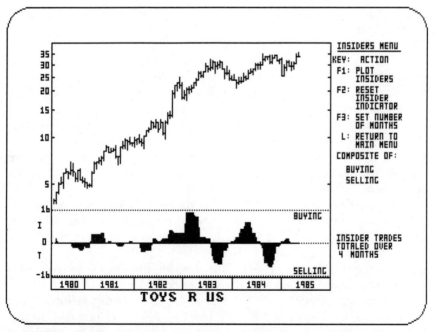

Figure 21.4. Insiders quite often have rotten luck buying and selling. This comes as a great surprise to some investors, perhaps because cynicism has come to prevail among us, but it is true. Telescan has created an indicator from insider data, which is conventionally distributed as a simple tabulation of transactions. The indicator can be plotted against a stock's price history as shown here, and this enables you to judge the judgment of the insiders. This is another Telescan exclusive.

selling. If they are consistently wrong, of course, the indicator is perfectly usable; just visualize it upside down.

Telescan provides options that enable you to view separately the buying, selling, and stock options transactions of insiders. These data are, incidentally, packaged for sale from other sources at rather fancy prices. Telescan includes this in its database at no extra charge.

Time Frames and the Cost of Telescan Data

Day 1 of the Telescan database is January 1, 1973. One year of daily data is kept on file. Prior to that, weekly data are maintained on file. To select the number of years you wish to view, just enter it from the keyboard. If you want more than nine years of data, the equal sign (=) will elicit a chart of data running all the way back to January 1973. If you are examining the current year only, you can stipulate the number of months constituting the time base by using the function keys. F1 retrieves a one-month chart, F6 retrieves a six-month chart, and so on up to ten months.

The long-term database, coupled with virtually instantaneous chart retrieval, makes this program very different from conventional programs that bring down data a day at a time. One would not out of casual curiosity drag down 12 years of data on a stock just to see what the chart looked like. In an extreme case you could spend $25 on such a chart using a conventional database service. If you were merely window-shopping for stocks, you could run up a very big bill at that rate. On Telescan, you can snick through several 12-year charts in a minute, as if you were turning the pages of a book of charts. This facility for browsing through charts is not accessible with any other type of program.

The off-prime-time cost of using the database is $15 an hour, or just 25 cents a minute. The prime-time cost is twice that. You can afford to log on to the database and luxuriate in it for an hour or so every now and then.

You can capture data as well. The program provides for rapid automatic retrieval and storage based on a preset (by you) list of stock charts. Each chart can be configured as you wish. The full capabilities of the program cannot be applied to saved charts, however. You can do just four things with them: moving-average smoothing, trend line drawing, momentum analysis, and cycle analysis. For any other sort of analysis, you should design the retrieval instructions to run the analysis on-line and then save the resulting chart. With care, you can get on-line and off-line in a fairly short time, but the program is not really designed for it. If you use Telescan, you will use its database quite a lot. That's why the program is priced virtually as a loss leader and why the per-time charges are so reasonable.

Technical Analysis

Figure 21.5 shows a standard chart of price and volume with smoothing trend lines drawn in by the program.

Telescan was originally introduced at $495, a full order of magnitude greater than its present price. At the higher price it would be regarded as priced on an equal footing with the other major technical analysis packages. Judged solely as a technical analysis program, it was probably about $150 high at $495, as it offers less comprehensive technical capability than Summa or Savant. It smooths prices with simple or exponential moving averages but not with weighted moving averages, and

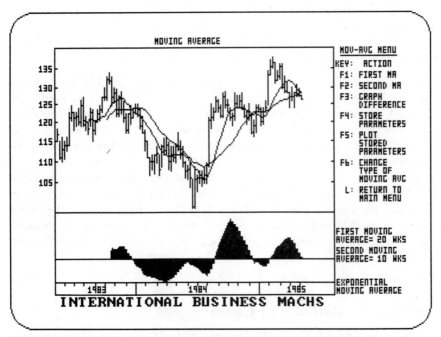

Figure 21.5. This is how the program handles two conventional technical charting techniques. The moving-average difference oscillator is particularly useful. The solid inlays help your eye. The moving-average curves are exponential. The program will do both simple and exponential averages but not weighted moving averages. It is about one notch less capable in every area than the $500 programs. It costs only $50, however, and provides fundamental and historical depth available from no other source.

smoothing can be applied only to price data. It will not draw envelopes. It draws point-to-point trend lines, linear regression lines, and parallel lines. It does not draw horizontal or vertical lines by specialized command, nor will it position lines using statistical relations (i.e., plus or minus one or two standard deviations). It has no provision for speed resistance lines.

Momentum and moving-average difference oscillators are easier to set up and prettier on display with this program than with any other. The program does not, however, enable you to superimpose families of curves. It runs conventional relative strength, but not in the J. Welles Wilder sense. One could go on in this vein, but the conclusion seems clear. The Telescan program will handle all the basic techniques of technical analysis. It does not offer the depth and detailing of the major $500 technical programs.

But Telescan costs $49.95, not $500. It offers capabilities you cannot obtain with the purely technical programs, including the freedom to browse through charts and the unique correlation with fundamental, short-selling, and insider data.

Groups and Indexes

The database includes about 175 groups and indexes. The indexes appear comprehensive and range from the obvious (the DJIA and the NASDAQ industrial index) to the not so obvious but useful-sounding yen exchange rate and municipal bond buyers' 20-bond index. All the standard stock groups are included, such as shoes, soaps, toys, semiconductors, homebuilding, and broadcasting.

It is in my view a great strength of the Dow Jones software that it enables you to construct indexes of your own. This is a valuable pursuit but a costly one compared with the standard offerings from Telescan. Because of the low price of the service, it would be economically feasible to browse through the charts of stock groups and inform yourself about where the action is.

Recommendation and Caveat

You would do well to buy this program first. If you already own a more conventional program package, you should buy this program second. At the price, it will get you off to a great start or nicely expand your existing capabilities. The caveat is this: At the end of your first year after purchase, Telescan may or may not ask for an annual maintenance fee for continuing the database service into subsequent years. The company has been discussing this. I don't see how the fee could exceed the going-in price of $49.95, however, lest we all just go and purchase the program anew.

And Wishful Thinking

Inherent in this program is the promise of a very helpful fundamental analysis tool: an earnings projector. Given the 12 years or more of data that already exist in the database and the linear regression utility that is already written into the program, it should be possible to write a rudimentary risk/reward evaluation program and include it with the Telescan program as a crowning touch.

Sources and Prices

TELESCAN
Telescan, Inc.
11011 Richmond Ave., Suite 600
Houston, TX 77042
(713) 952-1060

Price: $49.95

THE ACTIVE INVESTOR
Interactive Data Corporation
303 Wyman St.
Waltham, MA 02154
(617) 895-4300

Price: $495

PART 6

On-Line Services

22

How to Select and Use Financial Databases

Which Software Goes with Which Database:

Data for investors are made available by commercial databases. There are hundreds of databases to access in various fields, but when you select software, you perforce narrow the field to just those databases which are compatible with your program.

Here is a summary tabulation of the major software packages and the databases to which they provide access:

Anidata Market Analyst (no longer marketed)	Warner Computer Systems Compuserve
Dow Jones Market Analyzer Plus	Dow Jones
Interactive's Active Investor	Interactive (includes Value Line data)
Savant software	Warner Computer Systems Dow Jones
Summa software	Dial Data (Hale) Dow Jones

MetaStock

Compuserve
Commodity Systems Inc.
Hale Systems
IDS (Interactive Data)
I.P. Sharp
Nite Line
Warner

Trendline II

Warner

Telescan

Telescan

Many beginning users wonder whether they will be charged for long-distance connections to commercial databases. The answer is no. In most cities of any size the databases are accessible via local numbers. In the country and in the wilderness you can in most cases arrange for an 800-number connection.

The Four Kinds of Data You Actually Need

You need four kinds of data: current quotes, historical quotes, fundamental data, and news.

For current quotes, you should use an FM radio modem or TV cable service to monitor the market continuously. There is no database from which current quotes are drawn for quote broadcasts. The data come straight from the market. If you want to follow your stocks in real time, you must pay an exchange fee; otherwise, the stream is delayed 15 minutes before broadcast. In practice, when FM and TV cable services are first turned on, the data may take a bit longer to acquire and display.

The Impact of FM and TV Cable Quote and News Services

You can turn on an FM modem in the morning before the market opens and leave it on all day. It keeps a running track of current prices in its own memory so that you can use the computer for other things and access the modem whenever you grow curious about your portfolio. FM data cost a minimum of $20 per month. The modem can watch as many as 350 stocks simultaneously. The data are purchased from the company which supplies your FM modem. TV cable services are similar. They watch more stocks or deliver more news but tend to require the full-time attention of your computer for continuous monitoring. There are ways around this. See Chapters 6 and 7 for a comparison of the two types of services.

If you don't have FM or cable, it's time to get one or the other. In the meantime, you can use a phone modem to call Dow Jones for current (delayed 15 minutes) quotes. The Source also offers them, as does Compuserve. Some stocks, notably the OTC and OTC supplemental stocks, are not yet included in some FM ticker loops. The NASDAQ national market stocks are broadcast, but for information on the smaller OTC issues you still may have to use a dial-up service or call your broker for a quote, as of old.

For historical quotes, the best sources in my experience are Warner and Telescan. Their databases go back for over a decade, and they are inexpensive to use. Their transmission formats are compact so that data retrieval is speedy. Inefficient data transmission is notably a problem I experienced with the Dow Jones service. The data are neatly formatted into a tabulation of high, low, close, and volume, and as the data come down over the wire you can watch the neat columns of numbers as they soldier down your monitor screen. Unfortunately, it takes a great many blank spaces to separate and order these neat columns, and you are paying for the time it requires to transmit and receive the blank spaces. Warner sends data in a closely packed format, and Telescan uses a unique full-chart transmission system. Telescan is the only service you can use to casually browse through chart after chart without running up monstrous bills for data retrieval.

After a year or two with FM or TV cable, you may not require much in the way of historical data. If you specialize in a group, you can accumulate your own database from the daily closes as reported on the FM modem or TV decoder. You can accumulate quotes in a spreadsheet such as Lotus 1-2-3. A macro command which files each day's high, low, and closing prices is included in the sample FM portfolio-monitoring template shown in Figure 20.2. In practice, you push the Alt key and the A key simultaneously, and the day's closing results for all your stocks are added to the top of a stack of cumulative historical data.

To plot accumulated FM or TV cable data on a stock's history in a technical analysis program, use Lotus utilities to drop the broadcast data for that stock into a DIF file. The MetaStock program will pick up and plot this information, as will (perhaps rather surprisingly) the Dow Jones Market Analyzer Plus, at least in the version I have seen. Summa and Savant offer databridge programs to enable you to graph DIF files, but these programs are extra-cost items. Savant's, for example, costs $145 at this writing.

Fundamental Data On-Line

For substantial blocks of fundamental data, the only on-line source priced within reason for private investors and smaller institutional investors is the Value Line database. It is accessible via the Active Investor program only. With this single exception, I would suggest that you buy fundamental data on floppy disks (from Value Line, Savant, S&P, or Gibson) or enter the data yourself from printed sources. Floppy services cost about $25 to $100 per floppy. If you do screening work on floppy disk data and subsequently download fundamentals for a selected few stocks, the Savant Disclosure database is fine. But do not try to bring down data in quantity from any interactive (note the lowercase i) source. You can spend $6000 filling a single 360K floppy disk with data via modem from a top-quality on-line database. This is absurd even if you are an adviser or manager and can spread the cost across a large number of investors.

If you need a quick report on-line for a particular company, I suggest you use Warner Computer Systems or Schwab's Equalizer. Bear in mind, however, that Disclosure can send you photocopied reports overnight via Federal Express, and anyway, if you are examining fundamentals, you ought to be taking your time about it—musing.

On-Line News

The most popular dial-up news source is Dow Jones. You can gain access to this crucial database from most investment programs by selecting from the menu a terminal mode or a news mode. If your investment program does not have a terminal mode, you can use a separate communications package. I use Smart Com II, which came with my Hayes 1200B. There are many other popular communications packages. Crosstalk and PC Talk are favorites.

A subscription to the Standard & Poor's MarketScope costs $36 a year, and usage charges are based on the number of pages of data you bring down. The cost is $1.50 for 15 pages of data, with a $1.50 minimum per log-on. The service is particularly helpful in keeping up with market and specific stock trends in the course of a trading day. It also provides detailed historical data on 4600 stocks. I would dial this service first if anything abrupt and mysterious happened to the market or to one of my stocks.

The best broadcast news source is the X*Press TV cable service, though the other broadcast services provide limited news. X*Press enables your computer to run *live* key word searches as it monitors multiple news wires. You will get immediate notice whenever news about one of your stocks or groups appears. The cost is quite reasonable compared with that of dial-ups.

Don't Go On-Line without a Definite Plan

Know what you want before you venture on-line to any dial-up news or data service. Follow a specific research plan. Otherwise, imagine that you have taken a taxi to the back door of a major public library. You ask the cabby to wait and venture through the back door into the stacks. You wander about scanning book titles without the benefit of author, subject, or title cards. In the meantime, *the meter is running.*

I always keep a stopwatch next to my computer. When I log on to a commercial database, I start the watch. If too much time passes unfruitfully, I suddenly shut down the computer. I suppose this is the computerist's equivalent of slamming down the phone receiver. It's an expressive way to hang up.

Specialized Databases

There are two databases which are useful in tracking levels of institutional holdings in various stocks, potential takeover targets, and insider transactions. They are Vickers and Spectrum. Insider data are also provided in the Telescan database.

Hot Lines

Many investment advisory services provide, as part of their subscription packages, a telephone hot line. In the past this typically consisted of a recorded voice message from the adviser indicating portfolio changes or changes in stop-loss or target prices.

Some advisers now offer computer-direct hot lines via an on-line service called TeleShare. By making a local or 800-number call, investors can download hot line messages into their computers. The computer can capture and record the information more accurately than an investor making a quick handwritten transcript of a verbal telephone message. Some of the numerical data can be detailed and intricate. Same-day receipt of advisory information is definitely worth something. The value of the advice in an advisory newsletter tends to decay dramatically with each day it spends in the mail system. This is particularly true of letters which recommend high-volatility issues such as options or commodity futures.

TeleShare also provides a service of its own called the Investor's Resource. It is a sampling of commentary from various advisers, usually current to the day or, at most, the week.

Translation Programs

Some specialized programs are available to help you transfer database information into a spreadsheet by way of a DIF file. You can use the spreadsheet to operate on the data directly or simply as a way station for data in passage to one of the charting programs.

Savant and Summa, as noted, offer optional extra-cost programs that are supposed to function as bridges between their software and that of Lotus, Ashton-Tate, et al. The Dow Jones Market Analyzer Plus and MetaStock do not require these bridges to plot from DIF files.

To get data off the wire and into a spreadsheet, you need a communications package and some additional software, a converter, which makes the data you have brought down acceptable to a spreadsheet. One such program, LoadCalc by Micro Decision Systems, provides conversion capability only. Others combine communications with conversion programs in one package, including the Dow Jones Spreadsheet Link, the Data Connection from Quantitative Financial Services, and MQINT (you try to pronounce it) from Compuserve.

If you buy a charting package, there is little point purchasing a third-party conversion program. They are rather costly and have perhaps been made obsolete by the advent of specialized investment software.

If you intend to accumulate FM or TV cable data in a spreadsheet, you may wish to bring in a year's worth of data over the telephone to start the file. In this application it is helpful to have a spreadsheet link, but you probably will not use it much after the initial downloads.

If you are maintaining a portfolio manager on a spreadsheet, such as the Value/Screen Plus portfolio manager and you need only current quotes, you can bring them in with Market Link, an $85 program that accesses current quotes only (but no historical data) from Dow Jones or the Source.

Sources and Prices for Databases

COMPUSERVE
Information Services Division
5000 Arlington Centre Blvd.
Columbus, OH 43220
(614) 457-8600

Prices: Usage rates vary during the day, and there is a $100 minimum contractual obligation for business information service. At night, however, the rate is $6 an hour at 300 baud and $12.50 an hour at 1200 baud. A starter kit, which includes five hours of usage, is just $39.95. There are surcharges for Microquote. The Standard & Poor's CompuStat is accessible through this vendor. It is perhaps the premier fundamental database and is of interest chiefly to institutions. The rates are beyond the reach of most individual investors.

DIAL DATA
Hale Systems Inc.
Remote Computing Division
1044 Northern Blvd.
Roslyn, NY 11576
(516) 484-4545

Prices: About 2 cents per quote, with a $15 per month minimum charge. One stock for one year, $1.50.

DOW JONES NEWS RETRIEVAL
P.O. Box 300
Princeton, NJ 08540
(800) 452-2000

Prices: Prices range from 15 cents a minute for off-prime-time quotes to $1.20 per minute for prime-time news and other services. Varies with baud rate. Several pricing programs.

INTERACTIVE DATA
303 Wyman St.
Waltham, MA 02154
(617) 895-4300

Prices: Three cents per quote to the Active Investor program. Also provides Value Line data at prices set by Value Line. Currently these are $25 per month for fundamental data and $40 per month for fundamental data, plus Value Line's rankings and projections.

S&P MARKETSCOPE
Standard & Poor's Corporation
25 Broadway
New York, NY 10004
(800) 654-8855

Prices: Annual subscription, $36 per year. Cost per 15 billable pages is $1.50, and there is a $1.50 minimum each time you log on. Menus and other system pages are free.

TELESCAN
11011 Richmond Avenue, Suite 600
Houston, TX 77042
(713) 952-1060

Prices: $30 per hour for prime, $15 per hour for off-prime. Includes historical price and fundamental data, short interest, and insider transactions.

TELESHARE
1305 Duff Drive
Fort Collins, CO 80524
(303) 493-7304

Prices: 25 cents to 35 cents per minute off-prime. Distributed via Dialcom network. Individual advisers may charge premiums for their hot lines.

WARNER COMPUTER SYSTEMS
605 Third Avenue
New York, NY 10158
(212) 986-1919
(800) 626-4634

Prices: 60 cents for off-prime, $1.70 for prime at 1200 bps. At 300 baud, the corresponding rates are 30 cents and 85 cents. Compact transmission format means you don't download many blank spaces, as you do with some other services. A treasure trove of historical data back to 1975. Transmits fundamental data as well. Handles the Disclosure/Savant download, Exchange Master, and CompuStat at various prices.

VICKERS ON-LINE
226 New York Avenue
Huntington, NY 11743
(800) 645-5043
(516) 423-7710

Prices: $50 per year (includes 30 minutes of free usage), usage charge of $1 per minute. Maintains database on institutional holdings and insider transactions.

SPECTRUM
Computer Directions Advisors, Inc.
11501 Georgia Ave.
Silver Springs, MD 20902
(301) 942-1700

Price: Inquire. Database on institutional holdings.

Sources and Prices for Communications Software

Note: most modem manufacturers supply communications software free with the purchase of a modem.

PC TALK III
The Headlands Press Inc.
P.O. Box 862
Tiburon, CA 94920
(415) 435-0770

Price: Public domain. Contribute $35.

CROSSTALK XVI
Microstuf Inc.
1000 Holcomb Wood Parkway
Roswell, GA 30076
(404) 998-3998

Price: $195. Sample diskette available. Widely regarded as the state-of-the-art communications package.

THE DOWNLOADER
Computer Asset Management
P.O. Box 26743
Salt Lake City, UT 84126
(801) 964-0391

Price: $49 if purchased alone, $29 if purchased along with MetaStock. Provides MetaStock with access to Warner.

Communications plus Translation Software

DOW JONES SPREADSHEET LINK
Dow Jones
P.O. Box 300
Princeton, NJ 08540
(800) 257-5114

Price: $249. Loads Dow Jones into VisiCalc, Lotus 1-2-3, and Multiplan. Also acts as a communications program.

LOADCALC
Micro Decision Systems
P.O. Box 1392
Pittsburgh, PA 15230
(412) 854-4070

Price: $175. Converts files captured from any on-line database into formats that can be used by Lotus 1-2-3, Symphony, SuperCalc, Multiplan, VisiCalc, and other popular spreadsheets, databases, and graphics programs. Translation only; does not include communications capability.

THE DATA CONNECTION
Quantitative Financial Services
P.O. Box 565
Ardsley, NY 10502
(914) 591-6990

Price: $110. Downloads and converts Compuserve data into format for VisiCalc, Lotus 1-2-3, or Symphony. Also loads data for the Compu-Trac technical analysis program.

MARKET LINK
Smith Micro Software Inc.
P.O. Box 7137
Huntington Beach, CA 92615
(714) 964-0412

Price: $85. Recovers current price data from Dow Jones or the Source and loads the data into spreadsheets. A logical companion program to Value/Screen Plus for spreadsheet users.

SUMMA SWITCHBOARD
Summa Technologies, Inc.
P.O. Box 2046
Beaverton, OR 97075
(503) 644-3212

Price: $150. A family of programs that are advertised as links between the major database suppliers, the popular spreadsheets, dBASE II and WordStar, and Winning on Wall Street. One possible way to get accumulated FM or TV cable data into the Summa charting package.

THE TECHNICAL DATABRIDGE
THE FUNDAMENTAL DATABRIDGE
Savant Corporation
P.O. Box 440278
Houston, TX 77244
(800) 231-9900
(713) 556-8363

Price: $145 each. The Technical Databridge transfers price-volume data between the Savant Technical Investor and Lotus 1-2-3, SuperCalc, and other spreadsheet programs. This is one way to provide access to FM or TV cable data for the Savant program. The Fundamental Databridge transfers fundamental data between the Fundamental Investor and spreadsheets.

23
On-Line Brokerage Services

Why?

There are no important advantages to be gained by transmitting instructions to your broker via computer. Your orders will not be executed more quickly; you will not establish a "direct instantaneous link" to the exchange floor. What you will get in the final analysis is a means of communicating with your broker by typing over the phone instead of talking over the phone.

If you can talk better than you can type (and most people two-finger their computer keyboards), why use an on-line brokerage? Why peck away so diligently at the task of sending your broker a commission when a few carefully chosen words over the phone will suffice? Leaving aside the admitted conveniences of quick order confirmation and tidy record keeping, where is the main advantage?

The main advantage lies with the brokerage. An on-line brokerage service should be understood as a marketing device conceived by brokerages to gather in the business of computerized investors. Computerized investors are uniquely desirable customers. Among us are some of the heaviest, savviest, and most venturesome traders in the market. Viewed as a marketing target, we represent a large and easily found group of prequalified dream customers for any brokerage.

But the on-line brokerage service per se isn't much of a draw once you've looked past the technological novelty of it, and the brokerages know this. To make their basic buy and sell services attractive, they surround them with discounted information and analytical services. At a minimum, the service will offer a discounted stream of on-line quotes. The quote stream is in fact the centerpiece and main attraction for many traders, but there is more. A highly developed system, such as that offered by Security Pacific Brokers, Inc., may be used in lieu of purchased software for option analysis, intraday and historical charting, fundamental stock screens, and portfolio risk optimization. From most of the brokerages you can gain access to corporate news, market commentary and statistics, and research. One brokerage, Schwab, supplies communications and portfolio management software along with a nice collection of discounts and initial free-time packages (typically an hour) from the on-line news, commentary, and data services that support the software.

How to Select an On-Line Brokerage

It is the discounted, bonus, and extra services that make on-line brokerages worth a second look. In choosing between on-line brokers, first evaluate the commissions charged by the brokerages and then take a look at their menus of on-line services and charges.

To some degree, the on-line brokers are competing with one another for your business, but they are also competing with packaged software in the arena of decision support services such as portfolio management, option analysis, and fundamental stock screening. They are also competing in a minor way with the various on-line news and financial information resources, since these brokers typically offer discounted usage charges for access to quote streams and many of the basic services and databases. Access to brokerages is nevertheless available through Dow Jones, Compuserve, and the Source. Surprisingly, the discounted services (chiefly quotes) from brokers are provided over the same wire the database services might have used to convey their fully priced quotes.

If you have a steady requirement for analytical services, you will do better to purchase an appropriate dedicated analytical software package. If you have a heavy requirement for quotes, use FM or cable. Ditto the news. Fundamental financial databases are most reasonable via floppy subscriptions.

But for occasional requirements and for people who are just getting started, the brokers offer excellent alternatives to outright software, data, and hardware purchases. The hardware and software requirements are absolutely minimal. In communicating with the brokerage's mainframe-based service, your computer will in most cases act as a "dumb" terminal. It doesn't take much of a computer to do this, but you will require a modem. The only software required is a rudimentary communication program. Modem manufacturers typically include one along with the hardware, and there are nominally priced communications packages in circulation in the public domain. (Ask for one at a user group meeting.) Schwab's Equalizer is basically a specialized communications program with a portfolio manager appended. Security Pacific also offers a communication program, and although you could use a generalized program instead, you'll get more performance out of their service if you use their software.

As one might expect, if your initial commitment to hardware and software is low, the upkeep (usage charges) will be quite high. Most of the computer power you purchased a PC to obtain will simply sit idle if you use the computer as a dumb terminal. Over time, it will pay to upgrade from any "live" on-line services to software that goes on-line briefly, snatches data, and then goes off-line to analyze the data. This saves a tremendous amount of money in usage charges and puts your computer power to work.

Schwab's Financial Independence package includes some fundamental stock analysis and charting programs. Although I cannot recommend this particular package to serious private investors or professionals, it does point in the direction of a more attractive technology for brokerage services; the program puts your computer to work and saves you money in terms of usage charges. All the other brokerage services considered here—those of Quick & Reilly, Thomas F. White, C.D. Anderson, Security Pacific, Fidelity Brokerage, Charles Spear, and E.F. Hutton—are all dumb terminal services. They do almost everything on-line. Some are perhaps a little smarter than others, but the dumb terminal link is in general a rather primitive and costly form of technology for private investors and professionals to use as a steady resource.

Meanwhile, for solving occasional problems, the on-line brokerage services are great. For example, a fundamental stock screen is hardly a daily requirement for most individuals. For these investors, it makes better sense to go on-line to a brokerage such as Security Pacific. Security's On-Line Advantage service will let you use software resident in its mainframe to screen the Wilshire fundamental database.

If you need to run a screen only once a year or so, it makes sense to "borrow" the brokerage's mainframe software and database to get the job done. Chances are that the usage charge will be lower than the charge you would incur by calling a nonbrokerage on-line database.

The alternative is to purchase a screening package and maintain by downloading or floppy subscription a database of your own. The saving achieved by not purchasing fundamental analysis software can be as much as $500. If you do much screening, however (I do it every day, and other advisers, managers, and heavy traders do too), pick a package such as Savant's Fundamental Investor, Value Line's Value/Screen Plus, or the Standard & Poor's StockPak II.

On-line charges for fundamental screening, even at the reasonable rates available through the brokerages, can mount very quickly. I think I would spend about $100 on-line to run one of our typical screens. Once a year that would be fine. Once a day would be out of the question. If you screen frequently, you can do a better job at far lower cost over time with a dedicated screening software package fueled by floppies and an occasional highly selective or preprogrammed "whoosh" download (see Chapter 17).

Similarly, if you require lots of quotes, get FM or a cable link. The price per hour, per quote, per month, or any other way you may wish to calculate it deeply undercuts the price of dial-up quotes from any source, including the brokerages. Allow $20 per month for FM or cable versus $20 per hour or more for on-line quotes over the phone from your broker in prime time. But if you need to download only a few quotes occasionally—for example, once every Saturday morning—it makes sense to use the brokerage for quotes. It will probably cost a bit less than quotes from the more obvious dial-up sources (see the chapter on databases). The favorable pricing on quotes is made available because the brokerages want your trading business. If your requirement for quotes is modest, the price of installing FM or cable may not be justifiable.

The competition from FM and cable is relatively new, and it is causing more than a few traders to abruptly hang up on the dial-up services. Probably the majority of the traders using on-line brokerage services are interested in options. In fact, one brokerage spokesperson estimated that 80 percent of their on-line customers were options traders. For these people, a continuous stream of quotes is crucial. From the standpoint of cost, the FM and cable alternatives, coupled with off-line option analysis software, are nearly irresistible.

But for those who trade options only occasionally, the option analysis services available on-line from several of the brokerages are very attractive indeed. You can run Black-Scholes valuations on-line, using the brokerage's mainframe, and thus learn what the "correct" theoretical value of a given option might be. In this way you can avoid buying an options strategy evaluation software package and save a few hundred dollars.

It's a question of how involved you are in a particular field of investing. If you are a hard-core investor, by all means seek out dedicated software and hardware to support your activities. But if you are a novice or a dabbler in an area such as options trading or fundamental analysis, you can in effect rent the equipment from your broker, on-line, to try your hand. It costs more to rent if you do it indefinitely, but for occasional requirements this is the most sensible course.

Finally, you might as well take advantage of the special services an on-line brokerage will make available to you as a computerized investor. Chances are, you'll find something on the menu you can use in addition to the brokerage service itself, even if you dial up only occasionally.

What If Your Cat Jumps on the Keyboard?

Suppose in the calm of evening, several hours after the New York markets have closed, you elect to place an order with your 24-hour on-line discount broker. You seat yourself before the keyboard, trigger the autodial and automatic log-on functions in your communications package, and wait. Up comes an order menu from your brokerage. You enter an order for 100 shares of IBM.

Suddenly a child shrieks downstairs. You jump and run. It's okay; it turns out your children are just squabbling. You growl over them, right the wrongs, and counsel the wise, and in the meantime your enormously fat Persian cat stomps across the keyboard of the waiting computer on his way to a perch on the window seat. You return to log off. The cat purrs. It is not until late the next day that you learn that you somehow purchased, on the Tokyo exchange, an exceedingly odd number of Singapore hemp futures. In so doing, you (uncharacteristically) went to the absolute limit of your buying power, and in the course of the day's trading, as luck would have it, your newly acquired hemp futures plummeted through the floor of the Tokyo exchange. And here is your margin call, on-line. You owe your broker a zillion yen, but the Japanese are prepared to accept your kind computerized offer to pay them in rials at today's exchange rate. What day *is* it in Japan? Is there a way to undo all this? No? Yikes.

There are several reasons why this could not happen. The primary reason is that at the receiving end of the order is a live human broker— your broker—and it is unlikely that he would buy on your behalf something as weird as Singapore hemp futures without checking back with you first. Your order does not, in other words, go directly and automatically to be executed on any exchange floor or system. If you place it at night, your broker probably won't even look at it until the following morning. (There is one exception to this: Charles Spear.) Second, the system which accepts your order should have built-in safeguards. It will format an order on the screen and redisplay it to you for final proofreading and approval before releasing that order for transmission to the brokerage.

How to Buy a Stock with Your Computer

The entire sequence of operations involved in ordering 100 shares of Intergraph, an NASDAQ-listed security, is reproduced in Figures 23.1 through 23.3.

Figure 23.1 reproduces the main menu of a system called Trade Plus. It offers a basic range of services. This system is used by Quick & Reilly in New York and by Thomas F. White and C.D. Anderson in San Francisco. It is also the brokerage component of Covidea, a joint effort by Chemical Bank, the Bank of America, Time, and AT&T to provide home banking services. Trade Plus, a company based in Palo Alto, created and maintains the system for the brokerages that offer it. Until April 1986 Trade Plus was also the system used by Fidelity for the Fidelity Investor's Express. In the second quarter, Fidelity introduced a system of its own which is similar in kind. The Trade Plus system is used here to illustrate the on-line brokerage concept because it is straightforward, easy to use, and accessible via any standard communications program. No proprietary communication software is supplied by Trade Plus brokers or the new Fidelity Investor's Express service.

To bring up the main menu on your screen, you first dial a local number and log on to Compuserve and then bring up your chosen broker's Trade Plus menu. It is also possible to gain access to Trade Plus brokers' systems more directly by dialing a local Telenet number. The advantage of going in through Compuserve is that Compuserve provides access to major resources such as fundamental databases from Standard & Poor's and Value Line's Data Base II.

Unlike Security Pacific's On-Line Advantage, the Trade Plus system does not directly provide access to fundamental databases. Fidelity's Investor's Express now has a similar arrangement with the Dow Jones News Retrieval system. To reach the Fidelity Investor's Express, you can first log on to the Dow Jones service. Fundamental resources (e.g., Media General and the Dow Jones news services) are thus accessible on the

```
- 1 MAIN MENU -

 2 CHANGE PASSWORDS
 8 NEWS
 9 HELP
10 PRICE MENU
20 ORDER MENU
30 PORTFOLIO MENU
40 RECORD MENU
50 INFORMATION MENU
60 ANALYSIS MENU
 0 SIGN OFF



*** TYPE NUMBER TO SELECT  ...... 20


- 20 ORDER MENU -

21 STOCK ORDERS
22 OPTION ORDERS
29 HELP



*** TYPE NUMBER TO SELECT  ...... 21


- 21 STOCK ORDERS -

211 BUY OR SELL STOCKS
212 LIST STOCK ORDERS
213 CANCEL A STOCK ORDER
214 CANCEL ALL STOCK ORDERS
 29 HELP



*** TYPE NUMBER TO SELECT  ...... 211
```

Figure 23.1. The main menu of the Trade Plus system. The figure illustrates the procedure you would follow in initiating a trade with one of the discount brokers who offer Trade Plus. From the main menu, the selection of item 20 brings up the order menu. In this example a stock order is involved, so the next selection is item 21. Since the stock will be bought, the final menu selection is item 211.

Note that the system is designed for "point-to-point navigation." If you know the number of the service you wish to call up, you can enter it any time and move directly to that service. It is not necessary to work back and forth through a series of nested menus to get where you want to go unless, as a beginner, you find the menus helpful. In an on-line service, where you are being billed by the minute, point-to-point navigation is a particularly desirable feature.

same line you used to link with Fidelity. You are not required to pay the Dow Jones sign-up fees just to use Fidelity, however, and if you wish to use Trade Plus, you'll be given a waiver of the Compuserve sign-up fee. Charles Spear Securities is accessible via the Source, with similar benefits; the link to the Source surrounds the basic brokerage service with a wide range of news and financial information resources, including the extensive Media General database.

Refer to the main menu of the Trade Plus system in Figure 23.1. Since we wish to place an order, we select item 20 and enter the number 20 in response to the prompt "TYPE NUMBER TO SELECT . . ."

The system responds by displaying the order menu. We can now order a stock, order an option, or ask for help. To order a stock, we enter 21 at the prompt. The stock order menu is now displayed. Note that menu item 212 will list stock orders. If we have already placed some orders—particularly limit orders—we might check this item to see what orders have been executed. If we had placed some prior orders "at the market," we might learn from the list whether the order had been executed and, if so, how much we paid for the stocks. In this example we are about to place an order, so we enter 211 at the prompt, the selection which will enable us to buy or sell stocks.

What follows is a list of questions identical to those your broker might ask if the order were being placed over the telephone. They are reproduced in Figure 23.2. The system first asks which portfolio is involved and then lists the three possibilities on record. It asks the nature of the order. It could be a new order, a cancellation, or an "if nothing done" order. The last item refers to currently standing orders; it means, "If nothing has been done, proceed as follows." One might use this option to raise or lower a stop-loss price, for example. Finally, the system requests the ticker symbol of the stock. Intergraph's symbol, INGR, is entered at the prompt. The program instantly responds with the current quote on the stock and asks whether we want to buy or sell it. "The 20-minute price is . . ." means that the price quote is 20 minutes old. Real-time quotes are available through the system at extra cost.

The system now asks how many shares are to be purchased, whether the order is to be executed at the market or at a specified limit price, and how it is to be paid for. You elect to use the funds in the brokerage account. Finally, the system asks whether the securities are to be delivered or held in street name.

Now refer to Figure 23.3. Up to this point you have committed yourself to absolutely nothing. You could change your mind about any of it or simply dismiss the idea without entering the order. Before the order is transmitted, the system requests a password. For the demonstration, we

```
-- 211 BUY OR SELL STOCKS --
- Portfolio: AAII
-- Type CTRL/C to Escape --
> Short Name, or type RETURN




# SHORT NAME     BROKERAGE ACCT. NO.
  ----------     --------------------
1 A1             DM0089-0001
2 IRA            DM0089-0002
3 KEOGH          DM0089-0004
> Type # of the desired Portfolio.. 1


-- Portfolio: A1 DM0089-0001 --
  (N)ew Order, (C)ancel Former Order
  or (I)f Nothing Done Order...
> Order Type: (N,C,I) ...... n


> Stock Symbol ............. INGR


  INTERGRAPH CORP
  20-Minute Price is....  33 1/2
  Bid................  33 1/2
  Ask................  34
> (B)uy or (S)ell .......... B


  (C)ash or (M)argin Account
> Account (C,M) ............ C


> Number of Shares ......... 100


> Price:Your Limit or (M)kt. M


  (C)heck, (M)oney Fund,
  (F)unds in Acct
> Payment Method (C,M,F).... F


> Deliver Certificate: (Y,N) N
```

Figure 23.2. This is an interactive screen where you enter, in response to prompts, information of the type your broker would routinely ask of you if you were placing the order verbally. You select the portfolio in which you wish to trade and then indicate the nature of your order, the stock symbol, whether you intend to buy or sell, the number of shares involved, and so on. The only item on this panel of questions which is not self-explanatory is perhaps the "if nothing done" order. This refers to a limit order that may or may not still stand. You may wish to cancel or change the order.

339

```
> Password ................ SECRET


You have ORDERED the following:

Portfolio ..............A1 DM0089-0001
Stock Symbol .............        INGR
INTERGRAPH CORP
(B)uy or (S)ell ..........         Buy
Account ..................        Cash
Number of Shares .........         100
20-Minute Price..........      33 1/2
Price:Your Limit or (M)kt.         Mkt
Type of Order ............         Day
Payment Method ...........Funds in Acc
Deliver Certificate.......          No
Name ...                          AAII




WARNING: YOU ARE ENTERING A FIRM ORDER.

> Is this ORDER Correct: (Y,N)...... Y


Order placed at 01:00 PM EST  4/24/86

> Order again in this Portfolio: (Y,N)N


> Order in another Portfolio: (Y,N).. N




‡*‡  TYPE NUMBER TO SELECT  ......
```

Figure 23.3. Once you have answered all the pertinent questions in order to define your order, you will be asked to enter a password. In this demonstration the password "SECRET" was used. This is a safeguard to keep other people from transacting business in your account. When the system recognizes and approves the password, it transmits a tabulation of the information about your order. There follows a cautionary message: "WARNING: YOU ARE ENTERING A FIRM ORDER." If you approve the order as entered, that's it. You have finished. If it is a standing order, you can check on its status at any time after the order is entered by typing 212 for a listing of stock orders.

used "SECRET." The password will prevent unauthorized persons from trading in your account.

In response to the password, the system formats and displays all the pertinent facts it has recorded about your transaction and displays this statement: "WARNING: YOU ARE ENTERING A FIRM ORDER. Is this ORDER correct: (Y/N)." When you enter a Y for "yes," off it goes to Quick & Reilly, Thomas F. White, or C.D. Anderson. The inherent safeguards and precautions are evident. The order will be reviewed by your broker before it is executed. When the transaction is complete, a record of it will appear under menu item 211, for "List Stock Orders." Moreover, the new purchase will be automatically entered into your portfolio files on the system.

It is not apparent from the illustrations presented here on paper, but the information on the display scrolls up the page as it is downloaded or entered. On certain terminals the information does not scroll; instead, it is formatted into a neat page for display. The terminals include the DEC VT100, the DEC VT52, the Televideo 910, a Lear Seigler terminal, or a Quazon Quik-Link. If you are using a personal computer (which is more likely), you will require terminal emulation software to get these nicely page-formatted displays. Crosstalk will emulate a DEC VT100 on an IBM PC, and ASCII Express software will accomplish the same thing for an Apple II. This is primarily a matter of aesthetics. On the portfolio manager display, the valuation arrives and scrolls up the screen in a tabular format, but it would be helpful to have some ruled lines and borders to help you read it. Page formatting can establish such lines and provide entry points for data within tabulations. It's a nicety.

Your Files Are Kept on the Mainframe

Note that your portfolio will be kept on file on the mainframe, not on your own computer. You can view your account almost as your broker would, but not quite. The computation of buying power, which is important to margin traders, is not available from any of the brokerages through the Trade Plus system. Trade Plus has the software, but for some reason its brokers haven't implemented it. A competing system from Security Pacific, the On-Line Advantage, does offer the computation of buying power. C.D. Anderson, which is a Security Pacific subsidiary, offers both computerized services, so if you use this broker and trade on margin, you might prefer its On-Line Advantage service.

In addition to your portfolio, you may keep other Trade Plus files on the mainframe. Two of particular interest are called Option Watch and Stock Watch. If you are interested in following a particular collection of stocks, you might expect to phone the service, log on, and request quotes ticker by ticker. You are welcome to do this, but Stock Watch works better. Using Stock Watch, you enter your list of tickers just once. Then, whenever you like, you log on, and the mainframe will download to you the whole list of current quotes. The Option Watch features works the same way, based on a list of options you enter into a mainframe file. Your tax-related records and all trading records will also be kept in mainframe files. You can download and capture all this stuff for a slight premium charge over the normal usage charge.

If this makes you begin to wonder who has captured whom here, you're on the right track. It's actually quite pleasant to be locked up inside the cortex of a powerful mainframe computer. Given the range of services available to you in there, it is rather like being locked inside the candy store. Then comes the monthly invoice. Before long, I think you will find that you wish to buy some microcomputer investment software in order to break out of the "mainframe environment."

News, Information, and
Analytical Services

Trade Plus brokerages do not offer news wires or extensive fundamental databases under this system, but if you enter it through Compuserve, you will be able to use the other Compuserve menu services without hanging up. Compuserve has the Executive News Service (AP wire), S&P data on 3000 companies, and the Value Line II database on 1700 companies. Compuserve also has historical quotes, current quotes, and a ticker look-up, but these services are available within Trade Plus at a generally more attractive usage rate. In addition, Trade Plus presents earnings, dividend, and split announcements at no extra charge. There is a premium charge for retrieving and downloading historical price data on stocks and options. It is drawn from the IDSI (Interactive Data) database. No charting facility is provided to use these data, however, so you can't draw charts with the data unless you bring to bear some off-line software that can read these files.

Research from the Pershing Division of Donaldson, Lufkin, Jenrette Securities Corp. is available on-line at a premium. This is the sort of information you might ask of a full-service broker: research reports on specific companies and industry groups, technical analytical opinion, and observations on trends. The Pershing Instant Comment service also provides market commentary in the course of the trading day and makes specific recommendations.

As you might expect of a service which has drawn a customer base that consists primarily of options traders, the options analysis menu is extensive. The system will evaluate an option portfolio and analyze options leverage, options prices, call options, put options, spreads, and combinations. If you can't remember the symbol for a particular option, the system will fish out and display all the unexpired puts and calls on the underlying security, along with price and volume. When you select the option you're interested in from a numbered menu, the system displays a complete panel of information about that option: the current price (normally delayed 20 minutes), today's volume; the opening price; the high, low, and previous close; change; open interest; premium; the underlying stock's current price and its high, low, and change for today; the previous quarterly dividend; and the number of days to go before the option expires. The menu-type selection is much more convenient than using a code key to help determine each option's symbol. The menu is particularly helpful if you are choosing one option to buy from a large selection.

Security Pacific's On-Line Advantage

From the standpoint of analytical power, this is the best of the on-line brokerage systems evaluated here. I would be a little careful about using it, as it is possible to run up some whopping usage bills. It charts 6500 stocks intraday, daily, weekly, or monthly. Charting requires the On-Line Advantage communication software. On-line, you can do fundamental screening of the Wilshire database of 3500 stocks per 70 different criteria. Compare this with, say, the Value/Screen Plus software, which screens 1700 stocks per 35 different criteria. The system provides on-line portfolio management and analysis. It displays a complete accounting for your own brokerage account, including calculations of buying power. The analytical features associated with portfolio management are extensive. You can analyze real or hypothetical portfolios. In addition to the usual reports on unrealized and realized gains and losses and tax consequences, the system provides profiles of risk exposure. It displays and takes into account data such as the 52-week price range, earnings, P/E, the financial sector, and the volatility for each stock.

A complete option strategy analysis is available for existing and hypothetical positions. Black-Scholes valuations are included. If you want to look at the options available on a single stock, the system will provide a two-page report. The first page lists all available puts and calls, along with the change in price that would be required of the underlying security to bring the option to its breakeven point. The second page lists the theoretical value and the associated *delta,* or hedge ratio, for each option using the Black-Scholes valuation model.

If you are profoundly interested in the way a stock trades, you can follow the ticker trade by trade via the On-Line Advantage. This would be an absurdly expensive pursuit, since you can get the ticker over cable from FNN all day for a fraction of the cost. But if you want it, Security Pacific offers it. The system is under continuous development, and if you browse through the information file, you'll find a growing record of features and improvements that have been added over the past year and of any new features you might be unaware of.

Finally, the system offers quote streams, stock and option watch lists, buy and sell order entry, order monitoring, account status, and electronic mail to your broker. These features are common to most brokerage systems. Portfolio management screens and charts can be displayed in page formats if you have Security's software. The system will display exchange indexes and active stocks as menu selections (in competitive systems, you might have to enter a specific symbol in order to recover, say, the NYSE). Not all indexes, however, are available.

There are two "missing" elements that are available either directly or via most of the other on-line brokerages. One is a news wire. To get one, it's easy enough to separately access Dow Jones, for example. The other is packaged research. The system does not provide access to research reports, recommendations, or market commentary. The brokerage accepts orders on a 24-hour basis. If you transmit an order at night, it will be executed the following morning when the market opens. A quibble of my own was with the quote stream. I was unable to retrieve quotes on several NASDAQ stocks. They were relatively new issues but not brand-new issues.

Software from Charles Schwab & Co., Inc.

Of the two Schwab programs, the Equalizer and Financial Independence, the one of most interest to serious investors is the Equalizer. It is a communication package and portfolio manager on a single floppy disk. The Equalizer cannot be used like a generalized communication program (e.g., Crosstalk or Smart Com II) to access any and all on-line services. It is strictly for financial communications. The program will communicate with Schwab and with on-line financial information services: Warner, Dow Jones, and S&P's MarketScope. These services are at different phone numbers and respond to different user ID numbers and passwords.

The beauty of the Equalizer is that all you need do is select the service you want from a menu. The program then autodials, establishes the link, enters the passwords, and so on—behind the scenes. You see the menu, and then you see the prompt or menu of the service you have requested.

This is a more ambitious approach than that taken by several other brokerages, who simply provide you with a route of access to a single information utility: all financial services on Compuserve, for example, or on the Source. In short, Schwab gives you broader access to information services, and to some degree you can pick and choose among several databases to help control your costs. For example, I have used current quotes from Dow and historical quotes from Warner. For fundamentals I would have also had a choice of sources, but the system also offers a special approach to fundamental reporting. This is perhaps its most powerful and impressive feature.

The system not only can bring down data from several different sources, it can synthesize data from different sources into a single, comprehensive four-page company profile on a stock of interest. The report includes a stock chart (52 weeks, high, low, close, and volume in DOS graphics). The report is assembled with data from four sources: Standard & Poor's (company description and business summary), S&P's CompuStat (balance sheet and income statement data, valuation, profitability, and growth figures), Warner Computer Systems (price data), and Lynch, Jones & Ryan (estimates). The retrieval process is completely automated. You select a full Report from the main menu, and the program retrieves and files it for you. It can retrieve two at once, which will probably cost a bit less in usage charges than two separate runs. The cost per report will be about $3.50 base, plus the usage time charge on a network, which will run $12 an hour in prime time and half that in off-prime time. You would not want to use this full reporting feature casually. However, if you have by other means narrowed your choice to just two or three companies, this is a good way to gather up-to-the-minute data for a final decision.

The Equalizer provides access to S&P's MarketScope. This is an on-line source for specific research, daily market commentary, and specific recommendations. It is made up of two parts. The "active" section contains relatively hot information such as today's interest rates, a list of the best-performing stocks on a quarter-to-date basis, earnings estimates, specific investment ideas, and much more. The "reference" section is just that. It presents descriptive and statistical information on 4600 companies. The quickly changing statistics (price, P/E ratios) are updated daily. You may have noticed that Paul Kangas of the *Nightly Business Report* on PBS frequently cites MarketScope as one of his sources of explanations for sudden price changes or unusual volume activity. MarketScope costs $36 in annual subscription fees. For usage, MarketScope charges $1.50 for 15 pages. You will also pay network usage charges for connect time. Schwab provides an $18 saving on subscription and usage charges with the purchase of the Equalizer. Altogether, the package of discounted services and first-hour freebies available to you with the Equalizer is worth about $168.50.

The program includes a portfolio manager and creates off-line files to support it. It has specially designed screens to help you enter current prices manually from the newspaper. If you'd rather not do this by hand, you can of course download the price automatically from Warner or Dow. All the screens are neatly and logically page-formatted for the display and entry of financial information. The account records do include buying power if you trade on margin and need to know this.

The program offers the best access to financial information—meaning the widest selection of databases and other research sources—of all the brokerage services reviewed here. Its weakness is in the area of analysis. The Equalizer will value your portfolio and so on, but it doesn't do any serious calculating, sorting, or screening off-line. The program also has a technical peculiarity which may or may not affect you. It would not run at all on my IBM PC. I ran it instead on a Compaq.

My PC is fitted with a Paradise graphics card. Every time I turn on the computer, an autoexec.bat program calls a little utility program to bring the card into play. Until the program has run, the monitor displays illegible gibberish. Both the program and the autoexec.bat file that calls it run under the DOS operating system. The Equalizer was created to run under a different operating system, the UCSD p-system. I have no idea how to get my monitor to work under the p-system, and I don't particularly want to learn how. Assuming that there is a solution to this problem, a second problem arises. My PC has been upgraded to XT capability. It has a hard disk. In order to run two different operating systems on a hard disk, you must back up the disk, then partition it, and then restore the files before proceeding. This is an enormous project. Withal, I was glad I own a Compaq to test the Equalizer.

This business about the monitor not working is not just an isolated quirk of my own system, incidentally. It follows from the installation of the Paradise or Genoa cards, which are otherwise the best cards for IBM PCs that must run investment software. In any event, if you have an IBM computer with a hard disk or a monochrome graphics card (as opposed to a monochrome adapter card), you will find it hard to use the Equalizer. This is too bad, because it is a fine program. Schwab is very much aware of the problem, and perhaps the company will do something about the non-DOS operating system.

The cost is $199 plus $6.50 for shipping. At this writing the program is being offered at a discount for $99. This seems to be a fair price for the program, but bear in mind that several other brokerages will let you into their systems for the price of a modem, assuming that the modem comes, as most do, with free communications software.

Schwab offers in addition to the Equalizer another software package, Financial Independence. The stock management component of this 2.5-megabyte program slightly advances the technology available from brokerages by providing off-line dedicated software for charting, screening, and portfolio management. This program does not, however, attempt to compensate for the lack of analytical services in the Equalizer. Financial Independence runs under DOS, so the two programs are basically incompatible. The portfolio manager is a nice one, but the fundamental screening and especially the charting modules are very limited. The charting module will draw a chart and an n-day simple moving average, and that's about it. It is not fair, however, to compare this package with a full-blown dedicated fundamental screening and technical charting packages like that of Savant.

The purpose of Financial Independence is to provide a comprehensive personal tool for money management. It does budgeting, tax estimation, and personal financial planning. It therefore competes more directly with personal money management programs such as Andrew Tobias's or Sylvia Porter's than with any stock market package or on-line service. It is priced at $149.95. As a personal money management program, Financial Independence lies somewhere above the midpoint. In my view, it is better overall than the Porter program and not as good as the Tobias program, which is the best one in the field. In the specialized areas of stock market analysis and stock portfolio management, Schwab's program clearly does a better job than the other personal money management programs. It is not a full-blown stock market program, however, and is not marketed as one.

Financial Independence includes a nice portfolio manager and a built-in communications program. It downloads data from Compuserve and enables you to place orders with Schwab. To this extent, it overlaps the capabilities of the Equalizer, which also provides portfolio management and communications with the brokerage. The Equalizer, however, provides access to financial information databases which are inaccessible via the Financial Independence package. Perhaps this limitation on Financial Independence's ability to communicate is supposed to sharpen the marketing distinction between the two products. From a technical (programming) standpoint, I can't see any reason for it.

Spear Securities via the Source

You should scan the most current brokerage commission schedules before making a decision in favor of one broker or another. At the time of this writing, however, tabulations of comparative commission rates for various services would seem to favor Spear over several others. The quote streams, the business and market news, and the rest of financial information "surround" for the brokerage service are precisely those available on the Source. The fundamental database is Media General's and includes 3100 stocks traded on the NYSE, the AMEX, and OTC. The news wires are AP, UPI, and *The Washington Post* and are key word searchable. Research and recommendations, company profiles and growth forecasts, historical prices and industry overviews are all available on-line. The portfolio management and accounting services are similar in kind to those of the other brokerages, though Spear encourages putting nonstock assets on file as well; this is a nice convenience.

Two special features distinguish this service. First, it is a "real" 24-hour brokerage. Overnight, Spear essentially makes a market in certain exchange-listed and OTC stocks. They are, understandably, high-marketability issues. If you want to sell a stock in the middle of the night, Spear will buy it from you. If you want to buy one, he'll sell it to you. There is a limit of 500 shares per stock per 24-hour trading period. A premium over the previous day's close is charged to buyers. A discount under the previous day's close is charged to sellers. Spear publishes a schedule of premiums and discounts, but since he *is* the market at midnight, he retains the right to raise or lower prices in response to supply and demand or other factors. Basically, this is a nice service for people who simply have to get rid of a stock in order to get some sleep. Other brokerages are on-line 24 hours a day but do not make a market after hours. They simply hold the orders and buy or sell at the following day's opening prices.

The second special service is called the Spear Securities Commission Rebate Program. The SEC has recently cleared the purchase of qualifying computer software and hardware for investment management purposes using so-called soft dollars. Soft dollars are commission rebates. The Spear rebate program can help you with this. Spear will send you a list of eligible products and services which can be purchased under the program. Other brokers can do this as well, but Spear is vigorously promoting its program.

Computerized Investing Viewed as a Movement

Computerized investing virtually grew up in tandem with the discount brokerage industry. Some observers regard the march to computerized investing as something of a rebellion of private investors against the services of full-service brokerages. In another view, the computer revolution was launched as a palace revolution among brokers against in-house mainframes. However it may have begun, there is clearly a technological revolution in progress that pervades both the brokerage industry and its marketplace.

Most individual investors who use computers and many professionals will freely remark that they believe the research work of major brokerages to be automatically self-discounting in the market. Even a really excellent research idea, bruited across the country by an inspired team of hundreds of brokers, obviously loses its value as a hot tip. Most computerized investors feel that privately conducted research, even if it is inexpertly carried out, has a better chance of paying off.

The discount brokers may help you find research resources, but they won't do the research for you. They are able to discount, in fact, because they do not bear the overhead cost associated with research. If you do the research and analysis yourself, with the help of a computer, you are entitled to a discounted commission. You've earned it. For these reasons, computerized investors rarely use full-service brokerages. Here is a tabulation of commissions based on a telephone survey conducted last winter. The same prices will probably not obtain when you read this, but it may give you a feel for the politics of the situation. The yardstick trade was a 500-share block that moved at $52.

Company	Commission
E.F. Hutton	$395
Merrill Lynch	$394
Shearson/Amex	$420
Schwab	$136
Fidelity	$135
Spear	$123

The highest commission is more than triple the lowest, but commissions vary substantially at different price levels. On a smaller trade, e.g., 200 shares at $24, the cost of the highest was slightly less than twice the cost of the lowest ($111 and $62, respectively). Nevertheless, if you are paying full commissions for a full-service broker, why not just let the brokerage do the work? Forget all about computerized investing.

On-Line Full-Service Brokerages

Although computerized investors tend to seek out discount brokerages, E.F. Hutton offers its customers a very well designed and helpful on-line brokerage service. The customers can use it to keep in touch with the brokerages' thinking and to keep tabs on the status of their own accounts. HuttonLine is a typical computerized brokerage service that is somewhat reminiscent of Trade Plus. It's all on-line. It provides a 20-minute-delayed quote stream, an order entry and communication facility, stock watches, a portfolio manager, and access to the Moody fundamental database of 3500 companies. Appropriately, it seems to provide more advice than the discount brokerages. It offers market commentary three times a day, makes highly specific stock and strategy recommendations, and has an enormous menu of research reports on individual companies and industry groups. If I were a Hutton customer I would enjoy using the service even though it is difficult to justify paying a great deal of money for it. If I were paying for this research with my commissions, I would tend to feel entitled to get access to it for no more than the cost of the computer link time. Perhaps in recognition of this feeling, the services are quite reasonably priced. Sign-up is $25, and usage is 25 cents a minute in prime time and 10 cents a minute off-prime. Access is via Compuserve.

There are other software and database access services available from full-service brokerages. Merrill Lynch has a program available by subscription called the Merrill Lynch Equity Screen. The subscription price is $4000 annually. It is not a brokerage service per se but a stock-screening service. It is too expensive to be reviewed in detail in this book. However, Merrill Lynch is a participant in a low-priced quote and news delivery system via FNN's cable television network. See Chapter 7 for comments on this service.

Banks

Some banks are endeavoring to provide on-line brokerage services as one component of a selection of home banking services made available via computer. Chemical Bank and the Bank of America, as noted above, have contracted with Trade Plus for the Covidea project. Chase Manhattan owns Rose & Company, a discount brokerage, and offers customers of its Spectrum home banking service a 24-hour brokerage service on-line. Rose is based in Chicago and has offices in most major cities. Union Trust Company in Connecticut uses Dominick and Dominick in New York for discount brokerage services. The firm is said to be interested in licensing Chemical Bank's system, which would include Trade Plus.

Citicorp Information Services has advertised the CitiQuote Investor, an ambitious software package offering technical analysis, fundamental analysis, and portfolio management. The product has not appeared at this writing, nor does it seem to be forthcoming. However, you can get a communications program that provides access to Citicorp's enormous securities database. The program costs $395, but the price includes $200 worth of free access time. The database charges 40 cents per minute for off-prime time and 60 cents per minute for prime time. A spokesman told me this service is "intended to be affordable by an individual investor." One can afford it, yes. But is access to this excellent database worth committing $195, net, for a communications program? A professional would probably not fault this, but a private investor might.

What Next?

As for the future of these services, I think Charles Schwab & Co., Inc., has at least pointed the way with what I consider to be its unfortunately rather limited Financial Independence. From the customer's standpoint, on-line services work best and most economically in conjunction with off-line analytical software. The brokers can be forgiven for wanting to keep their customers on-line, since that very line is the conduit for their business. But "dial-up to order" as a menu item on an off-line program would really suffice.

No software for rapid downloading and comprehensive off-line analysis is available from brokerages at this time. Plenty of it is available from other suppliers, however, and I would suggest that serious investors use it in lieu of on-line brokerage services as their involvement in computerized investing grows.

One-way quote services via TV cable and FM are also more economical for traders and serious investors, and it would not be surprising if brokerages were to offer support for these services. Merrill Lynch is involved in one of the cable programs (FNN's), and pocket FM quote receivers have been used as premiums in special brokerage promotions. Now that some hardware can be qualified for purchase with soft dollars, brokers may begin to throw their weight behind the one-way quote services via FM and cable.

What's Best for You?

The brokerages all offer a similar range of on-line services. In making a selection, I would consider commission schedules first and information services second. These services should be used only on an occasional, as-needed basis. Accordingly, I would not attach too much importance to usage charges. If you begin to use these services heavily, it's time to switch to off-line software, FM, cable, floppy subscriptions, and so on. You will save a lot of money.

There is, incidentally, no reason why you should deal with just one brokerage, so the choice of a broker is not really a problem to labor over.

Fidelity's service is brand-new at this writing. The several Trade Plus brokerages and banks seem to offer the median, or standard, level of services. Security Pacific's On-Line Advantage is the most impressive in terms of analytical capability. It is a growing service that is under continuous development at Security Pacific and Wilshire.

Schwab's Equalizer offers the best range of information services, and the company's portfolio manager and account reports are excellent. Schwab went to some trouble technologically to synthesize information from diverse databases and resources into usefully integrated company reports. If you have a hard disk or a monochrome graphics card, however, *you* are going to go to some trouble technologically in order to run the Equalizer.

Spear is inventive at marketing and highly competitive on commissions. The company also offers the only real 24-hour buy and sell service and is aggressively marketing soft dollar (commission rebate) assistance with computer hardware and software purchases.

If you are an E.F. Hutton customer, you will find the HuttonLine helpful, and the prime-time rates are attractively priced.

Sources and Prices

THE ON-LINE ADVANTAGE
Security Pacific Brokers, Inc.
Electronic Services Division
297 N. Marengo Avenue
P.O. Box 7000
Pasadena, CA 91109-9990
(800) 272-4060, ext. 97

Pricing: Sign-up fee, $50. Includes manual, communications disk, demo disk. Connect time charges (West Coast time).

Weekdays:
6 a.m.–2 p.m.	$30 per hour
2 p.m.–10 p.m.	$20 per hour
10 p.m.–6 a.m.	$10 per hour

Weekends:
10 p.m. Friday until 6 a.m. Monday; $10 per hour

Quotes are delayed 20 minutes unless you stipulate real time. Real-time charges range from $7.50 a month for NYSE quotes down to $2.50 a month for live option quotes.

TRADE PLUS
480 California Avenue
Palo Alto, CA 94306
(800) 952-9900 (national)
(800) 972-9900 (California)

This service is provided through several brokers, including Quick & Reilly in New York, Thomas F. White in San Francisco, and C.D. Anderson in San Francisco. (Anderson also offers the On-Line Advantage service from Security Pacific.) Finally, Trade Plus is available as part of the Covidea home banking service of Chemical Bank and the Bank of America.

Pricing: Sign-up fee, $49.95. You will need communications software of your own to connect. Monthly charge of $15 includes one hour of connect time. Beyond that hour, the services costs 44 cents a minute in prime time and 10 cents a minute in off-prime time.

SPEAR ON-LINE INVESTOR SERVICES
Spear Securities Inc.
626 Wilshire Blvd.
Los Angeles, CA 90017
(800) 821-1902 (national)
(800) 321-6116 (California)

Pricing: The on-line services, other than the actual trading service, are those of the Source. The Source charges $10 a month minimum. There are premium charges associated with specific services for investors, but there is none associated with making transactions through Spear. At 1200 bps, the Source charges $25.75 an hour in prime time, and $10.75 after hours and on weekends. Prime time is 7 a.m. to 6 p.m. on weekdays. Real-time quotes are available for a premium of a flat $20 a month. Otherwise, quotes are delayed 20 minutes. Note that Spear offers a true 24-hour brokerage service by making a market in certain stocks after hours.

FIDELITY INVESTORS EXPRESS
Fidelity Brokerage Services Inc.
161 Devonshire St.
Boston, MA 02109
(800) 544-6666
(617) 523-1919

Pricing: For the most part, the services are those provided by Dow Jones News Retrieval. Quotes and transaction services are accessible to Fidelity customers via Fidelity's database at reduced rates. The Fidelity database is reached by logging on to Dow Jones and requesting Fidelity from the menu. Sign-up for Dow Jones is $75, and there can be various monthly service fees, depending on the Dow Jones plan you select. Connect time from Dow Jones costs 90 cents a minute in prime time, and 20 cents a minute off-prime. Prime is defined as 6 a.m. to 6 p.m. Eastern time on weekdays. For access to the Fidelity database, however, it's 30 cents a minute in prime time and 10 cents a minute off-prime.

HUTTONLINE
E.F. Hutton & Co. Inc.
One Battery Park Plaza
New York, NY 10004
(800) 334-2477

Pricing: Sign up, $25. Usage is $15 an hour in prime time and $6 an hour off-prime. Prime time is defined as 8 to 6 on weekdays, local time.

THE EQUALIZER
Charles Schwab & Co., Inc.
Schwab Technology Services
One Second Street
San Francisco, CA 94105
(800) 334-4455

Pricing: Schwab offers both services and software. The Equalizer program provides communications to Schwab for trading purposes. It also draws information from several different on-line sources and automatically creates a coherent, useful report on specific stocks. Finally, it is a portfolio manager. The program nominally costs $199 but has been offered at discount for $99. The on-line services it accesses include Dow Jones, Warner and (via Warner) the Standard & Poor's MarketScope, the Standard & Poor's CompuStat, Warner's historical pricing data, and earnings estimates from Lynch, Jones & Ryan.

The program is supplied with a tremendous amount of initial free access time on the various services it taps, $168.50 worth altogether. Sign-up fees are waived for the most part, although there is a $36 annual subscription charge if you want to sign up for S&P's MarketScope. Schwab acts as a billing agent for all the different services, so you will receive just one bill per month consolidating all the charges. There is no charge for communicating with Schwab's mainframe for trading purposes.

Index

About the Author

Michael C. Gianturco is president of High Technology
Investments (HTI), an investment advisory service
whose portfolios have in recent years been ranked at the
top of *Barron's* annual performance tabulations. In addition, HTI has been ranked No. 1 among all U.S. investment advisory services monitored by the Hulbert Service
for its portfolio performance over the three-year period
through September 1986. Mr. Gianturco personally di-
rected the development of computer software for his
firm, and he oversees the portfolios under its management. A regular contributor of reviews and articles
about investment software to *PC Magazine*, he is also a
frequent guest on Financial News Network.